MANOR THREAT

SNAKEPIT COMICS 2013-2015

BEN SNAKEP

MICROCOSM PUBLISHING
PORTLAND, OR

MANOR THREAT

SNAKEPIT COMICS 2013-2015

BY BEN SNAKEPIT, 2016

FIRST PRINTING, AUGUST 9, 2016

FOR A CATALOG, WRITE
MICROCOSM PUBLISHING
2752 N. WILLIAMS AVE
PORTLAND, OR 97227

OR VISIT MICROCOSMPUBLISHING.COM

ISBN 978-1-62106-381-0
THIS IS MICROCOSM #234

DISTRIBUTED WORLDWIDE BY LEGATO/PERSEUS
AND IN THE UK BY TURNAROUND

THIS BOOK WAS PRINTED ON POST-CONSUMER PAPER
IN THE UNITED STATES.

LIBRARY OF CONGRESS CATALOGING-IN-PUBLICATION DATA

NAMES: SNAKEPIT, BEN
TITLE: MANOR THREAT: SNAKEPIT COMICS 2013-2015 / BEN SNAKEPIT.
DESCRIPTION: FIRST EDITION. PORTLAND, OREGON: MICROCOSM PUBLISHING, 2016.
IDENTIFIERS: LCCN 2015048988 ISBN 9781621063810 (PBK.)
SUBJECTS: LCSH: SNAKEPIT, BEN - COMIC BOOKS, STRIPS, ETC. ROCK MUSICIANS - UNITED STATES - COMIC BOOKS, STRIPS, ETC. ROCK MUSICIANS - UNITED STATES - BIOGRAPHY. GRAPHIC NOVELS. GSAFD: COMIC BOOKS, STRIPS, ETC. LCGFT: BIOGRAPHIES. GRAPHIC NOVELS.
CLASSIFICATION: LCC ML419.S646 A3 2016 DDC 741.5/6973 - DC23
LC RECORD AVAILABLE AT HTTP://LCCN.LOC.GOV/2015048988

CONTACT ME AT BENSNAKEPIT@GMAIL.COM

SNAKEPIT IS, WAS, AND EVER SHALL BE INTENDED TO BE READ ON THE TOILET. IF YOU ACCIDENTALLY DROP IT IN, JUST LEAVE IT IN A BOWL OF RICE OVERNIGHT.

HELLO FRIENDS,

WELL, HERE WE ARE AGAIN. ANOTHER BOOK IN THE CAN, TO BE READ ON THE CAN. AS USUAL, WHEN PREPARING THESE COMICS FOR THIS COLLECTION, I WENT BACK AND REVISITED THE LAST THREE YEARS AND REFLECTED ON HOW I'VE CHANGED/GROWN OVER THAT TIME. I TURNED 40. THE OLD CLICHÉ IS THAT WHEN YOU TURN 40 YOU'RE SUPPOSED TO FEEL SAD ABOUT YOUR MIS-SPENT YOUTH AND BUY A SPORTS CAR. FORTUNATELY FOR ME, I DON'T FEEL LIKE I WASTED MY YOUTH. I SPENT TWO DECADES PARTYING, TRAVELLING, SHITTING MY PANTS AND PASSING OUT IN A DITCH. I FEEL LIKE I GOT IT OUT OF MY SYSTEM, AND INSTEAD OF A SPORTS CAR I BOUGHT A SENSIBLE ECONOMY CAR THAT GETS PRETTY GOOD GAS MILEAGE.

I HAVEN'T TOTALLY SOLD OUT, AT LEAST I HOPE NOT. I STILL PLAY MUSIC WITH MY FRIENDS, I'M JUST MORE REALISTIC ABOUT THE FACT THAT I'M NOT GOING TO MAKE A LIVING FROM IT. I STILL LIKE TO DRINK BEERS, I'VE JUST TONED IT DOWN FROM TWELVE A NIGHT TO TWO. WHO WANTS TO PARTY TIL THEY PUKE WHEN THEY'RE 41 YEARS OLD, ANY WAY?

AND OF COURSE, I STILL CAN'T FUCKING DRAW.

WHEN I WENT TO DETROIT IN 2014 TO SPEAK ABOUT COMICS AT MOCAD, SOMEBODY ASKED ME WHY I DON'T PENCIL MY COMICS BEFORE INKING THEM, LIKE REAL COMIC BOOK ARTISTS DO. THERE ARE TWO ANSWERS TO THIS QUESTION. FIRST: THE DEEP PHILOSOPHICAL ANSWER: FOR ME, DRAWING COMICS IS A LOT LIKE LIVING LIFE. I DO IT EVERYDAY, SO I BASICALLY KNOW WHAT TO EXPECT AND HOW TO DO IT, BUT SOMETIMES IT DOESN'T GO EXACTLY LIKE I PLANNED. OTHER ARTISTS WILL SKETCH OUT THEIR IDEA WITH A PENCIL, THEN ERASE IT AND REDO IT TO GET IT PERFECT. LIFE DOESN'T GO PERFECTLY AND YOU DON'T GET A SECOND CHANCE TO RE-DRAW THE LINES OF YOUR DAY. IF I THROW THAT FIRST LINE ONTO THE PAGE AND IT ISN'T IN THE EXACT SPOT I WANTED IT TO GO, TOUGH SHIT. I HAVE TO WORK WITH WHAT I'VE DONE, WHETHER IT CAME OUT THE WAY I WANTED IT TO OR NOT. ALL I CAN DO IS TRY AND REMEMBER WHAT WENT WRONG SO I DON'T DO IT AGAIN TOMORROW.

SECOND, THE REALISTIC, SIMPLE ANSWER: I'M LAZY. I DON'T WANT TO HAVE TO DRAW OUT AN ENTIRE COMIC STRIP AND THEN GO BACK AND DO IT *AGAIN*. I BARELY EVEN WANT TO DO IT THE FIRST TIME. NOWHERE IS THE COMBINATON OF THESE TWO ATTITUDES MORE PERFECTLY EXEMPLIFIED THAN ON THE LAST PAGE OF THIS BOOK. CONSIDER IT A "SURPRISE" ENDING.

IT CERTAINLY SURPRISED ME!

ENJOY THE COMICS,

♡

Bn

2013

OPERATION - THE UPSETTERS

1-1-13

IT'S A NEW YEAR AND I AM SUPER MOTIVATED!
I AM GOING TO LOSE FORTY POUNDS THIS YEAR!

I KNOW ITS NOT GOING TO BE EASY OR QUICK, BUT I'M GONNA DO IT!

MY FRIEND JOE POSTED A BEFORE/AFTER PIC OF HIMSELF AFTER LOSING 60LBS OVER 2012. IT'S SO INSPIRING!

I SPENT THE DAY PUTTING TOGETHER A DIET + EXERCISE PLAN.

SO I NEED TO REDUCE MY CALORIE INTAKE BY 500 PER DAY.

SURPRISE! YOU'RE DEAD - FAITH NO MORE

1-2-13

FIRST DAY AT WORK AFTER MY 2-YEAR TRIAL.
FINALLY ELIGIBLE FOR HEALTH INSURANCE AND 2 WEEKS PAID VACATION!

WHEN I GOT HOME, I BOUGHT AN EXERCISE BIKE ON THE INTERNET.

I KNOW I COULD JUST RIDE A REAL BIKE, BUT I'LL CRAP OUT IN THE SUMMER WHEN IT GETS TOO HOT.

KAREN MADE ME A HEALTHY MEAL WITH SMALL PORTIONS.

YOU'RE SO AWESOME AND SUPPORTIVE, THANK YOU!

PURE + BEAUTIFUL LOVE - SEWER TROUT.

1-3-13

WORK WAS SO COLD TODAY!
BRRR

HOME WAS ALSO COLD. EVEN PEEBER DIDN'T WANNA GO OUTSIDE.

GO ON, BOY!

ME + KAREN SNUGGLED ON THE COUCH.
PORTLANDIA

DIRTY ROBBER - THE SONICS

1-4-13

ANOTHER DAY AT WORK. MY NEW DIET MAKES ME KINDA GRUMPY BUT I DON'T MIND.
HARRUMPH

I PLAYED VIDEO GAMES WHILE KAREN MADE DINNER...

...A HEALTHY BOWL OF SOUP AND A SMALL SANDWICH!

SNAKEPIT 2013 IS SHAPING UP TO BE PRETTY EXCITING, HUH?

CALIFORNIA SUN- RAMONES

1-5-13

MY FIRST DAY OFF ALONE SINCE I STARTED MY DIET. I WAS NERVOUS.
WHAT IF I CAVE AND EAT SOMETHING BAD?

BUT I DID JUST FINE. I TOOK PEEBER ON A NICE LONG WALK.

LATER, KAREN TOOK ME OUT FOR SUSHI.

COUGH/COOL-MISFITS

1-6-13

KAREN+I BOUGHT GROCERIES TODAY. HEALTHY STUFF. I ACTUALLY READ LABELS AND COUNTED CALORIES.

THESE DRIED APRICOTS HAVE FEWER CALORIES THAN THIS OTHER BRAND OF DRIED APRICOTS.

WENT TO GHOST KNIFE PRACTICE...

AND WATCHED THE MOVIE "BERNIE" WITH KAREN.
BERNIE
HA HA! THIS MOVIE IS SO TEXAN!

MY OLD MAN'S A BUM- D.O.A.

1-7-13

BACK AT WORK TODAY...

WHEN I GOT HOME, MY EXERCISE BIKE HAD ARRIVED!
RAD!
625
FRAGILE
THIS END UP

I PUT IT TOGETHER AND TRIED IT OUT!
IT'S GONNA BE HARD, BUT I'M GONNA DO IT!
BEEP BEEP

I DON'T GIVE A FUCK- BOSS

1-8-13

WORK TODAY. I'VE FINALLY REACHED THE POINT WHERE I ENJOY IT.

CAME HOME AND WORKED OUT.
WOW, DRAWING YOURSELF ON AN EXERCISE BIKE IS HARD!

THEN I PLAYED VIDEO GAMES.
BUT DRAWING YOURSELF AS A GIANT TURD IS EASY!

TEARS OF A CLOWN- ENGLISH BEAT (OR IS IT MADNESS?) 1-9-13

WENT TO WORK TODAY...

...CAME HOME + EXERCIZED.

WOW, I WONDER HOW MANY ATTEMPTS IT WILL TAKE FOR ME TO DRAW THIS CORRELTLY?

THEN I DID A BUNCH OF WORK ON MY NEW BOOK.

SCAN

BETTER- HELMET 1-10-13

WORK WAS PLEASANT TODAY.

AS WAS MY WORKOUT.

I DRANK VODKA WITH KAREN. IT'S NICE TO DRINK.

WHERE DO YOU DRAW THE LINE- DEAD KENNEDYS 1-11-13

TODAY IS PAYDAY. I WANTED TO CELEBRATE TEN DAYS OF DIET AND WORKING OUT BY GOING OUT FOR AN INDULGANT DINNER.

ACCORDING TO THE INTERNET, ITS GOOD FOR MY METABOLISM TO HAVE A "CHEAT MEAL" EVERY ONCE IN A WHILE.

KAREN + I WENT OUT FOR TEX-MEX ENCHILADAS. I GOT A SMALLER MEAL THAN THE ONE I USUALLY GET.

CAREFUL SIR, HOT PLATE.

OH BOY! THIS LOOKS SO AWESOME!

BUT BOY DID I PAY FOR IT.

OW! OH MY GOD IT HURTS! I'M SWEATING AND I CAN'T STAY AWAKE. I CAN'T BELIEVE I USED TO EAT LIKE THIS ALL THE TIME!

BOMB- J CHURCH 1-12-13

RIGHT BACK ON THE HORSE AGAIN TODAY.
PUSHUPS IN THE MORNING, ONLY DRINKING WATER AND TEA, ONLY CONSUMING 1700 CALORIES ALL DAY.
A LOOK OF GRIM DETERMINATION
I EVEN DID AN EXTRA FIFTEEN MINUTES ON THE BIKE.
GRITTED TEETH
ALSO I FINISHED UP EVERYTHING FOR MY NEW BOOK.
I KNOW I COMPLAIN A LOT ABOUT HAVING TO DRAW MY COMICS, BUT EDITING THEM ON THE COMPUTER IS WAAAY MORE TEDIOUS.

TAKE ME- KISS

1-13-13

THIS MORNING I WENT TO GHOST KNIFE PRACTICE.

THEN I WENT ON A WALK WITH KAREN + PEEBER.

LATER WE ATE SALMON AND WATCHED STAR TREK.

SWEET SWEET MANDI- BAD SPORTS

1-14-13

WORK WAS NICE + STEADY TODAY.

CAME HOME AND DID MY WORKOUT.

KAREN STAYED OUT LATE WITH HER FRIENDS SO I DRANK VODKA + PLAYED VIDEO GAMES.

HIGGLE-DY PIGGLE-DY- THE MONKS

1-15-13

TODAY I WENT TO WORK.

DID A LITTLE EXTRA TIME ON THE BIKE.
I'M SUPPOSED TO BE GETTING BETTER AT DRAWING THIS WTF?

THEN I DRANK TOO MUCH VODKA AND ACTED LIKE A DICK.
I DON'T WANT TO GO TO TULSA THIS WEEK-END!
???

WORK TO RULE- NAPALM DEATH

1-16-13

THERE WERE MUFFINS + CUP CAKES IN THE BREAK ROOM AT WORK TODAY. IT WAS TOUGH, BUT I RESISTED.

I'M GONNA LOSE WEIGHT IF IT FUCKING KILLS ME!

I MADE UP WITH KAREN FOR BEING AN ASSHOLE.
I'M SORRY PUNKIN.

1-17-13

SMALL MAN, BIG MOUTH - MINOR THREAT

WORK WAS OKAY TODAY.

AFTER MY WORKOUT, I DRANK SOME VODKA.

I DRANK TOO MUCH OF IT AND GOT IN A FIGHT WITH KAREN.

1-18-13

PATHETIC - SWEET BABY

HOORAY FOR FRIDAY AT WORK!

KAREN + I GOT PACKED FOR OUR TRIP TO TULSA.

WE DROPPED PEEBER OFF AT AMY'S HOUSE. HE'S GONNA LOVE GETTING TO PLAY WITH ANOTHER DOG IN A YARD ALL WEEKEND.

1-19-13

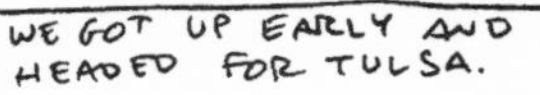
NO RAISE NO PRAISE - DERRICK MORGAN

WE GOT UP EARLY AND HEADED FOR TULSA.
NORTH
I 35

ABOUT AN HOUR INTO THE TRIP, MY "CHECK ENGINE" LIGHT CAME ON. I OPENED THE HOOD AND SAW OIL LEAKING OUT.
UH OH
! ! !

SO WE TURNED AROUND AND CAME HOME, TRIP ABORTED.

I'M SORRY. I PROMISE WE'LL VISIT TULSA AS SOON AS POSSIBLE.

SOB

1-20-13

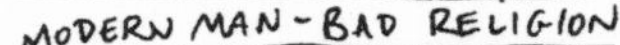
MODERN MAN - BAD RELIGION

KAREN + I ENJOYED OUR UNEXPECTED DAY OFF...
9:30

WE TOOK A LONG WALK.
I THINK I'M GONNA GO BACK AND FINISH ART SCHOOL.
AS MUCH AS I'M OPPOSED TO THE IDEA OF ART SCHOOL, I THINK YOU SHOULD.

WATCHED STAR TREK AND DRANK + TALKED. IT WAS NICE.

YOU DON'T WANNA KNOW - BAD SPORTS

1-21-13

THIS MORNING I TOOK THE CAR TO THE SHOP.
AUTO SHOPPE

THEY CALLED LATER WITH SOME AWFUL NEWS.
YOUR TRANSMISSION IS DYING. IT'LL COST MORE TO FIX THAN THE CAR IS WORTH.
ERP.

KAREN + I SURE HAD A LOT TO TALK ABOUT TONIGHT.
SHOULD WE GET A NEW CAR?
I DUNNO.

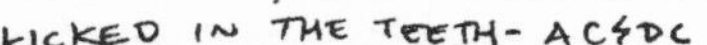
KICKED IN THE TEETH - AC/DC

1-22-13

WENT BACK TO WORK TODAY.

I CALLED MY DAD TO ASK HIS ADVICE.
DRIVE YOUR VAN UNTIL IT DIES. THEN GET A NEW CAR.

I THINK THAT'S WHAT I'M GONNA DO.
I HAVE TO PAY OFF THE LOAN ANYWAY.
HA HA HA THIS DRAWING IS SO FUCKING BAD.

CHICKEN TWIST - HASIL ADKINS

1-23-13

WORK WAS BUSY TODAY.

CAME HOME AND DID MY WORKOUT.
THE TOUGHEST PART OF DRAWING THIS IS GETTING THE FEET RIGHT.

I HAVE ANOTHER DEAD KENNEDYS COVER SHOW TOMORROW. I BAILED ON PRACTICE.
UH, YEAH. SORRY, I'M HAVING "CAR TROUBLE"

NIGHT PROWLER - AC/DC

1-24-13

WORK CALMED DOWN TODAY.

MY WORKOUT DID NOT.
YEAH, AND DON'T WORRY ABOUT DRAWING THE HEAD RIGHT. JUST CONCENTRATE ON THE FEET.

THE DEAD KENNEDYS BAND PLAYED A SLOPPY, FUN SET.

MAXWELL STREET STOMP - KING MUTT + HIS TENNESSEE THUMPERS 1-25-13

I'VE WORKED TWO YEARS AT MY JOB, AND I'M NOW ELIGIBLE FOR HEALTH INSURANCE. TODAY I MET WITH THE INSURANCE GUY.

TURNS OUT, ITS $240 OUT OF EVERY PAYCHECK! THAT IS TOTALLY INSANE.
WHAT?!

SO IT LOOKS LIKE AFTER ALL THAT WAITING, I STILL CANT AFFORD HEALTH INSURANCE ANYWAY.

I SURE HOPE I DON'T GET ANOTHER KIDNEY STONE ANYTIME SOON.

WHAT YOU'RE DOING - RUSH 1-26-13

A LAZY SATURDAY. I PLAYED VIDEO GAMES.

OF COURSE I DID MY WORKOUT, TOO.
WHEN I DRAW THE FEET FIRST, THE HEAD LOOKS WRONG. WHEN I DRAW THE HEAD FIRST, THE FEET SUCK.

WENT WITH KAREN TO SHOW HER TRAILER TO A POTENTIAL BUYER.

I'M SO PROUD OF YOU FOR FINALLY GETTING RID OF IT!

IN GOD WE TRUST - MENACE 1-27-13

STARTED THE MORNING WITH A GROCERY TRIP.

THEN GHOST KNIFE PRACTICE.

FOLLOWED BY A WALK WITH KAREN + PEEBER.

AT THE SEAMS - EPOXIES 1-28-13

MONDAY, BACK AT WORK.

I CAME HOME AND DID MY WORKOUT.

THEN I PICKED A FIGHT WITH KAREN. WHY AM I SUCH AN ASSHOLE?

?

EXPRESS YOURSELF-NWA

1-29-13

ANOTHER GODDAMNED DAY AT WORK.

FOLLOWED BY ANOTHER GOD DAMNED HOUR ON THE BIKE.

AT LEAST I GOT TO GO OUT FOR NOODLES WITH KAREN.

NOT FOR NOTHING- KNOCKOUT PILLS

1-30-13

IN THE INTEREST OF FULL DISCLOSURE, I FEEL I MUST SHARE SOMETHING WITH YOU, DEAR READER.
KAREN AND I ARE TRYING TO HAVE A BABY.
I KNOW I'VE SAID IN THE PAST THAT I DIDN'T WANT KIDS. BUT PEOPLE CHANGE.

AND WE'VE ACTUALLY BEEN TRYING FOR A WHILE.

SEVEN MONTHS, TO BE EXACT. GO BACK AND LOOK AT "SNAKEPIT GETS OLD." EVERY TIME I SAID WE WATCHED STAR TREK, THAT WAS CODE FOR TRYING TO MAKE A BABY.

EXCEPT FOR THE STAR TREK CONVENTION. THAT WAS REAL.

SNAKEPIT GETS OLD

THIS IS WHY I'VE QUIT WEED, CURBED MY DRINKING AND GONE ON A DIET, IN HOPES OF INCREASING MY SPERM COUNT.

AND AS A RESULT OF GIVING UP ALL THOSE THINGS I LIKE, I'M SUPER CRANKY AND IRRITABLE ALL THE TIME, AND THAT'S WHY I'VE BEEN FIGHTING WITH KAREN SO MUCH.

HORROR HOTEL- MISFITS

1-31-13

IT ACTUALLY FEELS PRETTY GOOD TO HAVE GOTTEN ALL THAT OFF MY CHEST YESTERDAY.
I'VE ALSO COME TO THE REALIZATION THAT I TAKE OUT A LOT OF MY FRUSTRATIONS FROM WORK ON KAREN, BECAUSE I CAN'T YELL AT MY CO-WORKERS. NO MORE OF THAT SHIT, ITS NOT COOL.

ANYWAY, BACK TO REGULARLY SCHEDULED SNAKEPIT. TODAY I WENT TO WORK.

THEN I WATCHED STAR TREK WITH KAREN. LIKE, WE ACTUALLY WATCHED THE TV SHOW. ITS NOT A METAPHOR OR ANYTHING.
STAR TREK
DEEP SPACE NINE

GUITAR SONG- RANDY HOLDEN

2-1-13

GLAD IT'S FRIDAY- THIS HAS BEEN A LONG WEEK.
WHEW

AFTER MY WORKOUT I TREATED MYSELF TO A SIX-PACK OF LITE BEER.
lite
26 YEAR-OLD-ME WOULD BE BUMMED!

KAREN+I WATCHED THE MOVIE "ORDINARY PEOPLE." WHAT A BUMMER!

BABY PLEASE DON'T GO - EDDIE "ONE-STRING" JONES

2-2-13

A LOVELY SATURDAY! I TOOK KAREN TO THE FANCY KITCHEN STORE TO USE HER GIFT CERTIFICATE.

THEN WE TOOK AN AWESOME HIKE THROUGH THE PARK.

AND HAD A NICE QUIET EVENING AT HOME.

PELLET - THE GOBLINS

2-3-13

A LOT OF SHIT DONE TODAY. I WENT TO BAND PRACTICE...

...CAUGHT UP ON A LOT OF DRAWING...

...AND ROUNDED OUT THE DAY WITH A WORKOUT.

I HATE MY FUCKING JOB - M.O.T.O.

2-4-13

TODAY AT WORK MY BOSS YELLED AT ME. I FUCKING HATE HIM.
HE'S A VERY LITTLE MAN

I FUCKING HATE MY GOD DAMNED FUCKING JOB.
FUCK.

I SURE DO WISH I COULD SMOKE SOME WEED TODAY.
72 DAYS CLEAN TODAY, FOR WHATEVER THAT'S WORTH.

500 MILES - TOY DOLLS

2-5-13

WORK WAS OKAY TODAY, I JUST AVOIDED MY SHITTY LITTLE BOSS.

I MADE A BAD CHOICE FOR DINNER + SLIPPED FROM MY DIET.
I'M REGRETTING THIS EVEN AS I EAT IT.

I DID AN EXTRA HOUR ON THE BIKE TO MAKE UP FOR IT. I CAN'T GET DISCOURAGED!

ROACHES- BOBBY JIMMY + THE CRITTERS

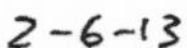
2-6-13

BACK ON TRACK AT WORK...

BACK ON TRACK WITH MY DIET...
BABY CARROTS
DRIED APRICOTS

I FEEL GREAT TODAY!

HYENA- RANCID

2-7-13

JUST ANOTHER DAY. WENT TO WORK.

CAME HOME AND EXERCISED

THEN PLAYED SOME VIDEO GAMES.

MERRY CHRISTMAS (I DON'T WANNA FIGHT TONIGHT) - RAMONES

2-8-13

PAYDAYS RULE EXTRA HARD NOW BECAUSE ITS ALSO DIET CHEAT DAY!

I ENJOYED A PEPPERONI AND JALAPENO PIZZA.

THEN KAREN + I WATCHED A MOVIE.
A MOVIE THAT I FORGOT THE NAME OF

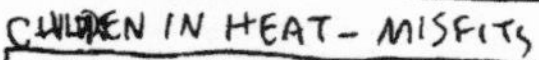
CHILDREN IN HEAT- MISFITS

2-9-13

WHAT A GREAT SATURDAY! I PLAYED VIDEO GAMES!

THEN GHOST KNIFE PLAYED A REALLY FUN SHOW.

I GOT REALLY, REALLY DRUNK.

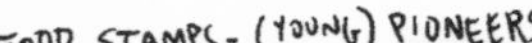
FOOD STAMPS - (YOUNG) PIONEERS

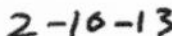
2-10-13

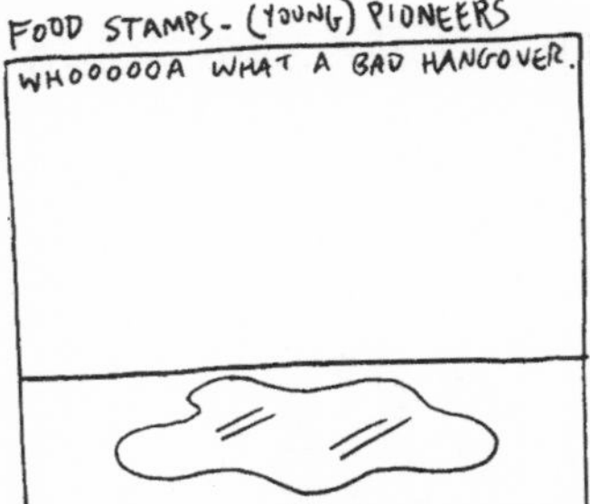
WHOOOOOA WHAT A BAD HANGOVER.

I LITERALLY DID NOTHING ALL DAY.
OWOWOWOWOWOW OH GOD OH GOD OH OWWOWWOWW GOD OH GOD OH

IT WAS 8PM BY THE TIME I FORCED MYSELF TO WORK OUT. IT ACTUALLY HELPED!
SWEAT IT OUT!

GARDEN OF SERENITY - RAMONES

2-11-13

BACK AT WORK, IT WAS PRETTY CHILL TODAY.

WENT GROCERY SHOPPING WITH KAREN.
HEB

THEN WE WATCHED STAR TREK.
WINK

LOVE HER ALL I CAN - KISS

2-12-13

WOW, KAREN + I HAVE BEEN MARRIED FOR A WHOLE YEAR!

WE WENT OUT FOR SUSHI AND I GAVE HER A LITTLE NECKLACE WITH THE DEAD MOON LOGO ON IT.

THEN WE ATE OUR YEAR-OLD WEDDING CAKE. IT WAS STILL GOOD!
MY BIG FAT ASS ONLY GETS A SMALL PIECE.

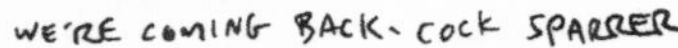
WE'RE COMING BACK - COCK SPARRER

2-13-13

THE ROACHES IN OUR APARTMENT HAVE BEEN GETTING REALLY BAD LATELY.
DAMMIT! HOW DID ONE GET INSIDE MY BAG OF BREAD?

TONIGHT WE GOT SOME HEAVY-DUTY BUG SPRAY.
SHOULD WE GET THIS ONE OR THAT ONE?
BOTH!
PEST CONTROL

IT LURED HUNDREDS OF THEM OUT OF HIDING. IT WAS HORRIBLE.

JESUS!

ROBOCOP – THE FOUR EYES

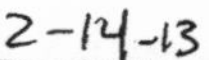
2-14-13

TODAY I TOOK PEEBER TO WORK WITH ME + WE SET OFF A BUG BOMB IN THE APARTMENT.

WHEN I GOT HOME I TALKED TO THE APARTMENT MANAGER.
DUDE, OUR BUG PROBLEM IS COMPLETELEY OUT OF CONTROL!
OKAY WE'LL SEND AN EXTERMINATOR.

KAREN + I WENT OUT FOR A NOT-VERY-ROMANTIC DINNER.
I SURE HOPE NO ROACHES GET IN TO OUR BED.

ARE YOU SINCERE – JEAN SHEPARD

2-15-13

WENT TO WORK TODAY...

CAME HOME TO A TOXIC SMELLING BUG-SPRAYED APARTMENT.
THE SMELL IS MAKING MY TEETH HURT!

WE ATE OUT AGAIN BECAUSE WE CAN'T USE THE KITCHEN.
IT'S KINDA TOUGH TO STICK TO A DIET WHILE EATING OUT BUT I FEEL PRETTY GOOD.

DEATH POD – GWAR

2-16-13

I THINK THE WORST OF THE BUG-POCALYPSE IS OVER.

KLIK

KAREN + I REASSEMBLED THE KITCHEN

LATER I PLAYED VIDEO GAMES.

INSANE SOCIETY – MENACE

2-17-13

I WOKE UP SUPER EARLY FOR SOME REASON TODAY.

NOT THAT I DID ANYTHING WORTHWHILE...

EXCEPT LAUNDRY.

DON'T TRY THIS AT HOME- HENRY FIAT'S OPEN SORE

2-18-13

MONDAY. BACK AT WORK.

I FINALLY BOUGHT SOME NEW PANTS. I WENT DOWN TWO SIZES!!
HOLY SHIT!
FITTING ROOM

I'M PRETTY PROUD OF MYSELF.
BUT NOT GONNA SLOW DOWN!

I'M DOWN- BEASTIE BOYS

2-19-13

WORK WAS CHILL TODAY.

I WENT TO THE POST OFFICE + PICKED UP SOME BOOKS FOR THE CONVENTION NEXT WEEKEND.
USPS

KAREN MADE CHICKEN FOR DINNER.

I WORRY- SCOTTY

2-20-13

WORK WAS EASY TODAY.

CAME HOME + WORKED OUT.

PLAYED VIDEO GAMES.

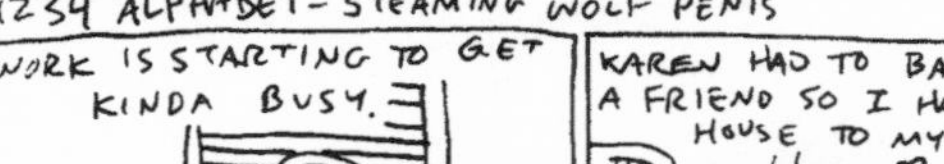
1234 ALPHABET- STEAMING WOLF PENIS

2-21-13

WORK IS STARTING TO GET KINDA BUSY.

KAREN HAD TO BABYSIT FOR A FRIEND SO I HAD THE HOUSE TO MYSELF.

I WATCHED A DOCUMENTARY ABOUT THE STANFORD PRISON EXPERIMENT. HOLY SHIT!

RAID ON KENSINGTON AVE - (YOUNG) PIONEERS

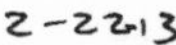
2-22-13

TODAY WAS PAYDAY AT WORK

NORMALLY, I LET PAYDAY BE MY DIET CHEAT DAY, SO I ORDERED A PIZZA.
HERE YA GO, MAN.
PIZZA
PIZZA
HIPPIE PIZZA

I WISH I HADN'T DONE IT.
DAMMIT, IT WASN'T EVEN THAT GREAT. I WANTED TO WAIT UNTIL SUNDAY AND GET SUPER BURRITO.
GUILT
GUILT

FUTURE HOMEMAKERS OF AMERICA - VINDICTIVES

2-23-13

A NICE SATURDAY OFF. I DID LAUNDRY...

...TOOK PEEBER FOR A WALK...

...AND HUNG OUT WITH KAREN.

SWEET SOUL SISTER - THE CULT

2-24-13

TODAY KAREN + I WENT TO THRIFT STORES...
BOOKS

AND I ATE AT SUPER BURRITO ANYWAY.
FUCK IT.

THEN I GOT A BUMMER PHONE CALL FROM MY DAD.
YOUR STEPMOM IS REALLY SICK AND NOT DOING WELL.
OH NO.

SHE SAID - THE CRAMPS

2-25-13

BACK TO WORK TODAY

AFTERWARD I WENT TO THE CRAFT STORE TO GET SOME STUFF FOR THE STAPLE CON THIS WEEKEND.

FABRIC

I ALSO PICKED UP MY NEW SNAKEPIT SHIRTS!

AMERICAN EYES - BANANAS

2-26-13

GOT A TEXT FROM KAREN WHILE AT WORK TODAY.
KAREN
I STARTED MY PERIOD TODAY :(

THIS MAKES 8 MONTHS OF TRYING AND FAILING TO GET PREGNANT.
I SURE HOPE I HAVEN'T PERMANENTLY SMOKED MYSELF IMPOTENT. I QUIT ALMOST 100 DAYS AGO.
CLICK
CLICK

IT'S WEIRD, TRYING TO GET PREGNANT AFTER YEARS AND YEARS OF THE EXACT OPPOSITE.
I GUESS ALL WE CAN DO IS TRY AGAIN NEXT MONTH.
YEP.

BRAINS - ACTION PATROL

2-27-13

TODAY I WENT TO WORK.

THEN I DROVE A 115 MINUTE COMMUTE FOR A 45 MINUTE BAND PRACTICE.
I HATE DRIVING IN AUSTIN!!!

WHEN I GOT HOME, KAREN WAS SUPER DRUNK!
WHISKEY TIME!

DADDY SANG BASS - JOHNNY CASH

2-28-13

WORK HAS BEEN PRETTY SHITTY LATELY. MY BOSS HAS BEEN CONSTANTLY BROWBEATING ME FOR NO REASON.
(HE'S A LITTLE GUY)

TONIGHT I TOOK A CHEAT DAY + HAD A CHEESEBURGER AND A BEER FOR DINNER.
FUGGIT!

BUT I STILL WORKED IT OFF AFTERWARDS.
WHEW!

3-1-13

A VERY TGIF DAY AT WORK.

CAME HOME AND HAD A NICE DINNER WITH KAREN.

THEN I GOT EVERYTHING READY FOR MY BIG DAY TOMORROW!
SHIRTS
BOOKS

SOMETHING MUST BREAK - JAWBOX
3-2-13
THIS MORNING I SET UP MY TABLE AT STAPLE.
SNAKE PIT
I'M SHARING IT WITH MITCH + AMANDA, IT WAS GOOD TO SEE THEM.
EPOXIES
BOY AM I TIRED!
WHEW! COMIC BOOK NERDS CAN WEAR A MOTHERFUCKER OUT!

SAME FEARS - SHELLSHAG
3-3-13
THIS MORNING KAREN + I DID AN EARLY GROCERY RUN.
HEB
THEN I WENT TO THE FINAL DAY OF STAPLE.
WHEN I GOT HOME AND COUNTED MY MONEY, I'D MADE A TOTAL PROFIT OF $18.00
WHAT A WASTE OF TIME.

SUPERNAUT - BLACK SABBATH
3-4-13
TODAY WAS BEAUTIFUL OUT! KAREN + PEEBER + I WENT TO THE PARK
WE HAD A NICE LITTLE PICNIC.
I'M SO GLAD I TOOK TODAY OFF WORK!
THEN I DID SOME DRAWING.
SEEING ALL THOSE COMIC ARTISTS THIS WEEKEND REALLY INSPIRED ME!

BURGER CITY - SHIT CREEK
3-5-13
BACK AT STUPID SHITTY WORK TODAY. I SO DIDN'T WANNA GO.
SIGH.
I THINK IT MIGHT BE TIME TO MOVE ON...
I'VE BEEN HERE LONG ENOUGH TO REALIZE THAT THIS COMPANY IS TOO SMALL FOR ME TO GET PROMOTED ANY HIGHER.
I'M JUST TOO LAZY TO BEGIN JOB HUNTING AGAIN.
I SHOULD UPDATE MY RESUME.. BUT LOOK! VINTAGE STAR TREK SHIRTS ON EBAY!

SHOWER DAYS- NOFX

3-6-13

WORK SUCKED TODAY. IT WAS REAL SLOW SO I HAD TO DO A BUNCH OF CLEANING.

WRRRRR!

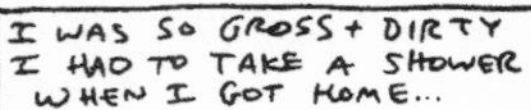
I WAS SO GROSS + DIRTY I HAD TO TAKE A SHOWER WHEN I GOT HOME...

AND THEN TAKE ANOTHER SHOWER AFTER MY WORK-OUT.

ACID- LIL WYTE

3-7-13

WORK WAS MUCH MORE NORMAL (AND CLEAN) TODAY.

I TOOK PEEBER TO THE VET TO GET HIS ANAL GLANDS EXPRESSED.

ANIMAL HOSPITAL

THEN KAREN TOOK ME OUT FOR GREEK FOOD.

ALCHEMY- SEXY

3-8-13

PAYDAY! WOO HOO!

I CAME HOME AND FELL ASLEEP ON THE COUCH.
ZZZ
ZZZ

THEN I TOOK KAREN OUT FOR TACOS.

WHEN IT'S OVER- WIPERS

3-9-13

A NICE SATURDAY OFF. I DID LAUNDRY.

INSTEAD OF MY NORMAL BIKE ROUTINE, I TRIED A NEW, MORE INTENSIVE WORKOUT TODAY.
OH MY GOD! AAAH!

HOLY SHIT IT KICKED MY ASS!
OW FUCK OW OW OW I CAN'T FUCKING MOVE OW OW OH MY GOD OW

07 - THE WIPERS

3-10-13

TODAY I DID A LOT OF DRAWING...

AND PLAYED GUITAR FOR A WHILE.
THIS IS ACTUALLY FUN WHEN I DON'T HAVE TO DO IT.

LATER I ATE NOODLES WITH KAREN.

THE NEXT IN LINE - JOHNNY CASH

3-11-13

BACK TO WORK. MONDAY.

I'VE FOUND SOMEBODY TO REPRINT MY FIRST BOOK, SO I RE-READ IT TO LOOK FOR MISTAKES.

MAN, I WAS A MISERABLE PIECE OF SHIT BACK THEN.

JESUS CHRIST, HOW DID I NOT DIE FROM DRINKING SO MUCH?

COWABUNGA SURF'S UP - SILLY SURFERS

3-12-13

I CALLED MY DAD TODAY TO SEE HOW MY STEPMOM IS DOING.
NOT GOOD. SHE'S GOING DOWNHILL REALLY FAST.

I FEEL AWFUL. I'VE NEVER BEEN VERY CLOSE WITH HER, BUT SHE'S ALWAYS BEEN REALLY SWEET.

SHE REALLY MADE MY DAD VERY HAPPY AT A TIME WHEN HE SEEMED VERY UNHAPPY WITH HIS LIFE.

I TOOK MY SUIT TO THE DRY CLEANERS. IT SEEMS PRETTY INEVITABLE THAT I'LL BE GOING TO VA. SOON.
DRY CLEANER

LAND OF CONFUSION - GENESIS

3-13-13

TODAY I WENT TO WORK.

AFTERWARDS I BOUGHT SOME NEW CLOTHES.
MEN'S PANTS

LOSING WEIGHT IS COOL.

PUBLIC SUICIDE- CHRONIC SICK

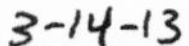
3-14-13

TODAY I GOT TO DRIVE THE WORK DELIVERY VAN TO CEDAR PARK. IT WAS NICE TO GET OUT.

ALSO, IT WAS SUCH A BEAUTIFUL DAY THAT KAREN AND I WENT OUT TO BILLY'S.

THEN WE SAT OUT ON OUR PORCH.

TEENAGERS FROM MARS- MISFITS

3-15-13

WORK WAS ENJOYABLE TODAY!

I GOT THE TABLET PC I ORDERED ON EBAY LAST WEEK.
IT WAS CHEAPER THAN A BAG OF WEED.

I HAVENT SMOKED WEED IN 110 DAYS.
NOT THAT I'M ALL THAT HAPPY ABOUT IT BUT GETTING PREGNANT IS MORE IMPORTANT TO ME THAN GETTING STONED.

THE STENCH OF BURNING DEATH- REPULSION

3-16-13

KIND OF A BORING SATURDAY. I TOOK PEEBER ON A LONG WALK.

I DID ANOTHER INSANE MUSCLE-TONING WORKOUT.
OH GOD!

SAT ON THE PORCH WITH KAREN.

911 IS A JOKE- PUBLIC ENEMY

3-17-13

SUNDAY WAS BORING TOO. NO CAR, NO MONEY, NOTHING TO DO.

I WORKED OUT.

I ATE SOUP FOR DINNER.
I HATE SOUP.

CAROL - GROOVIE GHOULIES

3-18-13

I HAD TO THROW A BUNCH OF BIG BOXES INTO A DUMPSTER AT WORK TODAY, IT WAS HARD.

KAREN TOOK ME OUT FOR DINNER.

THEN I CAME HOME AND PLAYED VIDEO GAMES.

VIETNAM SERENADE - CONFLICT

3-19-13

WORK WAS BACK TO NORMAL TODAY.

I WATCHED THE FIRST EPISODE OF GAME OF THRONES WITH KAREN.
I LOVE THESE BOOKS SO MUCH!
I LIKE IT SO FAR.

THEN SHE HEMMED MY NEW PANTS.

BEETHOVEN'S 9TH SYMPHONY

3-20-13

WORK WAS CHILL TODAY.

CAME HOME AND WORKED OUT.

TOOK KAREN OUT TO DINNER.

BOYS IN THE BRIGADE - YOUTH BRIGADE

3-21-13

ANOTHER DAY AT WORK...

ANOTHER NIGHT OF SOUP...
YEECCH!

ANOTHER EPISODE OF GAME OF THRONES.

SOMEBODY IS ALWAYS NOT HAPPY - GROOVIE GHOULIES

3-22-13

WORK WAS COOL BECAUSE IT WAS FRIDAY AND PAYDAY.

KAREN AND I WENT TO A PARTY! HOLY SHIT!

I GOT WAAAY TOO DRUNK.

JANELLE JANELLE - THE QUEERS

3-23-13

SUPER HUNGOVER TODAY. MY WORKOUT WAS HELL.

MUST... NOT... PUKE!

I HAVE NO IDEA WHY I DREW MYSELF SO SMALL.

I TOOK A BUS RIDE ACROSS TOWN. I WENT TO SUPER BURRITO.
I BOUGHT A T-SHIRT!
WANTED
SUPER BURRITO

AND I GOT TO MEET INDIE-COMIC LEGEND AL FRANK! COOL!!
WOW! THIS GUY'S COMICS HAVE INSPIRED ME FOR YEARS! SO COOL TO MEET HIM!

ROCK-N-ROLL PROBLEM - FUCKBOYZ

3-24-13

GOT GROCERIES WITH KAREN THIS MORNING.
HEB

WENT TO GHOST KNIFE PRACTICE.

CAME HOME AND WATCHED GAME OF THRONES.
I'M STARTING TO LEARN EVERYONE'S NAMES.

I HATE MY FUCKING JOB - M.O.T.O.

3-25-13

BACK TO WORK. SOMETIMES I HATE MY JOB.

I CAME HOME AND DID MY WORKOUT.

THEN I PLAYED VIDEO GAMES.

WANT SOME GAS, THAT'S ALL! - VANILLA MUFFINS

3-26-13

WENT TO WORK TODAY.

RAMPED UP MY WORKOUT A LITTLE BIT.
I'VE ONLY GOT 10 MORE POUNDS TO LOST TO REACH MY GOAL. THEY SAY THE LAST 10 ARE THE HARDEST TO LOSE.

THEN I WATCHED GAME OF THRONES WITH KAREN.
DAENERYS TARGARYEN IS MY FAVORITE.
MINE TOO!
HEY!

MY CONGRESSMAN - FIFTEEN

3-27-13

WORK WAS ALMOST ENJOYABLE TODAY.

KAREN TOOK ME OUT TO DINNER. I WAS PROUD OF MYSELF FOR GETTING A VERY SMALL MEAL.

CAME HOME AND PLAYED VIDEO GAMES.

LAST NAME - MAXIMILLIAN COLBY

3-28-13

TODAY AT WORK I STEPPED IN A PUDDLE OF INK AND TRACKED IT ALL OVER THE CARPET!
OH CRAP.

I CAME HOME AND TOLD KAREN ABOUT IT.
ARE THEY GONNA START CALLING YOU "EL ROJO"? HA HA HA!

THEN WE FINISHED SEASON 1 OF GAME OF THRONES.

FLASH OF THE BLADE - IRON MAIDEN

3-29-13

SO GLAD IT'S FRIDAY!
SIGH
WHAT'S UP "EL ROJO"?
I WENT OVER TO BRANDON'S + HUNG OUT.

THEN KAREN + I WATCHED A SUPER DEPRESSING MOVIE.
WHORES' GLORY

DEAR ABBY - DEAD KENNEDYS 3-30-13

THIS MORNING I RAN SOME ERRANDS WITH KAREN.
NORTH AUSTIN

THEN I WENT TO GHOST KNIFE PRACTICE.

I STAYED UP REALLY LATE PLAYING A DUMB VIDEO GAME.

BUNNIES - PANSY DIVISION. 3-31-13

TOOK PEEBER ON A LONG WALK TODAY.

DID AN INSANE WORKOUT
URRRGH

STARTED SEASON 2 OF GAME OF THRONES.

DEATH IN THE FAMILY - TENEMENT 4-1-13

I WAS ALL PREPARED TO DRAW A WACKY APRIL FOOLS STRIP TODAY.
HMM... UPSIDE DOWN AND BACKWARDS WITH MY LEFT HAND? I DID THAT LAST YEAR.

BUT INSTEAD I GOT THE CALL FROM MY STEP-BROTHER. MY STEPMOM PASSED AWAY THIS MORNING.
ULP.

I NEVER REALLY GOT TO KNOW HER VERY WELL, BUT SHE WAS A VERY NICE LADY.
R.I.P. BARB

GUITAR SONG - DEAD MILKMEN 4-2-13

TALKED TO MY DAD TODAY. THE FUNERAL IS ON FRIDAY.

I BOUGHT PLANE TICKETS AND MADE A LIST OF ALL THE STUFF I NEED TO DO.
SO MUCH TO DO AND SO LITTLE MONEY TO DO IT WITH.

THEN I WENT TO GHOST KNIFE PRACTICE.
SORRY GUYS, I KNOW WE'RE RECORDING NEXT WEEK AND NEED TO PRACTICE BUT I HAVE TO LEAVE TOWN.

BUILD TO BREAK - UNIFORM CHOICE

4-3-13

WENT TO WORK TODAY.

GOT A HAIRCUT AFTERWARD.

DROPPED PEEBEE OFF AT JOEYS AND GOT PACKED.

I PROMISE - SHELLSHAG

4-4-13

THIS MORNING WE TOOK THE BUS TO THE AIRPORT.

WE FLEW TO BALTIMORE

THEN DROVE THE RENTAL CAR TO RICHMOND.

TRAGEDY - WIPERS

4-5-13

GOT UP EARLY AND DROVE WAY OUT TO MY DAD'S LITTLE TOWN.

MY STEPMOTHER'S FUNERAL WAS SAD, BUT A NICE SERVICE.

SPENT THE EVENING DRINKING WITH MY DAD + HIS FAMILY AND FRIENDS.

NEW DAWN FADES - JOY DIVISION

4-6-13

WE HAD BREAKFAST WITH MY DAD THIS MORNING.

THEN WE DROVE BACK TO RICHMOND.

WE SAW DJANGO UNCHAINED AT THE BYRD THEATER.
THE MIGHTY WURLITZER

PROGNOSIS: NEGATIVE - NIGHT BIRDS
4-7-13
THIS MORNING I WENT WITH KAREN + MY MOM TO THE BELLWOOD FLEA MARKET.
THE COOLEST THING I SAW WAS A BLINGED-OUT PENDANT OF A GUY IN A SKI MASK.
THEN WE SAID GOODBYE AND DROVE BACK UP TO BALTIMORE.
WE STAYED IN THE SHITTIEST HOTEL EVER.
SHITTY INN
GOODSKY - SCARED OF CHAKA
4-8-13
WOKE UP AND HEADED TO THE AIRPORT
RENTAL CAR RETURN
FLYING FLYING FLYING.
WHEN WE GOT HOME, KAREN TREATED ME TO A DELICIOUS DINNER.
MIND RIDE - JEFF THE BROTHERHOOD
4-9-13
BACK AT WORK THIS MORNING.
WE NEED YOU TO COME IN EARLY TOMORROW.
THEN IMMEDIATELY TO GHOST KNIFE RECORDING.
WE WERE THERE TIL 11:00 PM!
FUCK, I GOTTA BE AT WORK AT 5:30.
I'M A TELLY ADDICT - TOY DOLLS
4-10-13
WORK SUPER FUCKING EARLY THIS MORNING.
GOT OUT AND FINISHED MY PARTS FOR THE GHOST KNIFE RECORD.
CAME HOME AND FELL ASLEEP.
I'M GETTING SICK, I CAN TELL.

TOO MUCH MONKEY BUSINESS - CHUCK BERRY

4-11-13

WHEN I WOKE UP THIS MORNING, MY TEMPERATURE WAS 102°.
BLAM!
UGH

I CALLED IN SICK TO WORK AND LAID ON THE COUCH WATCHING ADVENTURE TIME ALL DAY.

I FELT A LITTLE BETTER BY THE AFTERNOON.
KOFF
KOFF

GUILT FREE - ROCKET FROM THE CRYPT

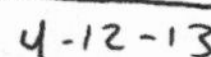
4-12-13

I FELT WELL ENOUGH TO GO TO WORK.

WHEN I GOT HOME, MY NEW BOOKS WERE WAITING FOR ME!!
SNAKE PIT GETS OLD

I TOOK KAREN OUT TO DINNER TO CELEBRATE!

MILK IT - WAD O'FUNK

4-13-13

TODAY I HAD MY BOOK RELEASE PARTY!

IT WENT WELL AND I SOLD A DECENT AMOUNT OF BOOKS.
SEE KIDS! IF YOU WORK HARD AND DRAW LOTS OF COMICS YOU MIGHT MAKE ALMOST $200!

KAREN WENT TO ALISON'S BACHELORETTE PARTY SO I STAYED HOME AND PLAYED VIDEO GAMES.

BESAME MUCHO - THE BEATLES

4-14-13

WHAT A NICE SUNDAY. KAREN + I BOILED CRAWFISH!

THEN WE TOOK PEEBER ON A LONG WALK.

AND HAD A NICE, LAZY NAP.
ZZZ

DOIN' MY TIME - JOHNNY CASH

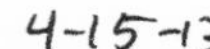

4-15-13

BACK TO WORK TODAY.

I WORKED OUT FOR THE FIRST TIME IN OVER A WEEK.

IT'S IMPORTANT THAT I GET MY DIET + EXCERCISE HABITS BACK TO NORMAL.
I'M SO CLOSE TO MY GOAL!

I HATE MY FUCKING JOB - M.O.T.O.

4-16-13

WORK SUCKED. MY BOSS YELLED AT ME FOR NO REASON.
*#@!!
LATER I DROVE AROUND TOWN, STOCKING MY NEW BOOK AT STORES.

THEN I HAD A QUIET EVENING WITH KAREN.

NEGATIVE APPROACH - NAPALM DEATH

4-17-13

WORK WAS A LOT MORE CHILL TODAY. MY COWORKER CALLED IN SICK SO I HAD THE OFFICE TO MYSELF.

I TOOK KAREN OUT TO DINNER.

THEN WE DRANK BEERS ON THE PORCH.

WALKIN' THE DOG - THE SONICS

4-18-13

TODAY I WENT TO WORK.

THEN I MADE A POT OF CHILI FOR DINNER.
I LIKE NEVER, EVER COOK, EVER. THIS IS PRETTY FUN.

KAREN + I ATE IT AND WATCHED "CARRIE."
THEY'RE ALL GONNA LAUGH AT YOU!

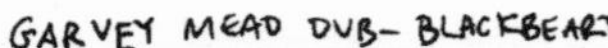
GARVEY MEAD DUB- BLACKBEARD

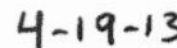
4-19-13

PAYDAY. AWESOME.
IT'S A "BENJAMIN." GET IT?

I TOOK KAREN OUT TO DINNER.

THEN WE WATCHED ALIEN. I HADN'T SEEN IT IN A LONG TIME.
WHERE DID THE CAT COME FROM? WHO WAS FEEDING IT WHEN THE CREW WAS IN HIBERNATION?

SONG #1 - FUGAZI

4-20-13

TODAY I RODE UP TO DALLAS WITH BRANDON.

DUDE, YOU SUCK AT DRAWING CARS.

YEAH I KNOW.

WE BOTH GOT SUPER BURRITO TATTOOS!
(DRAWN FROM MEMORY)

AFTER THAT I WENT TO A PARTY AT DARLENE'S HOUSE.
SHE TOLD ME TO DRAW HER EATING A GIANT PIECE OF CAKE.

CALIFORNIA FLASH - ATILLA

4-21-13

TODAY I TOOK A NICE LONG WALK AND ALSO BOUGHT A VIDEO GAME.

LATER I GOT GROCERIES WITH KAREN.

THEN I PLAYED MY NEW GAME.

777 - DANZIG

4-22-13

BACK AT WORK TODAY.

WHEN I GOT HOME, KAREN EXCITEDLY TOLD ME THAT HER PERIOD IS THREE DAYS LATE!
!!!
!!!

WE WENT TO THE DRUG STORE AND GOT A PREGNANCY TEST...
NOPE.

DEATH WISH KIDS - POISON IDEA

4-23-13

WE WERE BOTH PRETTY BUMMED OUT TODAY.

I CAME HOME AND WORKED OUT EXTRA HARD.
GAH!

THEN WE DROWNED OUR SORROWS BY FINISHING OFF THE LEFTOVER BEER FROM MY BOOK RELEASE.
YOU REALIZE YOU'RE UN-DOING YOUR WORKOUT?
YEP.

SWEET SONG FOR MY BABY - KEN BOOTHE

4-24-13

WORK WAS OKAY TODAY.

KAREN GOT EVEN MORE BAD NEWS.
I DIDN'T GET ACCEPTED AT U.T.

I FEEL SO BAD FOR HER.

MIKE ON THE MIC - BEASTIE BOYS

4-25-13

ANOTHER DAY AT WORK. THIS WEEK IS DRAGGING BY.

KAREN AND I WENT OUT FOR HAPPY HOUR...

...BUT I CAME HOME AND SWEATED IT OUT.
SERIOUSLY, WHY DO I DRAW SO FUCKING BAD?

ASTRA WALLY - ROSE TATTOO

4-26-13

SERIOUSLY, TGIF. FML.
NOT REALLY FML. MY L IS PRETTY GOOD, ACTUALLY. I HATE PEOPLE THAT SAY FML.

KAREN + I ATE PIZZA AND WATCHED STAR TREK.

THEN I PLAYED VIDEO GAMES ALL NIGHT.

WARNING - BLACK SABBATH

4-27-13

SATURDAY! I SLEPT IN SUPER LATE.
10:30
ZZZ

TOOK PEEBER ON A LONG WALK.

DID A HARD CORE WORK-OUT.
THEY SAY "IF IT DOESN'T HURT, IT DOESN'T COUNT. WELL THIS IS COUNTING LIKE A MOTHER FUCKER! OW!

SKIN-POPPIN' SLUT - THE DWARVES

4-28-13

A VERY LAZY SUNDAY. KAREN + I DIDN'T DO SHIT.

I DID ANOTHER INSANE WORKOUT. I THINK I'M GONNA HIT MY GOAL THIS WEEK.
HOLY SHIT! 203!

LATER I TOOK A NAP ON THE COUCH.
ZZZ

BAD REPUTATION - JOAN JETT

4-29-13

BACK AT STUPID DUMBASS WORK. I HATE MY JOB (SOMETIMES)
KAREN MADE A HEALTHY VEGETARIAN DINNER

THEN I WATCHED THE SOUND CITY DOCUMENTARY.
THE FIRST HALF OF THIS IS GREAT, BUT DAVE GROHL KINDA SUCKS.

HEEBY JEEBIES - LITTLE RICHARD

4-30-13

WORK WAS A LIL BETTER TODAY.

I'VE REALLY STEPPED UP MY WORKOUTS, I'M SO CLOSE TO MY GOAL!
GRR!

KAREN + I WATCHED STAR TREK (BOTH LITERALLY + FIGURITIVELY)
DO NOT DISTURB
PONN FAR IN PROGRESS

LOVE SONG - THE DAMNED

5-1-13

I DID IT!! I LOST 40 LBS IN JUST FOUR MONTHS!
200

I TOOK A PICTURE OF MYSELF TO COMPARE TO THE ONE I TOOK ON JAN. 1ST.

I CELEBRATED BY GOING OUT FOR CHEESEBURGERS AND BEER.
HAW HAW

ANGEL OF DEATH: SLAYER (R.I.P. JEFF HANNEMAN!)

5-2-13

WORK WAS OKAY TODAY.

I WAS A LITTLE HUNGOVER FROM CELEBRATING LAST NIGHT.
OW

SO I TOOK IT EASY.

LIVE UNDEAD - SLAYER

5-3-13

GOT OUT OF WORK EARLY TODAY!

KAREN + I WENT TO ALISON + BRYAN'S WEDDING.

IT WAS VERY NICE.

DEAD SKIN MASK - SLAYER

5-4-13

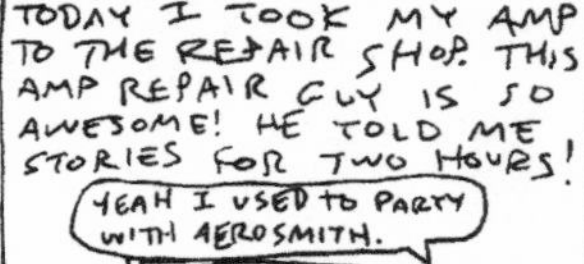
TODAY I TOOK MY AMP TO THE REPAIR SHOP. THIS AMP REPAIR GUY IS SO AWESOME! HE TOLD ME STORIES FOR TWO HOURS!

YEAH I USED TO PARTY WITH AEROSMITH.
AWESOME!

THEN I WENT TO SUPER BURRITO WITH BRANDON AND CHELSEA.

THEN KAREN + I WENT TO THE POODLE DOG AND SAW MY OLD FRIEND JEN + HER PAL JAMES.

CALLEY VERSION- THE AGGROVATORS

5-5-13

SLEPT IN SUPER LATE...

BOUGHT SOME NEW PANTS...

GOT SOME FANCY BEER.

THRASHARD- D.R.I.

5-6-13

BACK TO THE SAME OLD SHIT AT WORK.
I REALLY SHOULD TRY TO FIND A BETTER JOB.

I BOUGHT SOME NEW WEIGHTS YESTERDAY. MY WORKOUT WAS NUTS!

I'VE STARTED READING OLD ISSUES OF FANTASTIC FOUR AT NIGHT. IT WAS ACTUALLY REALLY GOOD BACK THEN.

THE GORGON- CORNELL CAMPBELL

5-7-13

ANOTHER DAY AT WORK.

CAME HOME AND BINGE-WATCHED MAD MEN WITH KAREN.
THEY'RE DOING A GREAT JOB OF TRANSITIONING INTO THE 70'S

THEN I READ SOME MORE FANTASTIC FOUR.

CHINA CLIPPER- SKATALITES

5-8-13

A DAY AT WORK,

FOLLOWED BY SOME VIDEO GAMING,

ROUNDED OUT WITH ANOTHER RIVETING F.F. TALE
OKAY SERIOUSLY HAVE YOU EVER TRIED TO DRAW THE HUMAN TORCH? HOW DO YOU DRAW A GUY MADE OUT OF FIRE?

BLACK MAN LAND - PRINCE FAR I

5-9-13

I LEFT WORK A LITTLE EARLY TODAY.

SPENT 3 HOURS DRIVING KAREN AROUND TO GET WEIRD FOODS.

SIGH

THEN I GOT DRUNK!

SIGH

THE GIRL WHO LIVES ON HEAVEN HILL - HUSKER DU

5-10-13

I'M SO GLAD TODAY IS FRIDAY.

KAREN TOOK ME OUT FOR ETHIOPIAN FOOD!

THEN I CAME HOME AND DID WHAT I DO BEST.

AND JUSTICE FOR ALL - METALLICA

5-11-13

SATURDAY! I TOOK PEEBER FOR A WALK

DID A CRAZY WORKOUT

AND WATCHED MAD MEN WITH KAREN.

I BET THE TWO FIRMS ARE GONNA MERGE

GOOD CALL!

BOOKS ABOUT UFOS - HUSKER DU

5-12-13

TODAY KAREN+I RAN SOME ERRANDS.
HEB

THEN WE HAD LUNCH WITH CHRIS, WHO'S IN TOWN FROM NEW MEXICO FOR A WEDDING.

I ATE A HUGE BURRITO SO I HAD TO DO AN EXTRA HARD WORKOUT.
YOU KNOW, IF I LIKED DRAWING COMICS AS MUCH AS I LIKE VIDEO GAMES, I MIGHT ACTUALLY BE GOOD AT IT.

THE LONELY ONE - WIPERS
5-13-13
BACK AT WORK TODAY. MEH.
KAREN MADE RIBS FOR DINNER + I DRANK FANCY BEERS.
FANCY BEER
WE WENT FOR A WALK AND SAW A DEER IN THE H.E.B. PARKING LOT!
MOMMY'S LITTLE MONSTER - SOCIAL DISTORTION
5-14-13
ANOTHER DUMBASS DAY AT MY DUMBASS JOB.
AFTER WORK I PICKED UP MY AMP FROM THE REPAIR GUY. IT SOUNDS AWESOME!
Marshall
THEN I DID A SUPER LONG WORKOUT.
WHEW!
SOCIETY IS A CARNIVOROUS FLOWER - J CHURCH
5-15-13
WORK WAS PRETTY NORMAL TODAY.
KAREN + I DRANK SOME BEER.
GLUG GLUG
GLUG GLUG
THEN WE WATCHED THE DOCUMENTARY ABOUT DANNY WAY.
SUNDAY YOU NEED LOVE - OBLIVIANS
5-16-13
I STAYED A LITTLE LATE AT WORK TODAY.
KAREN TOOK ME OUT TO DINNER.
GOD, THIS ALL LOOKS SO GOOD! I REALLY SHOULDN'T CHEAT ON MY DIET, BUT...
MENU
I ATE MORE THAN I SHOULD HAVE.
WHY DID I DO THAT?

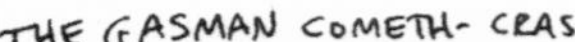
THE GASMAN COMETH- CRASS
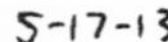
5-17-13

WORK WAS ALMOST ENJOYABLE TODAY.

KAREN+I WENT OUT TO DINNER WITH ALEX+ALYSE. IT WAS REALLY FUN!

I CAME HOME AND READ THE FANTASTIC FOUR.

SOMETIME IN THE MORNING- THE MONKEES

5-18-13

TODAY I FOUND A SET OF WEIGHTS BY THE DUMPSTER.
COOL! I'VE BEEN WANTING SOME HEAVIER ONES FOR MY WORKOUTS.

AFTER A HARDCORE WORKOUT, I WENT FOR THE FIRST SWIM OF THE YEAR.
IT'S STILL A LITTLE TOO COLD.

THEN I DRANK BEERS AND WATCHED A MOVIE WITH KAREN.

SOMEBODY IS ALWAYS NOT HAPPY- GROOVIE GHOULIES

5-19-13

DID AN EXTRA-LONG WORKOUT THIS MORNING.
CHECK OUT THESE SUPER-HUGE NEW WEIGHTS, BRO!

KAREN+ I WENT TO SEE THE NEW STAR TREK MOVIE.

IT WAS AWESOME!!!

I LOVED THAT IT WAS MORE TRUE TO CANON + KHAN WAS AWESOME AND SCIENCE OFFICER 0718 HAD A COOL VOICE AND ROBOCOP IS IN IT AND SCOTTY AND CHEKOV WERE AWESOME AND THE TWIST ON THE END OF WRATH OF KHAN AND SPOCK RULED AND THERE WAS LESS CRAPPY PARTS THAN THE FIRST ONE! IT WAS RAD!

SOCIETY- SCREECHING WEASEL

5-20-13

BACK AT WORK TODAY.

CAME HOME AND WATCHED THE NEW MAD MEN WITH KAREN.
THIS ONE IS WEIRD.
YEAH.

THEN I PLAYED VIDEO GAMES.

THE CLAW - MOTÖRHEAD
5-21-13
WORK WAS PRETTY COOL TODAY.
I PLAYED MUSIC WITH BRANDON AND BRAD. IT WENT GREAT.
I'M PRETTY EXCITED ABOUT STARTING A NEW BAND.
PRESSURE'S ON TO WRITE SONGS!
SCARE THEM - TOOTS + THE MAYTALS
5-22-13
WENT TO WORK AGAIN TODAY.
CAME HOME AND DID A WORKOUT.
THEN KAREN AND I WATCHED SERENITY. IT WAS A GREAT FOLLOW-UP TO FIREFLY.
I'M GONNA KILL HER - F.Y.P.
5-23-13
TODAY AT WORK WE GOT A NEW DIGITAL 4-COLOR ENVELOPE PRINTER. I GOT TRAINED TO RUN IT.
ON THE WAY HOME I WENT TO PLANNED PARENTHOOD TO GET A SEMEN ANALYSIS
HERE'S A CUP FOR YOU TO BEAT OFF INTO. YOU HAVE TO TAKE IT TO A LAB ACROSS TOWN WITHIN ONE HOUR. OH AND YOU HAVE TO BE THERE BEFORE 10 AM. THAT'LL BE 90 BUCKS.
KAREN TOOK ME OUT TO DINNER.
I'M PROUD OF YOU FOR TAKING STEPS TO TRY TO PLAN OUR PARENTHOOD.
THANKS.
KICK THE CAT - SQUIRREL BAIT
5-24-13
A NICE, RELAXED FRIDAY AT WORK
THIS THING IS COOL!
KAREN + I WATCHED STAR TREK.
THEN I STAYED UP LATE PLAYING VIDEO GAMES

MAMA'S BOY- RAMONES

5-25-13

KAREN HAD A SATURDAY OFF, WHICH IS RARE.

WE DIDN'T REALLY DO ANYTHING SPECIAL, JUST RAN SOME ERRANDS.

AND GOT A LITTLE DRUNK.
GIN
TONIC

ONE NIGHT IN BANGKOK- MURRAY HEAD

5-26-13

THIS MORNING I DID A REAL INTENSE WORKOUT.

THEN I ATE A TERRIBLE LUNCH THAT PRETTY MUCH UNDID IT.

LATER KAREN + I HAD AN 80'S DANCE PARTY.

BECOMING A GHOST- GROOVIE GHOULIES

5-27-13

TODAY KAREN + I WENT OVER TO BRANDON + CHELSEA'S FOR A COOKOUT.

THEN I HAD BAND PRACTICE WITH BRANDON AND BRAD.

I CAME HOME AND ATE PIZZA AND WATCHED MAD MEN WITH KAREN.

NOTHING- GROOVIE GHOULIES

5-28-13

AT WORK TODAY I GOT A PROMOTION TO THE ART DEPARTMENT!
YOU'RE GONNA BE IN HERE RUNNING THIS NEW MACHINE NOW.

I'M STOKED, THIS IS ACTUALLY THE KIND OF WORK I WENT TO COLLEGE FOR.
BUT BOY IT'S A LOT TO LEARN

I "CELEBRATED" BY COMING HOME AND DOING AN EXTRA-HARD WORKOUT.

NINE POUND HAMMER- JOHNNY CASH 5-29-13

TODAY I WENT TO WORK.

CAME HOME + WORKED OUT.

WATCHED STAR TREK WITH KAREN.
ITS THAT TIME OF THE MONTH WHEN WE WATCH A LOT OF STAR TREK.
WINK

HONKY TONK BLUES- HANK WILLIAMS 5-30-13

WORK AGAIN TODAY. I'M GETTING USED TO THE NEW JOB.
NOT QUITE USED TO DRAWING IT, THOUGH!

WORKED OUT FOR MY AFTER-WORK WORKOUT.

HAD A NICE DINNER WITH KAREN

STUCK UP BLUES- ROY ACUFF 5-31-13

TODAY I WENT ON A DELIVERY WITH MY BOSS. IT WASN'T AS BAD AS I THOUGHT IT WOULD BE.

I TOOK KAREN OUT FOR DINNER.

THEN I STAYED UP LATE PLAYING SKYRIM.

BLACK TRAIN- GUN CLUB 6-1-13

A NICE SATURDAY. I ATE VERY HEALTHY AND DID A LOT OF EXERCISING.
WATER
SALAD

KAREN + I HAD PERUVIAN FOOD FOR DINNER.
POOR OL' HIGHLAND MALL. IT JUST LOOKS WORSE AND WORSE.
FOR LEASE
FOR LEASE

THEN I ATE POPCORN AND WATCHED MOVIE MACABRE ON HULU.

RED + BLACK – ATHLETICO SPIZZ 80

6-2-13

THIS MORNING KAREN + I RAN SOME ERRANDS.
GROCERY STORE

THEN WE SAT BY THE POOL FOR A WHILE.

THEN WE ATE DINNER AND WATCHED A MOVIE.
SCREAM

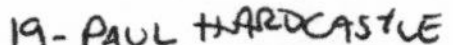
19 - PAUL HARDCASTLE

6-3-13

BACK AT WORK TODAY. I REALLY DIG MY JOB.

CAME HOME AND SWAM WITH KAREN.

THEN WE WENT FOR A WALK

YOUNG LIVERS – RFTC

6-4-13

WORK WAS COOL TODAY.

I CAME HOME AND GOT A LITTLE STONED FOR THE FIRST TIME IN MONTHS AND MONTHS.

IT WAS FUN, BUT I DON'T KNOW HOW I USED TO DO IT ALL THE TIME.
WHOA!

DON'T LOSE YOUR WAY – MONSULA

6-5-13

DID A LOT OF STUFF AT WORK TODAY.

CAME HOME AND WORKED OUT
MY WEIGHT HAS STOPPED DROPPING AND HAS BEEN THE SAME FOR A MONTH!
GOTTA WORK HARDER!

PLAYED WITH THE DOG.

SOLIDARITY - RANCID 6-6-13

TODAY AT WORK I HAD TO DRIVE THE COMPANY VAN TO BASTROP TO PICK UP SOME STUFF.

IT WAS KAREN'S PAYDAY AND SHE TOOK ME OUT FOR CHINESE FOOD.
HAVE YOU EVER TRIED TO DRAW A HAND HOLDING A PAIR OF CHOP-STICKS? ITS HARD.

THEN I PLAYED VIDEO GAMES.

GOIN' DOWN THIS ROAD FEELIN' BAD - WOODY GUTHRIE 6-7-13

ANOTHER DELIVERY AT WORK TODAY. IT'S NICE TO LEAVE THE OFFICE...

...BUT I STILL WANT TO LEARN ART DEPARTMENT STUFF.

DID A GNARLY WORKOUT THIS AFTERNOON.

GIMME GIMME GIMME - BLACK FLAG 6-8-13

SATURDAY! GOOD THING I'M TOO BROKE TO DO ANYTHING.

OTHERWISE I WOULD'VE SPLURGED ON BAD FOOD INSTEAD OF WORKING OUT.

AND WOULD'VE GONE TO A BAR INSTEAD OF PLAYING VIDEO GAMES.

KING OF THE NIGHT-TIME WORLD - KISS 6-9-13

RAN SOME ERRANDS WITH MY WIFE THIS MORNING.
STORE

THEN WENT TO PRACTICE WITH BRANDON + BRAD.

BRANDON GAVE ME A WEED COOKIE THAT WAS WAY TOO MUCH FOR ME TO HANDLE!
I'M FREAK-ING OUT!

HIGH SCHOOL HOP - HASIL ADKINS

6-10-13

BACK AT WORK TODAY. IT'S COOL.

CAME HOME AND DID A WORKOUT.

THEN I PLAYED WITH PEEBER

FEMME FATALE- VELVET UNDERGROUND

6-11-13

TODAY KAREN TOLD ME SHE GOT HER PERIOD.
SIGH.

THIS MAKES IT OFFICAL-LY ONE YEAR THAT WE HAVE BEEN TRYING TO HAVE A BABY.

I STILL HAVEN'T HEARD BACK FROM PLANNED PARENTHOOD YET.

I'M REALLY STARTING TO GET BUMMED OUT.
WHAT'S WRONG WITH ME?

MY SUMMER GIRL- THE RENTALS

6-12-13

WORK WAS COOL TODAY.

I WENT TO PLANNED PARENTHOOD AND GOT MY TEST RESULTS.

YEP. AS I THOUGHT, MY SPERM COUNT IS FUCKED UP. THERE'S NOTHING I CAN REALLY DO WITHOUT HEALTH INSURANCE. SIGH.

THEN I WENT TO GHOST KNIFE PRACTICE

UNCONTROLLABLE URGE- DEVO

6-13-13

WORK WAS GRUELING TODAY.
IN
OUT

I CAME HOME AND WORKED OUT...

...THE IMMEDIATELY UNDID IT BY DRINKING BEERS.

I'M A PRETENDER - EXPLODING HEARTS
6-14-13
TODAY IS MY 39TH BIRTHDAY. I WENT TO WORK.
KAREN TOOK ME OUT TO DINNER.
THEN WE DRANK BEERS AND WATCHED A MOVIE ON THE COUCH.
URGH! A MUSIC WAR
SET THE CONTROLS FOR THE HEART OF THE SUN - PINK FLOYD
6-15-13
TODAY I DID LAUNDRY.
THEN GHOST KNIFE JUST PLAYED A SUPER FUN SHOW!
PLAYING SHOWS IS WAY MORE FUN WHEN YOU DON'T DO IT ALL THE TIME.
THIS IS ONLY THE 3RD SHOW I'VE BEEN TO ALL YEAR!
COME TOOBIN - MEAN JEANS
6-16-13
TODAY I WENT TOOBIN'!
THEN I ATE AT SUPER BURRITO!
I'M SUNBURNED AND TIRED, BUT WHAT A PERFECT DAY!
Z Z Z
RUN - CAVES
6-17-13
I SLEPT 12 HOURS LAST NIGHT.
SUNBURN
HAD TO WORK LATE TODAY.
THEN GOT GROCERIES WITH KAREN.
CHIPS

'ELLO KIDDIES- CHEAP TRICK

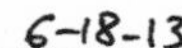
6-18-13

WE ARE TOTALLY SLAMMED AT WORK THIS WEEK.
GOOD GRIEF!

I WENT ON A DELIVERY WITH MY BOSS.
DON'T SAY ANYTHING DUMB.

THEN I CAME HOME AND WORKED OUT.
I TOTALLY SAID SOMETHING DUMB.

CREATION MYTH- TULSA

6-19-13

ANOTHER BRUTALLY LONG DAY AT WORK.

FOLLOWED BY ANOTHER BRUTAL WORKOUT.

I HAD WEIRD DREAMS.
(MY OLD VAN)

ANOTHER GIRL- SNUFF

6-20-13

WORK SUPER SUCKED TODAY. I WAS THERE FOR TEN HOURS.

I TOOK KAREN OUT FOR BURGERS + BEER.

WENT TO BED EARLY.
SO... TIRED.

I'M ON FIRE- DEAD MILKMEN

6-21-13

FINALLY GOT CAUGHT UP AT WORK, ONLY TO HEAR SOME CRUMMY NEWS.
WE'VE DECIDED TO GET RID OF THE NEW MACHINE. YOU'RE PROBABLY GONNA GO BACK TO YOUR OLD JOB.
CRAP.
BUT I CAME HOME AND WROTE A NEW SONG!
WHOA! INSPIRATION!

AND ITS FRIDAY!
IT'S THE WEEKEND!

WORDS I MIGHT HAVE ATE - GREEN DAY

6-22-13

TODAY WAS A NICE DAY OFF.

I DID A HARDY WORKOUT

THEN I ATE PIZZA WITH KAREN.

80,000 DUB - KING TUBBY

6-23-13

TODAY KAREN + I DROVE AROUND LOOKING AT HOUSES. WE'RE GETTING MORE SERIOUS ABOUT TRYING TO BUY ONE.
WE CAME HOME AND WENT FOR A SWIM.
THEN WE WATCHED THE AVENGERS. WHAT A SHITTY MOVIE.
IT'S THE SAME PLOT AS HOWARD THE DUCK.

JOHNNY BLADE - BLACK SABBATH

6-24-13

BACK AT WORK TODAY.

KAREN FOUND A CITY PROGRAM THAT WILL HELP US WITH A DOWN PAYMENT ON A HOUSE. WE APPLIED FOR IT.

THEN WE WATCHED THE SEASON FINALE OF MAD MEN.
IT WAS OKAY, BUT IT DIDN'T LIVE UP TO MY EXPECTATIONS.
I LIKED IT.
CREATED BY MATTHEW W

DEBBIE DUNLAP - THIS BIKE IS A PIPE BOMB

6-25-13

WORK WAS OKAY TODAY.

I GOT A CALL FROM THE CITY. WE ARE REGISTERED TO TAKE A HOME-BUYING CLASS. IT'S THE FIRST STEP!

AWESOME!

I CELEBRATED BY ORDERING A PIZZA.
AWESOME!

THE PRODUCT- MINUTEMEN
6-26-13
WENT TO WORK TODAY...
CAME HOME AND DID A KINDA HALF-ASS WORKOUT.
I'VE BEEN SLACKING LATELY, I GOTTA GET BACK TO WORK!
THEN I FUCKED AROUND ON THE INTERNET
DUH DUH DUH
STANDING BY THE SEA-HUSKER DU
6-27-13
WORK WAS LONG TODAY...
AFTERWARDS I HUNG OUT WITH JOE + CATIE + JOHN WHILE I GOT A HAIRCUT.
SNIP SNIP
I STAYED UP KINDA LATE PLAYING VIDEO GAMES.
RUINS-NILE
6-28-13
TODAY WAS ALL TGIF AS SHIT!
FUCK THIS!
I TOOK KAREN OUT TO DINNER.
THEN WE DRANK BEERS AND WATCHED STAR TREK.
STAR TREK
I GOT YOUR NUMBER-COCK SPARRER
6-29-13
TODAY KAREN + I DROVE AROUND LOOKING AT HOUSES.
THEN WE WENT SWIMMING
AFTER THAT WE WENT GROCERY SHOPPING.

OUTBREAK- GROOVIE GHOULIES

6-30-13

SUNDAY ERRANDS: LAUNDRY

DRAWING.

WORKOUT.
WHAT A TERRIBLE DRAWING. I SHOULD JUST QUIT.

ADVANTAGE IN HEIGHT- WIRE

7-1-13

I ARGUED WITH A GUY AT THE POST OFFICE FOR WORK TODAY.

KAREN HAD THE CAR, SO I HAD TO WALK A LONG WAY FROM THE BUS STOP.
GRUMBLE GRUMBLE

I "REWARDED" MYSELF WITH A SICKS PACK.

LA GRANGE- ZZ TOP

7-2-13

ANOTHER DAY OF DRIVING AROUND FOR WORK.
TEXAS

WATCHED A MOVIE WITH KAREN.

TOOK PEEBER FOR A WALK.

LONLINESS- DAVE BARKER

7-3-13

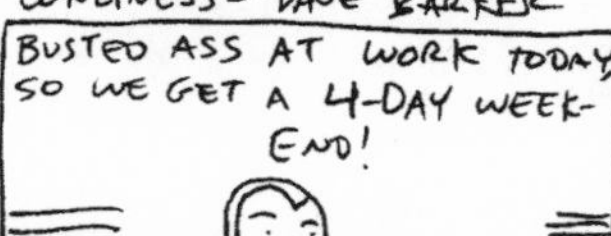
BUSTED ASS AT WORK TODAY, SO WE GET A 4-DAY WEEK-END!

KAREN + I WENT OUT FOR BURGERS + BEERS.

THEN WE HAD A LONG TALK ABOUT BUYING A HOUSE.
WE HAVE TO DECIDE BY AUGUST 15 IF WE WANNA STAY IN THIS APARTMENT.
EVERYTHING IS RIDING ON OUR DPA APPLICATION.

FUCK THE U.S.A. - EXPLOITED

7-4-13

I SPENT MY DAY OFF BY CLEANING THE HOUSE...

...DRINKING BEER...
GROSS
BUD LITE

...AND WATCHING THE FIREWORKS WITH KAREN.

7-5-13

CRABBY DAY - PANZY DIVISION

TODAY I GOT AN EMAIL SAYING THAT KAREN+I MAKE TOO MUCH MONEY TO QUALIFY FOR D.P.A.
WE'RE OVER THE LIMIT BY $200 A YEAR. FUCK.

THEN A BIG CHUNK OF ONE OF MY TEETH FELL OUT.
GAH!
CRUNCH

WHAT A SHITTY DAY.
GRUMBLE
GRUMBLE

RIGHT ON THRU - L7

7-6-13

FINISHED CLEANING THE HOUSE TODAY...

AND PLAYED VIDEO GAMES FOR A LONG TIME.

KAREN CAME HOME AND WE DRANK A BOTTLE OF RUM.
YO HO HO!

YOU CAN HEAR MY WHISTLE BLOW - WOODY GUTHRIE

7-7-13

SPENT THE MORNING KINDA HUNGOVER.
UGH.

THEN KAREN+I WENT TO A WRESTLING MATCH. IT WAS SUPER FUN!

AFTERWARD WE WENT OUT TO DINNER.

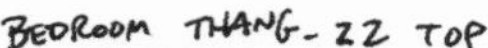
BEDROOM THANG - 22 TOP

7-8-13

THIS MORNING I CALLED AND MADE A DENTIST APPT. FOR TOMORROW.

WHEN I WAS LITTLE, I WAS SCARED OF THE DENTIST BECAUSE OF HOW MUCH IT WAS GONNA HURT.

NOW I'M SCARED OF THE DENTIST BECAUSE OF HOW MUCH ITS GONNA COST.
ACCOUNT BALANCE
$8.72

DROOM KIT - JEFF THE BROTHERHOOD

7-9-13

I WENT TO THE DENTIST THIS MORNING.

THE GOOD NEWS: I'M GETTING A GOLD TOOTH!

THE BAD NEWS: IT COST A THOUSAND DOLLARS!
AND IT'S STILL $200 CHEAPER THAN A WHITE TOOTH.

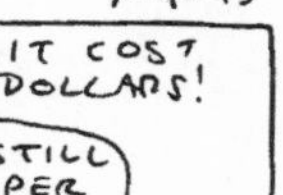

HOLLOW MAN - THE CULT

7-10-13

TODAY AT WORK I GOT AN IDEA.

I PUT A POST ON MY BLOG OFFERING TO DRAW PORTRAITS OF PEOPLE FOR TEN BUCKS.
THIS MIGHT WORK!

I GOT OVER 50 REQUESTS IN JUST A DAY!
OH MAN I HAVE A LOT OF WORK TO DO.
YOU HAVE 53 NEW EMAILS

PULL MY STRINGS - DEAD KENNEDYS

7-11-13

TODAY I WENT TO WORK.

THEN I GOT STARTED DRAWING PORTRAITS. IT'S ACTUALLY REALLY FUN!

I GOT HALF OF THEM DONE ALREADY.

CAUGHT... IN A DREAM- NAPALM DEATH

7-12-13

WORK WAS FRUSTRATING TODAY.

GHOST KNIFE PLAYED A FUN SHOW AT BEER LAND.

EVERYONE KEPT COMPLIMENTING ME ON MY WEIGHT LOSS.
AW SHUCKS.
DUDE! YOU LOOK GREAT!!

RAD 180- GODHEADSILO

7-13-13

TODAY WAS VERY PRODUCTIVE. I FINISHED ALL THE DRAWINGS

I DID LAUNDRY.

WENT FOR A SWIM.

THE FOGGY MOUNTAIN TOP- CARTER FAMILY

7-14-13

THIS MORNING WE WENT GROCERY SHOPPING.

I DID A HARD-ASS WORKOUT.
SO INSPIRED AFTER ALL THE COMPLIMENTS I GOT!

WATCHED A MOVIE WITH KAREN.
SPIES LIKE US

I'M A MILLIONAIRE- DR. HOOK

7-15-13

BACK AT WORK. ITS GONNA BE A LONG WEEK.

SENT EVERYONE'S DRAWINGS TO THEM. I'M ONLY A FEW BUCKS SHY OF PAYING FOR MY TOOTH!
RAD!

I WISH DRAWING WAS MY FULL-TIME JOB.
IF EACH OF MY FACEBOOK FRIENDS BOUGHT ONE DRAWING, I'D HAVE OVER $20,000!

FINGER LICKIN' GOOD- BEASTIE BOYS
7-16-13
I WORKED 9.25 HOURS TODAY.
AND PROBABLY WILL EVERY DAY THIS WEEK.
CAME HOME AND HAD DINNER WITH KAREN.
THEN WE WATCHED STAR TREK.
STAR TREK
DEEP SPACE NINE
KICKED OUT OF THE WEBELOS- TEENGENERATE
7-17-13
ANOTHER NINE AND A HALF HOUR WORKDAY.
LORD LOVES A WORKIN' MAN. DON'T TRUST WHITEY.
I WAS TOO TIRED TO DO ANYTHING.
ZZZ
VIOLENT WORLD- MISFITS
7-18-13
WORK CALMED DOWN A BIT TODAY
I CAME HOME DID A BUNCH OF DRAWING.
THEN I WATCHED VIDEOS ON MY COMPUTER.
HAW HAW HAW
KILL AGAIN- SLAYER
7-19-13
SO GLAD THIS WEEK IS OVER.
KAREN + I ORDERED A PIZZA.
ANOTHER WILD FRIDAY NIGHT.
ZZZ
ZZZ

ALL ABOUT NOTHING - FASTBACKS

7-20-13

THIS MORNING KAREN + I DID OUR SUNDAY GROCERY SHOPPING RITUAL.
FOOD STORE

THEN I REALIZED THAT TODAY IS SATURDAY.
ERM...

I RAN SOME ERRANDS AND WATCHED A RIDICULOUS MOVIE.
THE FP
WHOA!

HEART OF STONE - THE PAGANS

7-21-13

YEAH, I GOT THE COMICS FOR TODAY AND YESTERDAY MIXED UP.
HOW DO I DO SOMETHING THAT DUMB? I DON'T EVEN SMOKE WEED ANYMORE.

BUT ANYWAY TODAY KAREN AND I SPENT KINDA TOO MUCH MONEY ON FANCY BEER.
OOPS! I DIDN'T REALIZE HOW MUCH THESE WERE.
OH MY GOD!

BUT AT LEAST WE ENJOYED IT TOGETHER!

SLAUGHTER OF THE SOUL - AT THE GATES

7-22-13

MY COWORKER IS ON VACATION THIS WEEK. I'M RUNNING THE "DEPARTMENT" BY MYSELF.

I THINK I GOT A GOOD HANDLE ON IT.
JOBS

I CAME HOME AND WATCHED STAR TREK WITH KAREN.
SHOULD I PUT ON MY FERENGI MASK?
GROSS.
DEEP SPACE NINE

THE MODEL - BIG BLACK

7-23-13

WORK WAS CRAZY TODAY. I HAD A LOT TO DO.

I CAME HOME LATE AND TIRED.

BUT I STILL DID A WORKOUT.

JAILBAIT- MOTÖRHEAD 7-24-13

I HAD A BETTER HANDLE ON WORK TODAY.

KAREN + I WENT OUT FOR TACOS.

THEN I DID A BUNCH OF DRAWING.

UNACCEPTABLE- BAD RELIGION 7-25-13

WORK WAS OKAY TODAY.

I CAME HOME AND WORKED OUT...

AND HAD A SENSIBLE DINNER.

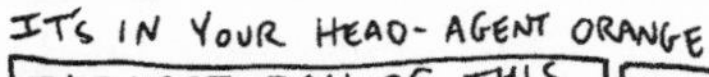
IT'S IN YOUR HEAD- AGENT ORANGE

7-26-13

THE LAST DAY OF THIS ROUGH WEEK IS OVER.
HONESTLY, I KINDA ENJOYED IT.

I TOOK KAREN OUT TO OUR NEIGHBORHOOD BAR.

LATER I SAT ON THE PORCH WITH PEEBEER, WATCHING A LIGHTNING STORM.
COOL!

REVENGE FANTASY #427- THE BANANAS 7-27-13

THIS MORNING I DID A HARD WORKOUT WHILE DOING LAUNDRY.

KAREN TOOK ME OUT TO DINNER.
WE EAT OUT TOO MUCH.
YEAH.

THEN I BOUGHT NEW SOCKS AND UNDERWEAR.
I'M BUYING SIZE "M" UNDERWEAR FOR THE FIRST TIME SINCE THE 90'S!
BOXER

POLICE HELICOPTER - RED HOT CHILI PEPPERS 7-28-13

GOT UP AND DID SUNDAY STUFF.
GROCERY STORE

KAREN + I BOUGHT A GROWLER AND GOT IT FILLED UP AT THE GROWLER ROOM.

THEN I GOT TOO DRUNK AND ATE COOKIES THAT I WASN'T SUPPOSED TO EAT.
I HATE MYSELF.

MONEY - EMBRACE 7-29-13

WORK SUCKED EXTRA HARD.
*!!#@#

KAREN + I RENEWED OUR LEASE.
STUPID D.P.A. SHIT MEANS WE CAN'T BUY A HOUSE TIL NEXT YEAR.

THEN WE GOT IN A FIGHT.
$

YOUR GENERATION - GENERATION X 7-30-13

ANOTHER TOUGH-ASS WORK DAY.

CAME HOME AND DREW A BUNCH OF PORTRAITS. MY TOOTH IS PAID FOR!
NOW I JUST WISH THE DENTIST WOULD CALL.

THEN KAREN + I WATCHED STAR TREK.
WILL YOU PUT ON THE FERENGI MASK?
GROSS, NO.
STAR TREK

COP AN ATTITUDE - POISON IDEA 7-31-13

WORK IS JUST TOTALLY KICKING MY ASS THIS WEEK.

CAME HOME AND DID A QUICK WORKOUT.

THEN I DRANK SOME BEERS.
OOPS I WASN'T GONNA DRINK THIS WEEK.
GLUG GLUG

THE PRISONER- IRON MAIDEN

8-1-13

TODAY WAS ANOTHER LONG-ASS WORK DAY.

I CAME HOME AND WORKED OUT.
OOOF!

THEN I TOOK PEEBER FOR A WALK.

YOU HIT THE NAIL ON THE HEAD- PARLIAMENT

8-2-13

I WAS SO GLAD THE WEEK IS OVER.

WHEN I GOT HOME FROM WORK, I FOUND THE WATER IN OUR APARTMENT WAS OFF.
AWW MAN!

APPARENTLY, A MAIN LINE BROKE AND THEY DON'T KNOW WHEN IT'LL BE FIXED.
CRAP.
DEAR TENANT

THE BALLAD OF LON STOKES- ARRIVALS

8-3-13

TODAY I HAD TO GO TO THE LAUNDROMAT, SINCE WE HAVE NO WATER.
LAUNDRO TERIA

KAREN + I WENT OUT TO DINNER.

THEN WE DRANK BEER AND WATCHED MOVIES.
I'M GOING TO PEE.
DON'T FORGET TO NOT FLUSH!
DEADLY PREY

WATER- WILD AMERICA

8-4-13

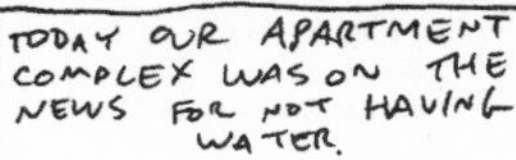
TODAY OUR APARTMENT COMPLEX WAS ON THE NEWS FOR NOT HAVING WATER.

COOL!
FOX 7
NW AUSTIN APARTMENTS WITHOUT WATER

KAREN + I WENT OVER TO BRANDON + CHELSEA'S TO TAKE SHOWERS.
THANKS FOR LETTING US GET NUDE IN YOUR HOUSE.
GROSS
UH, OKAY.

JUST BEFORE BEDTIME, THE WATER CAME BACK ON!

HALLELUJIA!

JAILBIRD - EXPLODING HEARTS

8-5-13

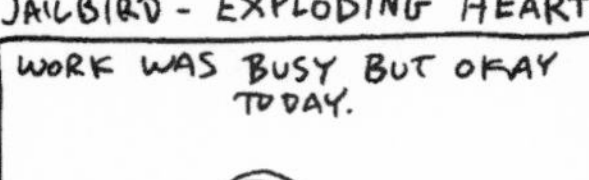
WORK WAS BUSY BUT OKAY TODAY.

I DID THE HARDEST WORKOUT EVER. I LET MYSELF SLIP OVER THE WATERLESS WEEKEND.
48... 49... 50!

NO DRINKING ALL WEEK EITHER!
TRUE TIL SATURDAY!

MR. SPEED- KISS

8-6-13

TODAY AT WORK, I LOST IT. I TOTALLY SCREAMED IN MY BOSS' FACE.

SURPRISINGLY, HE WAS COOL ABOUT IT. HE EVEN APOLOGIZED FOR BEING A DICK.
HUH?
YOU'RE RIGHT.

I CAME HOME AND WORKED OUT HARD.

PRECIOUS AND GRACE- ZZ TOP

8-7-13

ONLY WORKED A HALF-DAY TODAY.

I WENT TO THE DENTIST AND GOT MY NEW GOLD TOOTH.

THEN I WENT HOME AND WORKED THE FUCK OUT.

WOODPECKER FROM MARS- FAITH NO MORE

8-8-13

ANOTHER DINGDONG DAY AT WORK.

MY WORKOUTS HAVE BEEN MAKING ME SORE ALL WEEK. I LOVE IT.
COOL!

I FOUND SOMETHING ON EBAY THAT I REALLY WANT.
WOW!

DROOM KIT - JEFF THE BROTHERHOOD
8-9-13
TGIF AT WORK TODAY!
KAREN + I WENT OUT FOR BURGERS AND BEERS. AFTER A WEEK OF BEING SUPER-GOOD, ITS A GREAT REWARD!
AFTER DINNER WE MET UP WITH JAY + HIS FAMILY, VISITING AUSTIN AFTER THEY MOVED TO VA A FEW YEARS AGO.
JAY!
SARA!
OLIVE!
DREAD LION - LEE "SCRATCH" PERRY
8-10-13
IT'S SATURDAY! I DID LAUNDRY.
THEN I PLAYED MUSIC WITH BRANDON + SPENT. I'M STOKED ABOUT DOING A NEW BAND.
LATER I GOT MY GROWLER FILLED AND WATCHED MST3K.
HOBGOBLINS
FLAT EARTH SOCIETY - BAD RELIGION
8-11-13
KAREN + I DID OUR USUAL SUNDAY STUFF.. GROCERIES.
EER
BEER
BE
BEER
EER
BEER
WE WENT FOR A SWIM.
THEN WE BOUGHT A NEW TRASH CAN.
SORRY I BROKE THE OLD ONE.
WORKING - COCK SPARRER
8-12-13
WORK WAS AWESOME TODAY. MY SHITTY BOSS THAT I HATE IS ON VACATION.
I WON THE BASS I BID ON ON E BAY!!!
A 1981 ARIA PRO II CARDINAL CSB450! FUCK YES!
PEEBER GOT IN A FIGHT WITH A BIGGER DOG AT THE DOG PARK. HIS EYE GOT BLOODIED.

RESIST PSYCHIC DEATH - BIKINI KILL
8-13-13
ANOTHER FUN, EASY DAY AT WORK.
I HATE MY BOSS!
AFTER WORK I DID A BUNCH OF DRAWINGS
MY NEW BASS GETS HERE ON FRIDAY. I ORDERED SOME NEW STRINGS AND A STRAP FOR IT ON EBAY.
SO STOKED!
I REALLY GOT THE FEELING - DOLLY PARTON
8-14-13
WORK IS AWESOME WITH MY BOSS ON VACATION.
CAME HOME AND DID A WORKOUT.
THEN I ATE A CHEAPY PIZZA.
I'M BASICALLY UNDOING MY WORKOUT. OH WELL.
SHACATAC - DAVE BARKER
8-15-13
WORK WAS SUPER CHILL TODAY.
MY NEW WORKOUT REQUIRES THAT I "REST" ON TUESDAY AND THURSDAY. I DON'T LIKE IT.
I FEEL SO LAZY.
KAREN + I WENT AND SAW STARSHIP TROOPERS RIFFTRAX IN THE THEATER. IT WAS AWESOME!!
ELYSIUM - PORTISHEAD
8-16-13
I CALLED IN SICK TODAY.
ACTUALLY I TEXTED IN, BECAUSE THE FUTURE RULES!
MAINLY TO WAIT FOR THE UPS GUY.
UPS
HE BROUGHT ME MY NEW BASS!!!!

JOLENE - DOLLY PARTON

8-17-13

I SPENT ALL DAY PLAYING MY NEW BASS.
THE BRIDGE IS MUCH TIGHTER THAN MY EPIPHONE. IT'LL TAKE SOME GETTING USED TO AFTER PLAYING THE OTHER ONE FOR 15 YEARS.

I GOT OVERZEALOUS WITH MY WORKOUT TODAY AND HURT MY SHOULDER
OW!

KAREN TOOK ME OUT TO DINNER

RIVAL LEADERS - EXPLOITED

8-18-13

TODAY I WATCHED DAVID'S SURF BAND PLAY AT THE NEW H.E.B.

42¢

69¢

PRODUCE

I WAS SUPPOSED TO PLAY WITH BRANDON + SPENT, BUT BRANDON CRAPPED OUT.
DAMMIT, I WANNA PLAY MY NEW BASS LOUD!

I DIDN'T WORK OUT BECAUSE MY SHOULDER HURTS REAL BAD.
GRUMBLE GRUMBLE

SHAKE! - THE TIME

8-19-13

BACK AT WORK TODAY, I COULDN'T LIFT ANYTHING BECAUSE OF MY BUM SHOULDER.
COOL WITH ME!

I DID A STRICTLY-CARDIO WORKOUT ON THE BIKE.

PUT NEW STRINGS ON MY BASS.

THE DRIFTER - CORNELL CAMPBELL

8-20-13

ANOTHER DAY AT WORK.

I CAME HOME AND DID ANOTHER ALL-BIKE CARDIO WORKOUT.
I HOPE MY SHOULDER FEELS BETTER SOON.

THEN I WATCHED STAR TREK WITH KAREN.

ANOTHER DAY- THE MUFFS

8-21-13

WORK WAS NORMAL TODAY.

KAREN+I WENT OUT TO DINNER.

THEN WE GOT OUR GROWLER FILLED AND PLAYED DOMINOES.

DEATH'S DOOR-UNCLE ACID+THE DEADBEATS

8-22-13

ANOTHER DAY AT WORK.

MY SHOULDER IS FEELING BETTER, BUT I'M STILL WARY ABOUT LIFTING WEIGHTS

I PLAYED CANDY CRUSH ALL NIGHT.
SWEET!

WE AIN'T PLAYING - LIL WYTE

8-23-13

FRIDAY AT WORK IS NICE.

I CAME HOME AND FELT GOOD ENOUGH TO DO A FULL WORKOUT.
YEAH!

KAREN+I WERE SUPPOSED TO GO TO A PARTY, BUT WE GOT IN A FIGHT INSTEAD

SMOKING POPES- SEXY

8-24-13

TODAY I PLAYED MUSIC WITH SPENT+ BRANDON. SO STOKED TO PLAY MY NEW BASS LOUD!

I TOOK KAREN OUT FOR THAI FOOD SINCE I FELT BAD FOR BEING A DICK LAST NIGHT.

WE SAT ON THE PORCH AND DRANK BEER AND ATE PRETZELS. IT WAS AWESOME.

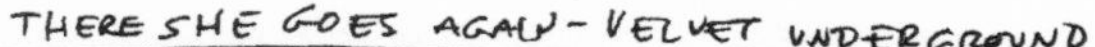
THERE SHE GOES AGAIN - VELVET UNDERGROUND

8-25-13

A VERY NORMAL SUNDAY. KAREN AND I WENT GROCERY SHOPPING.
I DID A HARD WORKOUT. IT'S NICE TO BE BACK!
THEN I PLAYED VIDEO GAMES.

DON'T TRY TO USE ME - HORACE ANDY

8-26-13

BACK AT WORK...

BACK TO WORKING OUT...

45... 46... 47...

I CHEATED AND DRANK A BEER.
I'M SO BAD.
SNAKEPIT 2013

SECOND GENERATION JUNKIES - CRIMPS*RINE

8-27-13

WORK WAS CHILL TODAY.

AFTERWARDS I WENT TO A SHOW AT TRAILER SPACE.

IT WAS SUPER FUN TO SEE A BUNCH OF FRIENDS I HAVEN'T SEEN IN A WHILE.

YOUR EMOTIONS - DEAD KENNEDYS

8-28-13

THIS MORNING PEEBER WAS REALLY REALLY SICK.
SPLOOCH
BLARF

I DROPPED HIM OFF AT THE VET BEFORE WORK.

HE'S GONNA BE OKAY, HE HAD AN INFECTION. IT WAS REALLY EXPENSIVE.

DAMMIT. I TOTALLY OVER-REACTED. HE'D PROBABLY HAD GOTTEN OVER IT ON HIS OWN.

FAINTED EYES - CELTIC FROST

8-29-13

I GAVE PEEBER HIS MEDICINE THIS MORNING.

WENT TO WORK.

CAME HOME AND DID LOTS AND LOTS OF DRAWING.
I GOTTA DO A LOT OF PORTRAITS TO PAY FOR THE VET BILL!

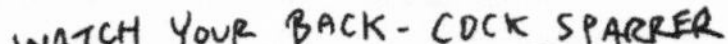
WATCH YOUR BACK - COCK SPARRER

8-30-13

FRIDAY AT WORK IS COOL

KAREN TOOK ME OUT TO DINNER.

THEN I STAYED UP LATE.

WILD CITY NIGHT - INEPSY

8-31-13

TODAY I DID SATURDAY STUFF: LAUNDRY AND SHIT.
SATUR-DAY STUFF

KAREN + I WENT TO A PARTY AT SPENT + WENDY'S HOUSE

I GOT REALLY SUPER-DRUNK!

9-1-13

FAT - VIOLENT FEMMES

I WAS HUNGOVER SO I TOOK IT EASY TODAY.
OW. MY HEAD.

KAREN + I WENT TO A WRESTLING MATCH. IT WAS SO FUN!
RAWR
RAWR!

I STAYED UP LATE AGAIN WATCHING STAR WARS

IN BLOOM - NIRVANA 9-2-13

TODAY I TOOK THE BUS TO THE COMIC BOOK STORE TO MEET GEORGE TAKEI!
CAPITAL METRO

I WAITED IN LINE FOR FOUR HOURS.
DR WHO
I GROK SPOCK

HE WAS REALLY NICE, BUT IN THE LONG RUN IT REALLY WASN'T WORTH THE TROUBLE.
I COULD'VE SPENT MY LABOR DAY DOING SOMETHING FUN.
OH, MY!

SCARBOROUGH FAIRE - SIMON + GARFUNKEL 9-3-13

BACK TO WORK WITH A VENGEANCE! I WAS THERE FOR TEN HOURS.

I CAME HOME AND STARTED A NEW AB WORKOUT.
OW!
CRUNCH CRUNCH

THEN I WAS A GOOD BOY AND DIDN'T DRINK ANY BEER.
SIGH. 25-YEAR-OLD ME WOULD BE SO BUMMED.
ALSO, 25-YEAR-OLD ME WEIGHED 20 POUNDS MORE THAN I DO

PURPLE HAZE - SNUFF 9-4-13

ANOTHER EXTRA-LONG DAY AT WORK. AT LEAST I'LL HAVE A GOOD PAYCHECK FOR KAREN'S BIRTHDAY.

DID MY WORKOUT. IT'S A TOUGH ONE!
OOF!

THEN I WATCHED A MOVIE WITH KAREN.
LIFE 2.0
THAT GAME LOOKS BORING.

BOYCHUCKER - RFTC 9-5-13

FINALLY A NORMAL-LENGTH WORK DAY.

I TOOK THE DOG FOR A NICE WALK

I WISH THE SUMMER WOULD HURRY UP AND END.
WHEW
TEMP

ATOM BOMB - NATION OF ULYSSES

9-6-13

TGIF + PAYDAY + I GOT TO LEAVE EARLY!
I GOT MY GROWLER FILLED UP AND BOUGHT SOME NEW PENS.
XXX
THEN I SAT ON THE PORCH WITH MY WIFE.

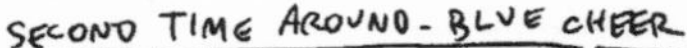

SECOND TIME AROUND - BLUE CHEER

9-7-13

TODAY I GOT A HAIRCUT.
THEN I DID A HARD WORKOUT. I'M DOWN TO 193!!!

KAREN + I WATCHED A MOVIE.
A MOVIE

PLASTER CASTER - KISS

9-8-13

SUPER LAZY SUNDAY. I WATCHED OLD EPISODES OF "IN SEARCH OF..." WITH KAREN.
UFOS BIGFOOT GHOSTS LOCH NESS MONSTER BERMUDA TRI-ANGLE CHUPA CABRA

AFTER THAT WE GOT GROCERIES.
REUSABLE BAGS

THEN WE WATCHED STAR TREK.

HARBOR RATS - NIGHT BIRDS

9-9-13

A CHILL MONDAY BACK AT THE SHIT FACTORY.

PEEBER AND I TOOK A WALK IN THE RAIN.

THEN I HUNG OUT WITH KAREN.

YOU SOUND LIKE YOU'RE SICK - RAMONES

9-10-13

WORK WAS SUPER CHILL TODAY.

KAREN + I WERE SUPPOSED TO GO TO THE OPENING OF HER FRIEND'S RESTAURANT, BUT THE LINE WAS CRAZY LONG.
NEW RESTAURANT

SO WE WENT TO BILLY'S INSTEAD

UNCLE CHARLEY - THE MELLOTUNES

9-11-13

I'M REALLY GETTING TO THE POINT WHERE I LIKE MY JOB.

KAREN + I WENT OUT FOR TACOS

THEN WE WENT TO RANDA'S GOING-AWAY PARTY. SHE'S MOVING TO CHICAGO.
BEN, THAT DOESN'T LOOK ANYTHING AT ALL LIKE RANDA.
DURP.

T.K.I.T. - SEXY

9-12-13

LAST NIGHT I HAD A REALLY GOOD IDEA IN A DREAM.
I'M GONNA MAKE A ZINE OF STORIES ABOUT MY TATTOOS!

I WENT TO WORK TODAY.

CAME HOME AND WATCHED STAR TREK WITH KAREN. ITS THE TIME OF THE MONTH WHERE WE WATCH AS MUCH STAR TREK AS WE CAN.
WINK

MAYBELLENE - CHUCK BERRY

9-13-13

OOOOH ITS FRIDAY THE 13TH! WORK WAS COOL.

I DRANK SOME BEER.

AND TOOK PEEBER FOR A WALK.

RAISANS - DINOSAUR JR. 9-14-13

SATURDAY! I GOT A TON OF WORK DONE.

KAREN + I WATCHED DR. STRANGELOVE. I CAN'T BELIEVE SHE'D NEVER SEEN IT!
WOO! HOO!

I GOT CAUGHT IN THE RAIN WALKING TO THE BEER STORE.

BRINGER OF DEATH - DANZIG 9-15-13

TODAY I GOT ALL OF MY NEW ZINE WRITTEN. OVER 10,000 WORDS!

ADDERALL HAZE

TAP TAP TAP

I ALSO TOOK PEEBER ON A LONG WALK.

THEN I WENT OVER TO MAX'S HOUSE AND WATCHED WRESTLING.

PARADE OF THE LIFELESS - ASSÜCK 9-16-13

IT'S MONDAY AND I'M BACK AT WORK.

I CAME HOME AND DID MY WORK OUT.

THEN I WORKED ON MY ZINE FOR A LONG TIME.

I KINDA MISS THE DAYS WHEN YOU HAD TO GO TO KINKO'S TO WORK ON A ZINE. BUT ONLY IN THEORY. IN REALITY ITS SO MUCH EASIER AND FASTER ON A COMPUTER.

CLICK CLICK

LIFE OF CRIME - THE SPITS 9-17-13

WENT TO WORK...

...DINNER WITH THE WIFE...

...DRANK A FANCY BEER WHILE WORKING ON MY ZINE. ALMOST DONE!
FAN C

WHAT WENT WRONG - METHADONES
9-18-13
WORK WAS CHILL TODAY.
I HURT MY SHOULDER AGAIN BY OVER-WORKING OUT.
OW!
AND I FINISHED MY ZINE!!
I WROTE IT ON ADDERALL AND THERE ARE TONS OF TYPOS!
SNAKEPIT TATTOO STORIES
BY HER OWN HAND - MUDHONEY
9-19-13
WORK GOT PRETTY BUSY. I WILL PROBABLY HAVE TO WORK THIS WEEKEND.
I CAME HOME AND DID A BIG MESS OF PORTRAITS.
I HAVE SO MUCH WORK TO CATCH UP ON!
MAKING THAT ZINE TOOK TOO LONG.
TO DO
MAKIN' LOVE - SASS DRAGONS
9-20-13
IT WAS CRAZY RAINY TODAY.
I TOOK KAREN OUT TO DINNER.
THEN WE WATCHED FUNNY VIDEOS ON YOUTUBE.
PITTSBURGH TO LEBANON - BUTTHOLE SURFERS
9-21-13
SATURDAY. I HAD TO GO IN TO WORK FOR A COUPLE HOURS.
THEN I PLAYED MUSIC WITH BRANDON + SPENT.
KAREN + I DRANK BEER AND ATE CHEESE.
FROMAGE

WE CARE A LOT - FAITH NO MORE
9-22-13
THIS MORNING I TOOK KAREN AND PEEBER ON A NATURE HIKE.
THEN WE RAN OUR NORMAL WEEKEND ERRANDS.
GROCERIES!
LAUNDRY!
POTATOS
THEN ANOTHER ONE OF MY TEETH BROKE OFF!
FUCK! I JUST FINISHED PAYING FOR THE LAST ONE!
MISSISSIPPI HEAVY WATER BLUES - ROBERT HICKS
9-23-13
THIS MORNING I WENT TO WORK.
I REALLY CAN'T AFFORD TO GET MY TOOTH FIXED. I JUST GOTTA WAIT, FOR NOW.
CAME HOME AND DID MY WORKOUT.
LATER KAREN + I HUNG OUT WITH JAMES AT BILLY'S.
UNITY - OPERATION IVY
9-24-13
WORK WAS BUSY BUT ENJOYABLE TODAY.
I GOT A LOT OF DRAWING DONE WHEN I GOT HOME.
KAREN HAD BAD NEWS.
I GOT MY PERIOD.
SIGH.
WIN OR LOSE - THE STRIKE
9-25-13
ANOTHER BUSY DAY AT WORK.
CAME HOME AND WORKED OUT.
DID A LOOOOOT OF DRAWING.
AAAH!

GOD'S PHONE NUMBER- THE BANANAS

9-26-13

LAST NIGHT I GOT GTA 5 FROM A REDBOX!
OH SHIT!
GTA 5

ALL DAY AT WORK ALL I COULD THINK ABOUT WAS PLAYING IT.

I'M GLAD I'VE ONLY GOT IT FOR A FEW DAYS.
OTHERWISE I'LL NEVER GET ANY WORK DONE.

GOT ME UNDER PRESSURE- ZZ TOP

9-27-13

A BUSY FRIDAY AT WORK.

KAREN + I WENT OUT FOR BURGERS.

THEN I DRANK OATMEAL STOUT AND PLAYED GTA 5.
BLAM BLAM

NO COSTUME, NO CANDY- SWINGIN' NECKBREAKERS

9-28-13

SPENT MY SATURDAY PLAYING GTA 5 BEFORE I HAD TO RETURN IT.

I TOOK KAREN OUT TO A FANCY FRENCH REST-AURANT FOR HER BIRTHDAY.

WE CAME HOME AND WATCHED BEHIND THE CANDELABRA.

LIVING IN THE URBAN UK- CHELSEA

9-29-13

HAD A NICE, LAZY, HUNGOVER MORNING.
ZZZ

TOOK PEEBER ON A LONG WALK.
SNORT SNORT

ATE PIZZA WITH MY WIFE.
PIZZA!

DOWNPRESSOR MAN- THE STRIKE

9-30-13

WORK SUCKED TODAY. I WAS THERE FOR 10 HOURS.

I WAS TOO TIRED TO WORK OUT.

I HAD CRAZY DREAMS.
zzz

BURN DOWN THE FOREST- CRINGER

10-1-13

TODAY KAREN FOUND OUT THAT HER SISTER IS PREGNANT.

I'M HAPPY FOR HER, BUT I'M SO FRUSTRATED THAT WE CAN'T SEEM TO GET PREGNANT.

I'M KINDA STOKED ON THE IDEA OF BEING AN UNCLE.

UNCLE BEN.
"Perfect every time"

BACKLASH- MARKED MEN

10-2-13

ANOTHER LONG DAY AT WORK.
THIS IS THE BUSIEST OUR COMPANY HAS BEEN SINCE THE 1980'S.

I DID A NICE LONG WORKOUT

THEN WATCHED A MOVIE WITH KAREN.
ROOM 237

GARBAGE IN GARBAGE OUT- SEWER TROUT

10-3-13

WORK HAS JUST BEEN SO FUCKING BRUTAL THIS WEEK.

KAREN+I WENT OUT TO OUR FAVORITE TEX-MEX JOINT.

THEN WE TOOK PEEBER ON A SUPER-LONG WALK.

TAKE ACTION – THE STRIKE

10-4-13

FOR THE MONTH OF OCTOBER, I'M DOING A SPLIT COMIC WITH MITCH.

HE'S A WAY BETTER ARTIST THAN ME, SO I FIGURED I REALLY NEED TO BRING MY A-GAME THIS MONTH.

TODAY HE SENT ME A MESSAGE.
OH SHIT I FORGOT WE'RE DOING THIS SPLIT!
HAHA
FACEBOOK

I DRINK BLOOD – ROCKET FROM THE CRYPT

10-5-13

I DID A SHITLOAD OF DRAWING TODAY.

I ALSO MANAGED TO DO A GOOD WORKOUT,

ONLY TO UNDO IT BY EATING FRIED CHICKEN FOR DINNER.
I'M A BIG FAT GREASY CHICKEN PIG!

GOO GOO ITCH – DEVO

10-6-13

TODAY I BOUGHT NEW PANTS SIZE 34. I HAVEN'T BEEN ABLE TO FIT IN SIZE 34 SINCE I WAS A TEENAGER!
HOLY SHIT!

I GOT ALL MY NEW ZINES STAPLED AND FOLDED, READY FOR HOUSTON.

THEN I WATCHED STAR TREK WITH KAREN.

PRE-PAST TENSE – MONSULA

10-7-13

IT'S DUMBASS MONDAY AND I AM BACK AT WORK.

I WENT TO GHOST KNIFE PRACTICE FOR THE FIRST TIME IN MONTHS.
MY FIRST TIME GETTING TO PLAY MY NEW BASS!

THEN I WAS A GOOD BOY AND DIDN'T DRINK ANY BEER.
MEH.

EYES OF WAR- NO HOPE FOR THE KIDS

10-8-13

I HAD TO WORK TEN HOURS TODAY.

I WAS TIRED BUT STILL MANAGED TO DO A WORK OUT.

KAREN WENT OUT WITH HER FRIENDS SO I DRANK BEER ALONE.

IT'S YOU- SNUFF

10-9-13

ANOTHER LONG, SHITTY DAY AT WORK.

CAME HOME AND LIFTED WEIGHTS.
BRO, DO YOU EVEN LIFT?

THEN I UNDID MY WORK-OUT BY EATING CHICKEN WINGS AND DRINKING BEER.
I HAVE TONS OF WILLPOWER WHEN IT COMES TO EXERCISE, BUT NONE FOR DIETING.

NO FAIR- WIPERS

10-10-13

WORK WAS LONG AND TOUGH TODAY.

KAREN TOOK ME OUT TO DINNER.

THEN WE SPENT SOME QUALITY TIME WATCHING STAR TREK.

SHOOT THE SHIT- BELTONES

10-11-13

FRIDAY AT WORK, MY BOSS ASKED ME TO WORK THE WEEKEND.
SORRY, I'M GOING OUT OF TOWN.

I CAME HOME AND GOT PACKED + READY FOR HOUSTON.
T-SHIRTS
ZINES
BOOKS

ON THE WAY HOME FROM WORK, MY CAR'S ODOMETER HIT 100,000 MILES.
I'M A GROWN-UP NOW!

CHICKEN WALK - HASIL ADKINS

10-12-13

TODAY I WENT TO THE ZINE FEST IN HOUSTON. I SHARED A TABLE WITH MITCH.

AFTERWARDS, WE WENT TO GET PIZZA AND MY KNEE SNAPPED AND GAVE OUT!!!
OW!
POP!

I LIMPED BACK TO MY CAR AND DROVE HOME TO AUSTIN IN TORRENTIAL RAIN AT 2:00 AM.

LAST DAYS OF MAN ON EARTH - THE URINALS

10-13-13

THIS MORNING I TRIED TO LOOK ON THE INTERNET TO ASSESS THE DAMAGE TO MY KNEE.
THE INTERNET ROUTER IS BROKEN!
KAREN'S LAPTOP

I WENT TO MY COMPUTER TO OPEN THE REPAIR TOOL
MY COMPUTER GOT A VIRUS!
MY LAPTOP

KAREN GOT ME SOME CRUTCHES AT GOODWILL AND WE WENT TO SEE WRESTLING.

DREAMING OUT LOUD - TENEMENT

10-14-13

I HOBBLED IN TO WORK ON MY CRUTCHES TODAY, AND THE COMPANY VAN WOULDN'T START!
I'M GLAD. MY LEG HURTS TOO MUCH TO DRIVE
PUTT PUTT PUTT

THEN MY WORK COMPUTER FUCKING CRASHED AND DIED!
DID SOMEBODY PUT A CURSE ON ME?

I JUST LAYED ON THE COUCH FOR THE REST OF THE NIGHT.
WHOA! IS ME

SURFIN' BIRD - RAMONES

10-15-13

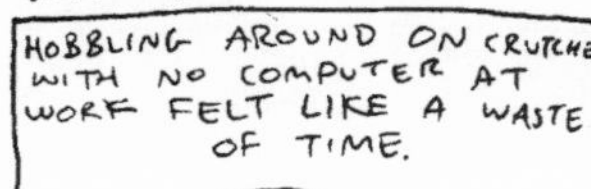

HOBBLING AROUND ON CRUTCHES WITH NO COMPUTER AT WORK FELT LIKE A WASTE OF TIME.
SIGH.

I THINK MY KNEE INJURY WAS JUST A SPRAIN. IT'S ALREADY STARTING TO FEEL BETTER.
I REALLY HOPE I CAN GET BACK TO WORKING OUT SOON.
STANDING UP

I EVEN WENT DOWN THE STAIRS AND BACK UP WITH NO CRUTCHES!
MEIN FUHRER! I CAN WALK!

SCREAM - BLITZ

10-16-13

I TOOK THE DAY OFF WORK SINCE I HAD NO COMPUTER AND NO LEGS.
NOT COMING IN

I SPENT THE DAY WATCHING NETFLIX WITH PEEBER.

THEN I HUNG OUT WITH KAREN WHILE SHE GOT READY FOR HER TRIP.
IM GONNA MISS YOU.
ME TOO

REAL WILD CHILD - IVAN

10-17-13

I DROPPED KAREN OFF AT THE AIRPORT THIS MORNING.

TO TERMINAL ←

BYE

SEE YOU ON MONDAY!

I HAD TO WORK LATE AND KINDA WORRIED ABOUT PEEBER.
HE HASNT BEEN OUT SINCE 5 AM!

WALKING A SUPER-HYPER DOG THAT HAS TOO PEE DOWN THE STAIRS WHILE ON CRUTCHES IS SERIOUSLY THE HARDEST THING TO DO.

WHOA DUDE!

KISS ME HARDER - SHELLSHAG

10-18-13

WENT TO WORK THIS MORNING, IT WAS PAYDAY!

YOU GOTTA WORK TOMORROW!

I CELEBRATED BY BUYING A VIDEO GAME...
GTA 5

...SINCE I GOTTA STAY OFF MY FEET FOR A WHILE.

CITALIVENDED - CARRIE NATIONS

10-19-13

I WENT IN TO WORK TODAY (SATURDAY) BUT I BROUGHT PEEBER WITH ME.

I STOPPED AT THE STORE ON THE WAY HOME AND GOT SOME BEER.
I HOPE THIS IS ENOUGH BEER

APPARENTLY, IT WAS TOO MUCH BEER.

CHINESE FOOD - ALISON GOLD
10-20-13
WOKE UP IN MY CLOTHES WITH THE LIGHTS ON.
WHOA! WHA...
SPENT THE DAY GETTING MELLOW ON THE COUCH.
AND ORDERED SOME CHINESE FOOD.
GROWING - JEFF THE BROTHERHOOD
10-21-13
BACK AT WORK THIS MORNING, I'M DOWN TO ONLY 1 CRUTCH.
I PICKED UP KAREN FROM THE AIRPORT.
AUSTIN BERGSTROM
WE WENT TO BILLYS. BILLY MADE US GET UP AND MOVE BECAUSE WE WERE SITTING AT HIS TABLE.
BOULEVARD TRASH - EXPLODING HEARTS
10-22-13
I REALIZED THE LAST TIME I HURT MY KNEE WAS OCTOBER 2005, EIGHT YEARS AGO.
FIVE YEARS AGO...
I LOOKED, AND BY THIS TIME AFTER THE 2005 ACCIDENT, I WAS TOTALLY NORMAL AGAIN.
I STILL CAN'T STRAIGHTEN MY LEG OUT.
I REALLY CAN'T AFFORD TO GO TO THE DOCTOR, I HOPE IT HEALS ON ITS OWN.
FUCK THIS SUCKS
PRECIOUS ROSE - EDDY CURRENT SUPRESSION RING
10-23-13
WENT TO WORK TODAY. I THINK I WAS OVER-REACTING ABOUT MY KNEE.
IT'S STILL HEALING.
I PLAYED GTA 5 FOR A LONG TIME.
I ALSO WENT TO THE GROCERY STORE FOR KAREN.
CHIPS
CHIPS
CHIPS
CHIPS
CHIPS
CHIPS
CHIPS
CHIPS

SURPRISE! YOU'RE DEAD- FAITH NO MORE

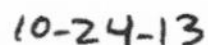
10-24-13

ANOTHER LIMPY DAY AT WORK.

CAME HOME AND TRIED TO FIX MY BUSTED COMPUTER, TO NO AVAIL.
BLEAH!

THEN I HAD A LONG HEART-TO-HEART WITH KAREN.
I'M SORRY YOU'RE HAVING TO DO SO MUCH EXTRA WORK BECAUSE OF MY KNEE. I FEEL LIKE SUCH A BURDEN.
ITS OKAY.

BLUE HIT- SCARED OF CHAKA

10-25-13

I WAS SO GRUMPY AT WORK TODAY.
I'M SICK OF NOT BEING ABLE TO WALK!

I DRANK SOME STRONG BEERS WITH KAREN, IT MADE ME FEEL BETTER.
"THE YETI" FROM GREAT DIVIDE.
YETI

I DECIDED TO GET A NEW COMPUTER

NO PARTY FOR YOU- HOLY MOUNTAIN

10-26-13

I STARTED DOING SOME WORKOUTS THAT DONT TAX MY KNEE. I'M STARTING TO GET FAT AGAIN!!
NEVER AGAIN!

I ALSO MADE AN EFFORT TO REALLY STAY OFF MY BAD KNEE TODAY. IT STILL NEEDS TO HEAL.
IT CAN TAKE UP TO SIX WEEKS!

SO I SPENT MOST OF THE DAY ON MY ASS PLAYING VIDEO GAMES.

ALL THIS AND MORE- DEAD BOYS

10-27-13

I'M STARTING TO GET TO THE POINT WHERE I CAN SORTA WALK.

TODAY I DID SOME DRAWING AND WATCHED TV. IT WAS PRETTY BORING.
THE THORIUM DREAM

I WENT TO BED EARLY JUST BECAUSE I WAS SO BORED.
THIS SUCKS

MINDLESS FEW - CHRON GEN
10-28-13
TODAY I WORKED WITH NO CRUTCHES OR BRACES AT ALL!
I'M ALMOST HUMAN!
WHEN I GOT HOME I CLEANED THE BATHROOM.
BLEAH!
GROSS
KAREN'S BEEN IN A BAD MOOD LATELY.
ADDICTED - THE SCUDS
10-29-13
WORK WAS OKAY TODAY.
I DID A LITTLE NO-LEG WORKOUT.
KAREN BOUGHT ME SOME FANCY BEER TO MAKE UP FOR LAST NIGHT.
AWW THANK YOU SWEETIE!
SMOOCH
SANCTUARY - CRIMPSHRINE
10-30-13
TODAY I HAD TO DELIVER BOXES IN THE RAIN FOR WORK.
ITS BEEN CRAZY RAINING AND FLOODING IN AUSTIN THE LAST COUPLE OF DAYS.
EMERGENCY!
FLOOD WARNING
I THINK THE RAIN IS NICE.
HALLOWEEN - MISFITS
10-31-13
WORK WAS MUCH MORE CHILL TODAY.
KATE + ZAC CAME OVER FOR DINNER, THEY'RE IN TOWN FOR THE WEEK END.
WE HUNG OUT AND WATCHED HORROR MOVIES.
TRICK OR TREAT

BÖRJE - KLAMYDIA
11-1-13
SUPER EASY DAY AT WORK, ALL MY BOSSES ARE ON VACATION.
WENT OUT TO DINNER WITH KATE AND ZAC.
THEN WE CAME BACK TO THE APARTMENT AND DRANK SOME BEERS.
KATE DIDNT DRINK BECAUSE SHE'S PREGNANT.
THE CLAW - MOTORHEAD
11-2-13
MY NEW COMPUTER GOT HERE TODAY!
RAD!
NEW P.C.
I SPENT THE DAY SETTING EVERYTHING UP ON IT.
NOW INSTALLING
LATER I ATE SUSHI WITH KAREN.
CITY OF MUD - DEAD MILKMEN
11-3-13
TODAY I FOUND OUT THAT GHOST KNIFE IS GOING TO OPEN FOR THE DEAD MILKMEN IN DECEMBER.
NO WAY!
I HONESTLY DON'T THINK I'VE EVER BEEN EXCITED ABOUT ANYTHING IN YEARS, IF EVER!
BIG LIZARD IN MY BACK YARD
HOLY FUCKING SHIT.
SERIOUSLY, I CAN QUIT PLAYING MUSIC AFTER THIS. THERE'S NOTHING LEFT TO ACHIEVE.
SWAMPLAND OF DESIRE - DEAD MILKMEN
11-4-13
BACK AT WORK. THE BOSS IS STILL ON VACATION SO IT'S CHILL.
CAME HOME AND DID MY NEW MODIFIED KNEE-FRIENDLY WORKOUT.
KAREN + I BUILT A FIRE IN THE FIREPLACE.

VINCE LOMBARDI SERVICE CENTER - DEAD MILKMEN 11-5-13

WORK WASN'T TOO BAD TODAY.

I PICKED KAREN UP FROM WORK AND WE WENT TO VOTE.

IF THE AFFORDABLE HOUSING BOND PASSES, IT MIGHT BE EASIER FOR US TO BUY A HOUSE NEXT YEAR!

THEN WE DRANK SOME BEERS AND WATCHED STAR TREK.
IF THIS SHUTTLECRAFT'S A-ROCKIN, DON'T COME A-KNOCKIN!

VFW - DEAD MILKMEN 11-6-13

WORK WAS SO SLOW AND BORING IT KINDA SUCKED.

AFTERWARD I WENT TO GHOST KNIFE PRACTICE.

I ♡ MY NEW BASS

I WAS SUPPOSED TO MEET UP WITH MITCH AT TRAILER SPACE BUT I PEEPAW'ED OUT.

I SHOULD SEND HIM A TEXT. WAIT, WHAT'S A TEXT? WAIT WHERE AM I?

STUART - DEAD MILKMEN 11-7-13

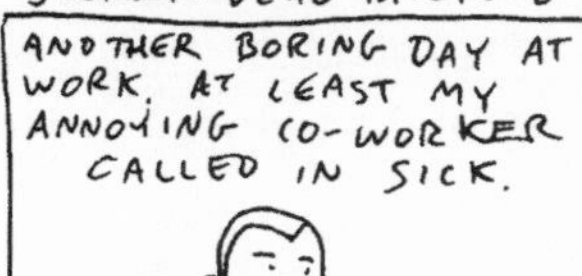
ANOTHER BORING DAY AT WORK. AT LEAST MY ANNOYING CO-WORKER CALLED IN SICK.

I CAME HOME AND DREW A FEW PORTRAITS. MY REQUESTS HAVE REALLY SLOWED DOWN

I WISH I HAD A STEADY INFLUX OF THEM. I COULD ALMOST QUIT MY JOB IF I DID.

MORE *STAR TREK* WITH KAREN.

I GROK SPOCK

SERRATED EDGE - DEAD MILKMEN 11-8-13

WORK WAS SLOW AGAIN SO I LEFT EARLY.

I CAME HOME AND STARTED PLAYING CIV 5 ON MY SUPER-FAST NEW COMPUTER.

THIS WENT LONG INTO THE NIGHT.
ARE YOU COMING TO BED?
AS SOON AS I CONQUER BABYLON.

KKSUCK2 - DEAD MILKMEN

11-9-13

THIS MORNING I DID LAUNDRY AND BOUGHT A BIRTHDAY CARD FOR MY MOM.
THIS ONE LOOKS GOOD.
MOM

I FINALLY FELT HEALED ENOUGH TO DO A REAL WORKOUT ON MY BIKE.

KAREN CAME HOME AND WE ATE NACHOS.
NACHOOOOOOOOS!

JELLYFISH HEAVEN - DEAD MILKMEN

11-10-13

IN THE PAST FEW MONTHS, KAREN + I HAVE BEGUN A TRADITION OF GETTING FANCY BEER ON SUNDAYS.
OR "CRAFT BEER" AS THE FANCY PEOPLE CALL IT.
FLAG STORE

THE ONE WE GOT TODAY WAS 12% ABV.
DOGFISH HEAD
PALO SANTO MARRON

KAREN COULDN'T HANG.
OUT LIKE A LIGHT BY 7PM
ZZZ

THE PIT - DEAD MILKMEN

11-11-13

WORK WAS SO SLOW TODAY THAT I ONLY WORKED FOUR HOURS.

I CAME HOME AND TOOK PEEBER ON A LONG WALK.

THEN I ATE A PIZZA WITH KAREN.

BLOOD ORGY OF THE ATOMIC FERN - DEAD MILKMEN.

ELEVEN TWELVE THIRTEEN!

THIS MORNING I CALLED MY MOM AND WISHED HER A HAPPY 66TH BIRTHDAY!
DID YOU KNOW YOU HAVE THE SAME BIRTHDAY AS CHARLES MANSON?
YES.

AFTER WORK I PLAYED VIDEO GAMES.

THEN I WATCHED A MOVIE WITH KAREN.
MOVIE

FIFTY THINGS- DEAD MILKMEN

11-13-13

WORK HAS BEEN SO SLOW LATELY, IT KINDA SUCKS.
ZZZ

WORKED OUT WHEN I GOT HOME. I'VE BEEN REALLY DISCOURAGED SINCE I HURT MY KNEE
SIGH
SCALE REMAINS UNCHANGED

I DIDN'T REALLY DO ANYTHING AFTER THAT.

TVGENA - DEAD MILKMEN

11-14-13

ANOTHER GOD DAMNED DAY AT WORK.

I DID ANOTHER WORKOUT, BUT I THINK I MIGHT BE GOING TOO HARD ON MY KNEE.
OW!

LATER I DID SOME DRAWING.

SPIT SINK - DEAD MILKMEN

11-15-13

WORK WAS COOL TODAY, MY CO WORKER WAS GONE SO I HAD THE OFFICE TO MYSELF.
DEVIL MUSIC

I ATE CHINESE FOOD WITH KAREN.

THEN WE HUNG OUT AND WATCHED FUNNY VIDEOS ON THE COMPUTER ALL NIGHT.
HA HA!
POOT

TINY TOWN - DEAD MILKMEN

11-16-13

TODAY WAS SUPER PRODUCTIVE. I DID LAUNDRY AND PUT A NEW TURN SIGNAL BULB IN MY VAN.

THEN I RESTOCKED BOOKS ALL OVER TOWN, GOT A HAIRCUT AND GOT MY GROWLER FILLED.
XXX

TOOK KAREN OUT TO DINNER AND DREW A BUNCH OF PORTRAITS.

BRAT IN THE FRAT - DEAD MILKMEN

11-17-13

TODAY I GOT GROCERIES WITH KAREN.

THEN I DOWNLOADED A SUPER-NERDY VIDEO GAME.
GALACTIC CIVILIZATIO
II

THEN KAREN & I WATCHED THE RIFFTRAXED STAR WARS HOLIDAY SPECIAL.
WHEW, NOT EVEN RIFFTRAX CAN SAVE THIS STINK-BOMB!

TACOLAND - DEAD MILKMEN

11-18-13

WORK WAS EXTRA-CHILL TODAY.

WHEN I GOT HOME, KAREN WAS BAKING A CAKE.

I DRANK TOO MUCH WINE.

PUNK ROCK GIRL - DEAD MILKMEN

11-19-13

WORK HAS BEEN BRUTALLY SLOW ALL MONTH. I KEEP GOING HOME EARLY BECAUSE THERE'S NOTHING TO DO.
MY CHECK IS GONNA SUCK.

I CAME HOME AND DID A WORKOUT.
GAH!

I CAN'T DECIDE WHETHER TO SELL MY TATTOO ZINE ONLINE OR NOT. I'M NOT HAPPY WITH IT.
DO I WANT TO SELL AN INFERIOR PRODUCT? WHY DO I CARE SO MUCH?
SNAKE PIT TATTOO TORIES

HEARD IT THRU THE GRAPEVINE - DEAD MILKMEN

11-20-13

ANOTHER DRAG-ASS DAY AT WORK.

KAREN GOT A PIZZA AND I GOT SOME BEER.
PIZZA
12 PAK

THEN KAREN GOT TOO DRUNK AND WE GOT IN AN ARGUEMENT OVER A STAR TREK EPISODE.
"CHIMERA" IS SUPPOSED TO BE A METAPHOR FOR ODO EXPERIMENTING WITH HOMOSEXUALITY.
NO IT ISN'T!

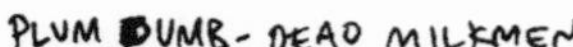
PLUM DUMB - DEAD MILKMEN

WORK WAS STILL SLOW TODAY.

KAREN TOOK ME OUT TO DINNER.

11-21-13
THEN I PLAYED VIDEO GAMES.

I TRIPPED OVER THE OTTOMAN - DEAD MILKMEN

11-22-13

AT THE END OF THE DAY TODAY MY BOSS GAVE ME A THANKSGIVING TURKEY!
WOW! THANKS!
BUTTER BALL

IT WAS SUPER COLD AND SHITTY OUT, SO KAREN AND I BUILT A FIRE.

WE HAD A NICE COZY NIGHT IN.

MEANINGLESS UPBEAT HAPPY SONG - DEAD MILKMEN

11-23-13

KAREN HAD SATURDAY OFF INSTEAD OF SUNDAY THIS WEEK SO WE DID OUR SUNDAY ERRANDS
H·E·B

KAREN MADE A BIG POT OF CHILI AND WE BUILT ANOTHER FIRE.

THEN WE WATCHED A FOUR-EPISODE MINI-MARATHON OF STAR TREK.
TAKE THAT HOWEVER YOU LIKE. HA HA.

THE THING THAT ONLY EATS HIPPIES - DEAD MILKMEN

11-24-13

THIS MORNING AS SHE WAS LEAVING FOR WORK, KAREN SUPER-GUILT TRIPPED ME.
HAVE FUN PLAYING YOUR VIDEO GAME ALL DAY.

SO INSTEAD OF PLAYING IT, I CLEANED THE APARTMENT.
RRRRRR

SHE KNOWS ME TOO WELL.
WOW THE APARTMENT LOOKS SO NICE! WHAT A NICE SURPRISE!
UH HUH.

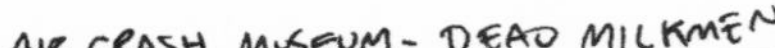
AIR CRASH MUSEUM - DEAD MILKMEN

11-25-13

BACK AT WORK TODAY, ITS GONNA BE A SHORT WEEK.

I CAME HOME AND DID A WORKOUT.
GUH!

AND BOUGHT CHRISTMAS PRESENTS FOR MY FAMILY ON EBAY.

SMOKIN' BANANA PEELS - DEAD MILKMEN

11-26-13

WORK WAS TEDIOUS.

AFTERWARDS I HAD GHOST KNIFE PRACTICE.

THEN I RAN SOME SANTA-CLAUS ERRANDS.

RASTABILLY - DEAD MILKMEN

11-27-13

TODAY WAS LIKE THE SLACKERIEST DAY AT WORK.

EVERYONE LEFT EARLY.
FIVE-DAY WEEKEND STARTS NOW!
WORK

I STAYED UP LATE PLAYING VIDEO GAMES.

DEPRESSION DAY DINNER - DEAD MILKMEN

11-28-13

TODAY IS THANKSGIVING. I WATCHED THE PARADE WHILE KAREN COOKED.

WE ATE A HUGE, FANTASTIC MEAL.

THEN WE PUT UP OUR CHRISTMAS TREE.

I HATE MYSELF- DEAD MILKMEN

11-29-13

KAREN MADE THIS INSANE PIE YESTERDAY, ITS THE BEST THING I'VE EVER EATEN IN MY LIFE...
OOOH.

I DID AN EXTRA-LONG WORKOUT TODAY BUT THAT GODDAMNED PIE IS JUST LOOKING AT ME.

I HATE THIS FUCKING AWESOME DELICIOUS PIE.

BLEACH BOYS - DEAD MILKMEN

11-30-13

DAY THREE OF MY 5-DAY WEEKEND.

I GOT A LOT OF DRAWING DONE.

OUT

IN

BUT I ALSO SPENT THE DAY WORKING OUT AND EATING PIE.

ONE STEP FORWARD, THREE STEPS BACK.

UR FAT

BEACH SONG - DEAD MILKMEN

12-1-13

THIS MORNING I DREW SOME PORTRAITS.

THEN KAREN+I WENT TO ALISON+BRYAN'S PARTY.

I GOT WAYWAY WAY TOO DRUNK!

I WALK THE THINNEST LINE- DEAD MILKMEN

12-2-13

DESPITE THE DAY'S HANGOVER, I GOT SOME STUFF DONE TODAY...

PICKED UP MY CHECK+TOOK IT TO THE BANK, GOT SOME GROCERIES AND PAID RENT.
HERE, WILL YOU THROW THIS AWAY FOR ME?
BOSS
PAYCHECK

THEN I DREW TONS AND TONS OF PORTRAIT$!
COWABUNGA!

SRI LANKA SEX HOTEL - DEAD MILKMEN
12-3-13
BACK AT WORK AFTER FIVE DAYS OFF WASN'T AS HARD AS I WAS EXPECTING.
AFTERWARD I WENT TO GHOST KNIFE PRACTICE.
SO STOKED ABOUT THE SHOWS WE HAVE COMMING UP!
MY KNEE HAS BEEN KINDA HURTING AGAIN LATELY. I HOPE ITS JUST THE COLD WEATHER.
OW!
INSTANT CLUB HIT (YOU'LL DANCE TO ANYTHING) - DEAD MILKMEN
12-4-13
WORK WAS COOL TODAY.
I CAME HOME AND DID A WORK OUT.
THEN I WATCHED NETFLIX WITH KAREN.
A MOVIE OR A DOCUMENTARY OR SOME SHIT.
NUTRITION - DEAD MILKMEN
12-5-13
I ACTUALLY ENJOYED WORK TODAY.
ON THE WAY TO BAND PRACTICE I SAW A SEMI TRUCK THAT HAD DRIVEN INTO A BUILDING!
WHOA!
IT WAS COLD TONIGHT SO KAREN + I BUILT A SNUGGLEFIRE.
MORON - DEAD MILKMEN
12-6-13
RUSHED THROUGH WORK AND LEFT EARLY TODAY.
IT'S DEAD MILKMEN DAY!
THE DRIVE UP TO DALLAS DURING AN ICE STORM WAS KINDA SCARY.
WOW BEN, YOU CAN'T DRAW!
BUT WE MADE IT RIGHT IN TIME AND OPENED FOR THE DEAD MILKMEN
JOE!
DEAN!
RODNEY!
NOT DAVE BLOOD

BITCHIN' CAMARO- DEAD MILKMEN
12-7-13
IT WAS AN ICY DRIVE BACK TO AUSTIN THIS MORNING.
I SPENT MY DAY LAZILY.
AFTER THAT I WENT AND PLAYED WITH THE DEAD MILKMEN AGAIN!!
THIS IS ONE OF THE GREATEST HONORS OF MY LIFE! I WOULD'VE NEVER PICKED UP A BASS IF IT WASN'T FOR DAVE BLOOD!
SOME HEADS ARE GONNA ROLL- JUDAS PRIEST
12-8-13
TWO NIGHTS OF BACK-TO-BACK PARTYING DID ME IN.
I CAN'T BELIEVE I USED TO LIVE LIKE THIS!
I LAYED ON THE COUCH RECUPERATING FOR MOST OF THE DAY...
I FEEL AWFUL.
ACTUALLY, I LAYED ON THE COUCH RECUPERATING FOR THE ENTIRE DAY.
PROGNOSIS NEGATIVE- NIGHT BIRDS
12-9-13
BACK AT WORK TODAY, IT WAS CHILL.
WHEN I GOT HOME, MY SNAKEPIT BOOK 10th ANNIVERSARY REPRINTS WERE WAITING FOR ME!
RAD!
SNAKEPIT
SNAKEPIT
SNAKEPIT
WOW, THEY LOOK SO NICE!
THE SNAKE PIT BOOK
I'M BRANDED- LINK WRAY
12-10-13
WORK WASN'T BAD, SINCE ITS ALREADY "HUMP DAY".
CAME HOME AND DID A HARD WORKOUT.
WATCHED A MOVIE AND TOOK IT EASY
STAR TREK IV THE VOYAGE HOME

TWIN CITIES BRIDGE IS FALLING DOWN - BIRTHDAY SUITS
12-11-13
RUSHED THROUGH WORK TODAY.
FOUR-DAY WEEKEND STARTS... NOW!
GHOST KNIFE PLAYED A SHOW AT RED 7
WITH DILLINGER FOUR!
I IDOLIZE YOU - WAILERS
12-12-13
OW. HANGOVER. OW. OW.
OW
I LITERALLY LAYED AROUND THE HOUSE ALL DAY DOING NOTHING.
OW
ABSOLUTELY NOTHING.
WHAT THE HELL IS WRONG WITH ME?
PROBLEM - GRIMPLE
12-13-13
TODAY WAS PAYDAY AND I GOT A BUNCH OF ERRANDS DONE.
POST OFFICE
GHOST KNIFE PLAYED A SHOW AT TRAILER SPACE, BRINGING OUR LITTLE RUN OF SHOWS TO A CLOSE.
I HAD A REALLY GOOD TIME.
ANODIZER - FU MANCHU
12-14-13
MY BODY HATES ME. AND IT HAS EVERY REASON TO.
HOW ABOUT I SPEND AN ENTIRE YEAR EATING RIGHT AND EXERCISING, THEN THE LAST MONTH OF THE YEAR I TAKE NO CARE OF MYSELF AND GET SUPER WASTED LIKE FOUR TIMES IN A WEEK?
I'M TEN POUNDS BACK UP.
DAMMIT! I'LL GET BACK ON THIS HORSE.
I MEAN, AFTER THE HOLIDAYS ARE OVER.
COOKIES
BEER
NUTS

WHAT YOU WANT - RADIOACTIVITY
12-15-13
DID SUNDAY STUFF WITH KAREN.
GROCERIES
LAUNDRY
DREW A FEW PORTRAITS..
I WISH I DIDN'T HAVE TO GO BACK TO WORK TOMORROW.
HAVING FOUR DAYS OFF MADE IT WORSE.
ME + THE BOYS - HARD SKIN
12-16-13
BACK AT WORK, IT WASN'T TOO BAD.
I CAME HOME AND WORKED OUT...
URGH!
WHICH I IMMEDIATELY UNDID BECAUSE KAREN MADE XMAS COOKIES!
URGH!
ALL RIGHT WITH THE BOYS - JOAN JETT
12-17-13
WORK WAS FINE TODAY, CONSIDERING ITS ALREADY "HUMP DAY"
IN CASE YOU'RE WONDERING, I HAD TO USE UP A BUNCH OF VACATION DAYS BEFORE THE END OF THE YEAR.
KAREN MADE TACOS FOR DINNER.
WE DRANK BEERS AND WATCHED A MOVIE TOGETHER
GREMLINS 2
SOMEBODY'S WATCHING ME - ROCKWELL
12-18-13
TGIW!
I DID A SOLID WORKOUT THIS AFTERNOON.
23...
24...
25...
I STAYED UP LATE. I WATCHED "THE EMPIRE STRIKES BACK" WHILE WEARING NOISE-CANCELING HEADPHONES.
IT'S LIKE A COMPLETE OTHER MOVIE!

CRY MIAMI - DRUG CZARS

12-19-13

TODAY BEGINS MY SECOND 4-DAY-WEEKEND IN A ROW.
IT'S GONNA SUCK IN JANUARY WHEN I HAVE TO GO BACK TO WORKING NORMAL HOURS
DECEMBER

I TOOK PEEBER ON A LONG WALK

AND HAD A NICE TIME WITH KAREN.
STAR TREK
VOYAGER

RADIO RADIO RADIO - RANCID

12-20-13

I GOT A LOT OF DRAWING DONE TODAY, PROJECTS I'D BEEN PUTTING OFF.

I JUST REALIZED I ALWAYS DRAW MYSELF AS LEFT-HANDED. OOPS. I'M ACTUALLY RIGHT-HANDED.

PEEBER AND I HAD A PICNIC LUNCH.

WHEN KAREN GOT HOME WE HUNG OUT TOGETHER.

IN THE SHADOW OF THE HORNS - DARKTHRONE

12-21-13

THIS MORNING WE MADE A SPUR-OF-THE-MOMENT DECISION
LET'S DRIVE DOWN TO SAN ANTONIO AND GET PUFFY TACOS FOR LUNCH!!
YES!

WE WENT TO RAY'S DRIVE INN. IT WAS SO AWESOME!
Ray's
DRIVE INN
HOME OF THE ORIGINAL
PUFFY TACO
OOH!

THEN WE WENT TO SOME THRIFT STORES.
WOW THE THRIFT STORES HERE PUT AUSTIN TO SHAME!

SEEK AND DESTROY - METALLICA

12-22-13

I'VE REALLY FALLEN OFF THE WAGON AS FAR AS EATING RIGHT AND EXERCISING.
I JUST CAN'T SEEM TO GET BACK WHERE I WAS BEFORE I HURT MY KNEE.

TODAY I GOT BACK ON IT WITH A VENGEANCE!
RAWR!

LATER I HUNG OUT WITH JAMES AT BARFLY.

HUMAN SPINE - ROCKET FROM THE CRYPT

12-23-13

BACK AT WORK TODAY. MY VACATION IS NOW OVER.
EXCEPT I GET XMAS OFF IN TWO DAYS!

CAME HOME AND DID ANOTHER HARDCORE WORKOUT.
OH WOW. THIS DRAWING CAME OUT REALLY GOOD. GREAT JOB, BEN.

THEN I WATCHED STAR TREK WITH KAREN.
STAR TREK
VOYAGER

IN NEW ORLEANS - LEAD BELLY

12-24-13

XMAS EVE. WORK CLOSED EARLY AND MY BOSS GAVE ME A $50 BONUS!
$50.00

I BOUGHT A MINI-KEG OF CHRISTMAS ALE.
THIS IS GONNA BE FUN!
CHRISTMA ALE

KAREN + I DRANK IT AND WATCHED DIE HARD.

WOW, HE'S WEARING A GUN ON THE PLANE, AND SMOKING IN THE AIRPORT. AND WHEN THE COPS GET A CALL ABOUT TERRORISTS, THEY THINK ITS A JOKE AND SEND ONE COP TO CHECK IT OUT.

THIS IS FUN!

MERRY MUTHAPHUKKIN CHRISTMAS - EAZY E

HOLY SHIT ITS CHRISTMAS!

KAREN + I EXCHANGED GIFTS.
RAD!
RAD!
HOME BREW BEER KIT
BATH ROBE
JAPANESE COOKING

12-25-13

WE ATE A DUCK AND WATCHED MST3K ALL DAY!

RAMBLE TAMBLE - CREEDENCE CLEARWATER REVIVAL

WENT TO WORK TODAY. IT WAS PRETTY SLOW.

KAREN TOOK ME OUT TO DINNER.
SHE'S BEEN WEARING HER HAIR DIFFERENT

12-26-13

WE WERE PRETTY TIRED AND WENT TO BED SUPER EARLY.
9:30
Z Z Z

PINEAPPLE FACE - LARD

12-27-13

PAYDAY AT WORK, AND MY CRAPPY CO-WORKER CALLED IN SICK!
WHAT A GREAT DAY!

THEN I GOT CONFIRMATION THAT I'LL HAVE A TABLE AT SAN ANTONIO COMIC CON IN 2014!
WHAT AN AWESOME DAY!

I CELEBRATED BY TAKING KAREN OUT TO A FANCY DINNER.

GEE BUT I LOVE YOU - HASIL ADKINS

12-28-13

RAN A BUNCH OF ERRANDS WITH KAREN TODAY.

I GOT HER A JAPANESE COOKBOOK FOR CHRISTMAS, SO WE WENT TO THE ASIAN MARKET TO GET INGREDIENTS.
THEY'RE HAVING A SALE ON PORK BLOOD.
LOOK! AN EMU EGG.

WE DRANK CHAMPAGNE AND WATCHED NETFLIX.
NETFLIX
YOU'RE MY LITTLE EMU EGG.

SERIOUS - SLOPPY SECONDS

12-29-13

LAST DAY OFF OF 2013. I SPENT IT ACCORDINGLY.
SKRATCH
SKRATCH

I DID MANAGE TO GET A HARD WORKOUT DONE.
I HATE TUMMY-TUCKS!

I ALSO STARTED MY FIRST BATCH OF HOME BREW!
OH BOY! JUST SIX MORE WEEKS!

MOVE ON - THE RENTALS

12-30-13

WORK WAS VERY UNUSUAL TODAY. I WAS SENT TO A TRAINING FACILITY TO LEARN A NEW MACHINE.
RICOH

IT WAS COOL BECAUSE IT TOOK ALL DAY AND THERE WAS A FREE LUNCH.
TRAINING VIDEO

KAREN MADE A HEALTHY DINNER AND WE SNUGGLED ON THE COUCH.

HARDLIGHT- PEGBOY 12-31-13

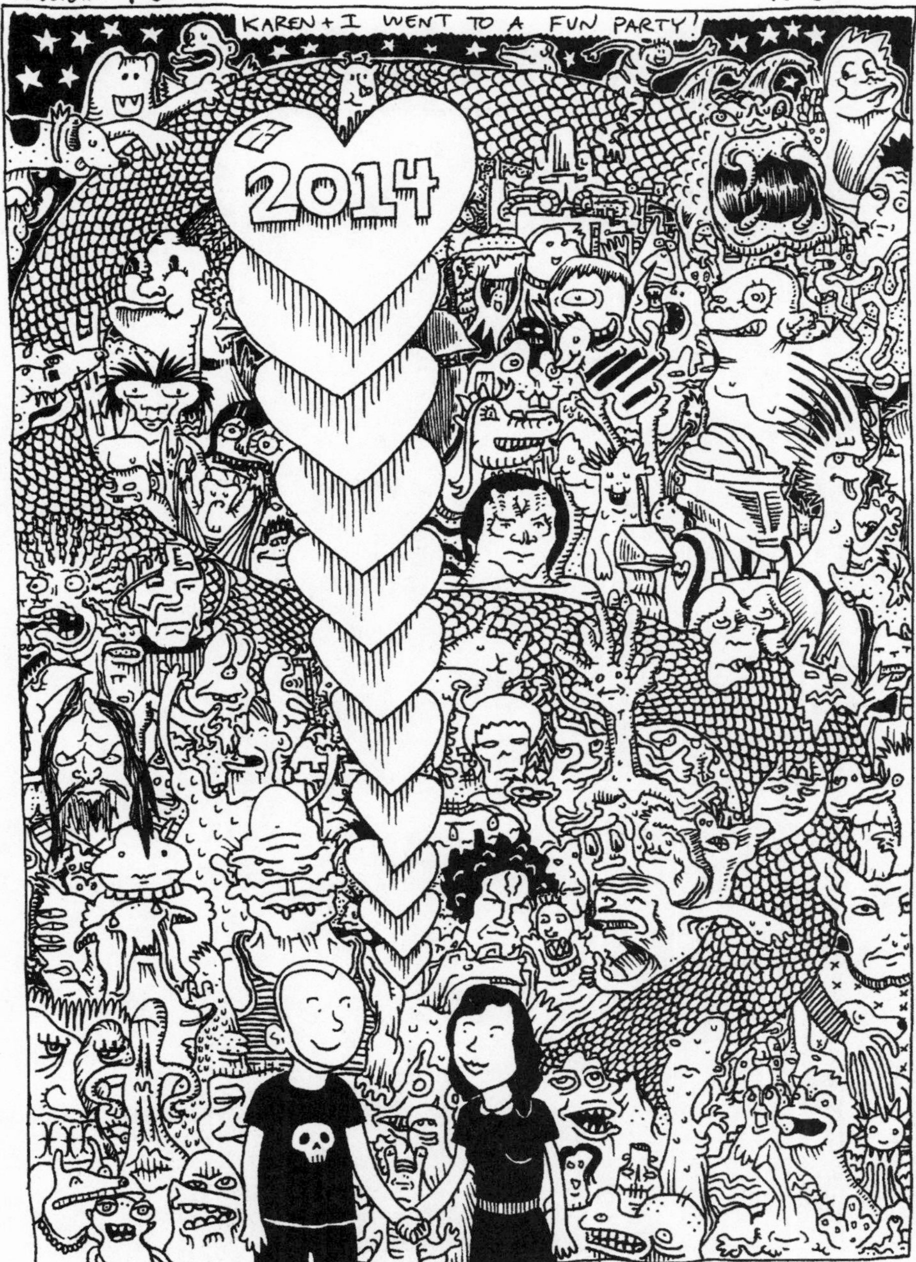
KAREN + I WENT TO A FUN PARTY!
2014

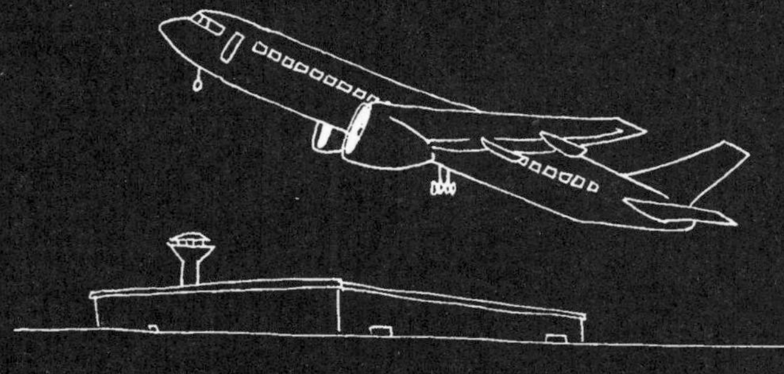

2014

WAR TORN - ASSUCK 1-1-14

I STARTED THE NEW YEAR PRETTY HUNGOVER.
BLEAH

UNDAUNTED, I MANAGED TO DO AN INTENSE WORKOUT.
26... 27... 28...

AND TOOK PEEBER FOR A LONG WALK.

FADING FAST- THE GO-GO'S 1-2-14

BACK TO WORK TODAY. WE ARE STARTING TO GET BUSY AGAIN SO I DON'T MIND IT.

KAREN MADE CRAB LEGS FOR DINNER. THEY WERE PRETTY GOOD.
ABOUT AS GOOD AS CRAB LEGS CAN BE IN CENTRAL TEXAS.

I DECIDED TO OPEN THE PIGGY BANK I'VE BEEN FILLING FOR THE LAST THREE YEARS.
HOLY SHIT! THERE'S ALMOST $250 HERE!
(IT'S ACTUALLY A GORILLA, NOT A PIG)

CONCRETE JUNGLE- THE SPECIALS 1-3-14

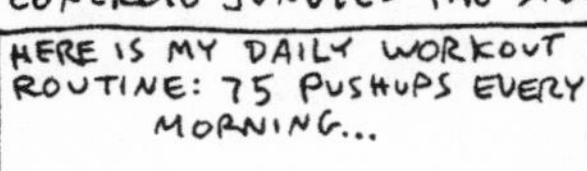
HERE IS MY DAILY WORKOUT ROUTINE: 75 PUSHUPS EVERY MORNING...

45... 46.. 47...

AFTER WORK: 15 MINUTES OF AB CRUNCHES, 15 MORE MINUTES OF DUMBELL LIFTING...
14... 15... 16...

THEN 45 MINUTES ON THE BIKE.
I'M STILL NOT BACK TO WHERE I WAS BEFORE MY KNEE INJURY BACK IN OCTOBER...
(YOU'D THINK WITH ALL THIS TIME, I'D FIND THE TIME TO PRACTICE DRAWING)

WIZ KID- FU MANCHU 1-4-14

TODAY I TOOK KAREN TO IKEA TO BUY A DESK
IKEA

THEN I PUT IT TOGETHER FOR HER.
???

AFTER THAT I DID A BUNCH OF DRAWING.

KISSIMMEE- BENT OUTTA SHAPE
1-5-14
TOOK CARE OF A LOT OF ERRANDS THIS MORNING.
WENT OVER AND HUNG OUT AT BRANDON'S.
HUH HUH HUH.
THEN WENT TO SEE WRESTLING!!!
RAWR!
RAWR!
DUST PNEUMONIA BLUES- WOODY GUTHRIE
1-6-14
TODAY STARTS MY FIRST FULL WEEK OF WORK IN 44 DAYS.
WHEW! I HOPE I CAN STILL HANG.
CAME HOME AND DID A GOOD WORKOUT.
EVERYTIME I SEE WRESTLING, IT "INSPIRES" ME TO GET IN SHAPE! HAW HAW!
I HAD A DREAM THAT MY GRANDMA WAS A NOTORIOUS ECO-CRIMINAL.
POLLUTION JAIL
ZZZ
NEVER ENOUGH NECK (PT 1) - THE FUCKING CHAMPS
1-7-14
TODAY AT WORK I PULLED OFF SOME AMAZING SAVE-THE-COMPANY TYPE SHIT.
THE ONLY BAD PART IS THAT I GOTTA WORK A SUPER-LONG DAY TOMORROW.
KAREN GOT AN ISRAELI COOKBOOK, SO SHE'S BEEN MAKING AMAZING MEALS ALL WEEK.
I DUNNO HOW TO PRONOUNCE THIS, BUT IT RULES!
I WENT TO BED REALLY EARLY TO PREPARE FOR TOMORROW.
I DON'T ACTUALLY SLEEP IN MY CLOTHES, I JUST STARTED DRAWING MYSELF LIKE THAT UNCONCIOUSLY. AND IT WAS TOO LATE TO FIX IT. ONE OF THE (DIS)ADVANTAGES OF NOT DRAWING IN PENCIL FIRST.
TURN OFF YOUR MIND- ELECTRIC WIZARD
1-8-14
TODAY I WORKED A SHIFT THAT LASTED 13.5 HOURS!
I TREATED MYSELF TO A SUPER-FANCY BEER AFTERWARD.
SIXTEEN BUCKS FOR A SINGLE BOTTLE. THIS SHIT BETTER TASTE LIKE MAGIC.
TOMORROW AT WORK IS GONNA SUCK TOO.
FUCK IT. GETTING DRUNK TONIGHT!!

DUB TO AFRICA - PRINCE FAR I

1-9-14

KAREN GOT HER PERIOD THIS MORNING.

ITS PARTICULARLY A BUMMER THIS MONTH BECAUSE SHE'D BEEN A FEW DAYS LATE AND WE WERE STARTING TO GET EXCITED

JANUARY

I WISH WE COULD SEE A DOCTOR ABOUT FERTILITY TREATMENT, BUT WE'RE PUTTING OFF GETTING HEALTH INSURANCE AS LONG AS WE CAN BECAUSE ITS SO EXPENSIVE.

ONCE MY CAR IS PAID OFF WE'LL BE ABLE TO AFFORD IT. THAT'S ONLY SEVEN MONTHS AWAY.

LITTLE MAGGIE - RED ALLEN

1-10-14

OH YEAH I FORGOT TO COMPLAIN ABOUT MY 14-HOUR SHIFT YESTERDAY.

WAAAH! I WENT TO MY JOB AND THEY MADE ME DO WORK!

ANYWAY, TODAY I BOTTLED MY FIRST BATCH OF HOMEBREW!

JUST A FEW MORE WEEKS!

THEN I TOOK KAREN OUT FOR A NICE DINNER.

BLINDED BY SCIENCE - FLUX OF PINK INDIANS

1-11-14

DID A BADASS WORKOUT TODAY.

LATER I MET UP WITH DAREN FOR SOME BEERS. HE JUST MOVED INTO MY NEIGHBORHOOD.

FYP

AFTER THAT I STARTED WORKING ON AN EPIC RECORD COVER FOR GHOST KNIFE

IF I DON'T FUCK THIS UP, IT'LL BE THE BEST THING I'VE EVER DRAWN!

HOOK IT UP - THE DONNAS

1-12-14

TODAY KAREN AND I WENT TO TEN DIFFERENT STORES TO FIND ME A NEW HOODIE.

CAMPING GEAR

SPORTING GOODS

THRIFT SHOP

CLOTHES STORE

STRANGELY ENOUGH, WE HAD NO SUCCESS.

HOW HARD IS IT TO FIND ONE THAT ISN'T CAMOFLAUGE OR HAS A SPORTS TEAM ON IT?

LATER I DID LAUNDRY.

THE FAMILY GHOST- KING DIAMOND
1-13-14
WE GOT A NEW PRINTER AT WORK TODAY.
GONNA TAKE A FEW TRIES TO LEARN HOW TO DRAW IT.
CAME HOME AND DID A HARD-ASS WORKOUT
THEN I FINISHED THE GHOST KNIFE RECORD COVER.
CLICK CLIK CLICK
THE CROWD- OPERATION IVY
1-14-14
ITS SHAPING UP TO BE A VERY BUSY WEEK AT WORK
LATER I WATCHED STAR TREK WITH KAREN
AND I PLAYED VIDEO GAMES ON MY COMPUTER.
NEED MORE TIME- EPOXIES
1-15-14
TODAY I DROPPED KAREN OFF FOR HER FIRST DAY OF SCHOOL.
AUSTIN COMMUNITY COLLEGE
WORK WAS STUPID CRAZY BUSY
I DRANK SOME NICE BEERS AFTERWARD.
MMM!
KNOCK ME DOWN- RED HOT CHILI PEPPERS
1-16-14
ANOTHER INSANE DAY AT WORK. I'M PROBABLY GONNA HAVE TO GO IN THIS WEEKEND.
I DIDNT REALLY DO MUCH OF ANYTHING TONIGHT.
CLICK, CLICK

I AM A CAT - SHONEN KNIFE

1-17-14

WORK JUST WON'T SLOW DOWN.
YOU MIGHT HAVE TO WORK ON SATURDAY. I'LL TEXT YOU TONIGHT AND LET YOU KNOW

KAREN + I HAD DINNER AT BILLY'S WITH BRANDON + CHELSEA

JUST BEFORE BED I GOT A GOOD NEWS TEXT!
WORK
YOU DON'T HAVE TO WORK TOMORROW

INTRO TO REALITY/BELLY OF THE BEAST - ANTHRAX

1-18-14

THIS MORNING I TOOK THE DOG ON A NICE LONG WALK.

THEN I STARTED MY SECOND BATCH OF HOMEBREW.
MY FIRST BATCH STILL WON'T BE READY FOR THREE MORE WEEKS

THEN I DID A SUPER LONG WORKOUT
16... 17... 18... UGH! THESE FUCKING BURPEES!

PRAYING TO THE ALIENS - TUBEWAY ARMY

1-19-14

KAREN + I BOTH HAD THE DAY OFF. WE WENT + GOT TACOS.

THEN WE DROVE AROUND AND LOOKED AT HOUSES FOR FUN.
WE COULD TOTALLY AFFORD THAT!
FOR SALE

THEN WE GOT GROCERIES.
HEB
HEB

KENTUCKY - LOUVIN BROS.

1-20-14

TODAY I WENT BACK TO WORK.

CAME HOME AND DID A WORKOUT.

OH, BUT BEFORE THAT I TOOK MY CAR IN TO GET THE BRAKES FIXED.
YOST
AUTOMOTIVE

WE'RE SO SMALL - THE EPOXIES

1-21-14

WORK WAS COOL TODAY. I'M STARTING TO GET THE HANG OF THE NEW MACHINE.

I TOOK THE BUS TO GO PICK UP MY CAR FROM THE SHOP.
CAPITOL METRO

THEY HAD A SNAKEPIT BOOK IN THE WAITING ROOM!
COOL!

KICKS - PAUL REVERE + THE RAIDERS

1-22-14

ANOTHER PLEASENT DAY AT WORK.

CAME HOME AND DID A WORKOUT.

NOW THAT KAREN HAS LATE SCHOOL ON WEDNESDAYS, SHE TAKES ME OUT TO DINNER!

DRUNK AS SHIT - MUNICIPAL WASTE

1-23-14

I'VE HIT A GREAT STRIDE AT WORK. I'M VERY CONTENT.

IT GOT SUPER COLD THIS AFTERNOON.
CHATTER CHATTER CHATTER
(HOW DO YOU DRAW WIND?)

KAREN + I HUNKERED DOWN WITH A 12-PACK OF WINTER STOUT.

THE NIGHT - MERCYFUL FATE

1-24-14

EVERYTHING WAS COVERED IN ICE THIS MORNING!
WOW COOL!

THE DRIVE TO WORK WAS ACTUALLY PRETTY SCARY.
(CRASHED CARS)

EVERYTHING MELTED BY THE AFTERNOON.
I LOVE TEXAS!

HELL AGE- FUNERAL ORATION

1-25-14

I SPENT MY DAY OFF DRIVING ALL OVER TOWN VISITING BEER STORES.
PAINFULLY HIP LOCAL MARKET #1
PAINFULLY HIP LOCAL MARKET #2

I FINALLY FOUND THE GINGERBREAD STOUT I WAS LOOKING FOR.
RAD!
GINGER BREAD STOUT

I'M GONNA SEND IT TO JAY IN VIRGINIA IN TRADE FOR SOME KBS!
THAT'S KENTUCKY BREAKFAST STOUT. I'M JUST LETTING GO AND TOTALLY IMMERSING MYSELF IN THIS CRAFT BEER CULTURE.

Q. AND CHILDREN? A. AND CHILDREN.- DISCHARGE

1-26-14

I WOKE UP SUPER EARLY TODAY AND GOT A BUNCH OF DRAWING DONE.

THEN KAREN AND I WENT ON A SUNDAY DRIVE.

IT WAS GORGEOUS OUT, SO WE SAT ON THE PORCH.

CAPTOR OF SIN - AT THE GATES

1-27-14

BACK AT WORK TODAY, IT WAS JUST FINE.

IT STARTED GETTING COLD AGAIN, ITS SUPPOSED TO ICE OVER AGAIN TONIGHT.
I WISH THE GOD DAMNED WEATHER WOULD MAKE UP ITS FUCKING MIND!

I SPENT THE EVENING PLAYING VIDEO GAMES.

I LOVE TO SINGA - OWL JOLSON

1-28-14

ANOTHER CHILL DAY AT WORK.

KAREN + I DID OUR TAXES
CLIK CLIK

WITH THIS TAX RETURN, WE FINALLY HAVE ENOUGH MONEY SAVED TO PUT A DOWN PAYMENT ON A HOUSE!!!
HOLY SHIT! IT SEEMS LIKE WE'VE BEEN SAVING FOR YEARS!
WE HAVE

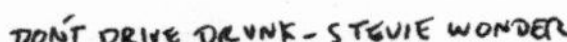
DON'T DRIVE DRUNK - STEVIE WONDER

1-29-14

WORK IS STARTING TO SLOW DOWN AGAIN.

AFTER WORK I WENT TO SPENT + WENDY'S. SPENT HAS BREWED SOME NEW BEERS.

CHEERZ!

I HAD TO LEAVE EARLY TO PICK UP KAREN, BUT I GOT PRETTY DRUNK ANYWAY!
OOPS

EXTRA GOOD - JEFF THE BROTHERHOOD

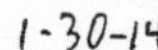
1-30-14

WORK WAS THE SAME AS ALWAYS.

KAREN STAYED HOME SICK TODAY. I CAME HOME AND TOOK CARE OF HER.
HERE SWEETIE, I MADE YOU SOME TEA.
SNIF THANKS.

THEN I PLAYED VIDEO GAMES BEFORE BED.
PEW! PEW!

METASTASIS - NAKED RAYGUN

1-31-14

IT WAS A BEAUTIFUL DAY TODAY. THEY SHUT DOWN WORK EARLY.
PRINT SHOP

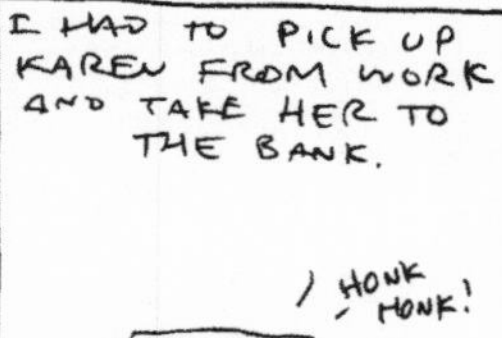
I HAD TO PICK UP KAREN FROM WORK AND TAKE HER TO THE BANK.

HONK HONK!

THEN I WASHED A BUNCH OF BOTTLES. MY NEXT BATCH OF HOME BREW IS DONE FERMENTING.
STOKED!

RED EYE - DEVO

2-1-14

TODAY KAREN + I TOOK A DAY TRIP OUT TO THE JESTER KING BREWERY!
WHOA!

WE TRIED LOTS OF DELICIOUS BEERS AND HAD FUN, BUT THE PLACE WAS INSANELY CROWDED
THIS IS GOOD
WHAT!

I GOT ALL STOKED TO BOTTLE MY HOMEBREW WHEN WE GOT HOME, BUT IT'S NOT READY YET.

TASTES SWEET. THERES STILL SOME SUGAR LEFT.

SUNSHINE SHOWDOWN - THE UPSETTERS

2-2-14

I GOT A LOT DONE TODAY. WORKOUT, LAUNDRY, DRAWING.

WHEN KAREN GOT HOME FROM WORK, WE DRANK SOME OF THE BEERS WE GOT YESTERDAY.

CHEERS!

I DRANK TOO MUCH. I GOT KINDA DRUNK AND WAS MEAN TO KAREN.

???

YELLIN' IN MY EAR - OPERATION IVY

2-3-14

I APOLOGIZED TO KAREN FOR BEING SUCH A DICK LAST NIGHT.

YOU'RE AN AWFULLY GOOD WOMAN TO PUT UP WITH ME SOMETIMES.

I KNOW

THEN I WENT TO WORK

WHEN I GOT HOME I STARTED READING THE NEW BOOK I GOT.

GO AHEAD AND TALK SHIT. I DON'T CARE.

TASTING BEER

RANDY MOSHER

SLIPKNOT - WOODY GUTHRIE

2-4-14

WORK WAS COOL TODAY.

I CAME HOME ALL READY TO BOTTLE MY NEXT BATCH OF HOMEBREW, BUT IT'S NOT READY.

TOO SWEET.

SO I PLAYED VIDEO GAMES INSTEAD.

WALK IN COLD - NAKED RAYGUN

2-5-14

SO MUCH AWESOME GOOD NEWS TODAY!!!
SHELLSHAG INVITED ME TO NYC TO BE ON THEIR NEW TV SHOW!!
IT JUST NEVER STOPPED COMING!
I'VE BEEN CONFIRMED AS THE SPECIAL GUEST AT THE MOCAD COMIC JAM IN DETROIT!!!
I WISH THIS DAY WOULD NEVER END.
MY TAX RETURN POSTED TO MY BANK ACCOUNT. WE NOW HAVE ENOUGH FOR A DOWN PAYMENT ON A HOUSE!!!!

MODERN MAN - BAD RELIGION

2-6-14

WORK WAS PRETTY COOL TODAY.

I CAME HOME AND BOTTLED MY BATCH OF PILSNER.

I BOUGHT A BOTTLE-CAPPER, ITS REALLY NEAT!
COOL!
KA-CHUNK!

BATHROOM AT AMELIAS - TRAGIC MULATTO

2-7-14

WORK WAS PRETTY BUSY. I'M GONNA HAVE TO WORK ON SATURDAY.
GRR

AFTER I GOT OFF, I BREWED A NEW BATCH OF BEER.

HOMEBREWING IS SUPER FUN!
KAMPAI!

VACUUM - FOURTH ROTOR

2-8-14

SPENT A GOOD CHUNK OF THE DAY LAYING OUT MY SPLIT COMIC WITH MITCH.

I PICKED UP KAREN FROM WORK AND WE WENT TO THE FANCY CHEESE STORE.
HERE, TRY THIS ONE

WE DRANK AND ATE AND LAUGHED, AND EVEN DECIDED TO EXCHANGE OUR ANNIVERSARY GIFTS FOUR DAYS EARLY.
HOMEBREW RECIPE JOURNAL

GLAD TO SEE YOU GO - RAMONES

2-9-14

RAN LOTS OF ERRANDS TODAY.
THIS PLACE
THAT PLACE →

IT WAS NICE OUT, SO KAREN + I READ ON THE PORCH.
zzz

TOMORROW WE'RE GOING TO TALK TO THE BANK ABOUT A MORTGAGE!
DO YOU THINK WE'RE READY?
I THINK WE'RE READY!

REJECTED - RANCID
2-10-14
THIS MORNING I PUT ON MY NICEST SHIRT.
I THINK WE'RE READY!
I LEFT WORK EARLY AND PICKED KAREN UP FROM SCHOOL.
DO YOU THINK WE'RE READY?
I THINK WE'RE READY!
WE WENT TO THE BANK.
YOU'RE NOT READY.
WE DIDN'T GET THE NEWS WE WANTED.
DIGITAL - JOY DIVISION
2-11-14
PRETTY BUMMED OUT AT WORK TODAY.
SIGH
I CAME HOME AND DID A WORKOUT.
GRRR! I'M A BIG TOUGH MAN!
THEN I PICKED KAREN UP FROM WORK BECAUSE IT WAS COLD + SHITTY OUT.
LIKE A REFRIDGERATOR FULL OF POOP!
GROSS.
HAPPY ANNIVERSARY - THE QUADRATICS
2-12-14
WENT TO WORK TODAY.
PICKED KAREN UP FROM WORK. SHE HAD TO WORK TWO HOURS LATER THAN SHE WAS SUPPOSED TO.
WE WENT AND GOT SUSHI.
HERE'S TO TWO AWESOME YEARS!
CHEVROLET - ZZ TOP
2-13-14
WORK WAS BUSY BUT COMFORTABLE.
LOOKING AROUND ON THE INTERNET, I FOUND A STATE DPA PROGRAM THAT I THINK WE QUALIFY FOR.
TSAHC
HMMM
I SENT A FEW EMAILS OUT TO SEE WHAT HAPPENS.
I'M NOT GONNA LET MYSELF GET DISCOURAGED.
KLIK KLIK

FOCUS POCUS - BIG BUSINESS

2-14-14

I GOT LOTS OF CALLS BACK FROM THE LENDERS I EMAILED YESTERDAY.

HELLO!

THE OVERWHELMING MESSAGE I GOT FROM ALL OF THEM IS THAT WE CAN DO THIS!!!

KAREN + I EXCITEDLY DISCUSSED IT OVER A VALENTINE PIZZA.

BALLAD OF A HANDGUN - CRINGER (HAPPY BIRTHDAY LANCE)

2-15-14

TODAY I FILLED OUT AND SUBMITTED THREE MORTGAGE APPLICATIONS.

THEN I DID LAUNDRY AND CLEANED THE APARTMENT.

REMEMBER WHEN I USED TO BE PUNK?

LAST NIGHT I SHIT MY PANTS AND PASSED OUT IN A DITCH

ZZZ

TINY TOWN - DEAD MILKMEN

2-16-14

TODAY KAREN AND I TOOK A DRIVE UP TO CEDAR PARK.

THE MORTGAGE PEOPLE SAID WE'D GET A MUCH BETTER DEAL OUT HERE.

BOONIES THIS WAY

BUT I DON'T THINK WE'D FIT IN WELL THERE.

TEA PARTY

PROLIFE!

JESUS DIED4U

IMPEACH OBAMA

ULP!

SO MAYBE WE WON'T GET THE BEST DEAL IN AUSTIN, BUT IT'S STILL WORTH IT.

I WANNA STAY IN AUSTIN, WHERE WE CAN FORGET THAT WE'RE IN TEXAS!

ME TOO!

MONEY - EMBRACE

2-17-14

BACK TO WORK TODAY.

I GOT AN EMAIL FROM ONE OF THE MORTGAGE PEOPLE, WE'RE APPROVED FOR A REASONABLE AMOUNT!!!

FUCK YEAH! SUCK IT, LADY FROM LAST WEEK!

KAREN + I CELEBRATED WITH FINE BEER AND CHEESE.

HERE'S TO THE BEGINNING OF LOTS OF HEADACHES!

OXIDYZED RAZOR MASTICATOR - CARCASS 2-18-14

I GOT MORE MORTGAGE ESTIMATES TODAY.
HMM

KAREN AND I LOOKED OVER EVERYTHING AND SHE SUDDENLY GOT COLD FEET.
WE'RE NOT READY!

I KIND OF AGREE WITH HER THOUGH, WE SHOULD WAIT A FEW MORE MONTHS.
OKAY, YOU'RE RIGHT.

LAST MORNIN' - DR. HOOK 2-19-14

WENT TO WORK TODAY.

DID A WORKOUT WHEN I GOT HOME.

KAREN WORKED SUPER LATE TONIGHT. I HAD TO PICK HER UP AT 10:30!

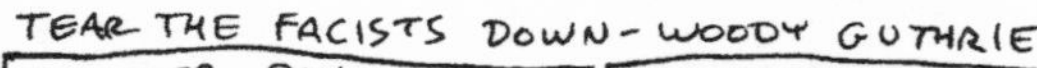
TEAR THE FACISTS DOWN - WOODY GUTHRIE

2-20-14

ANOTHER DAY AT WORK.

CAME HOME AND WORKED ON THE SPLIT ZINE I'M DOING WITH MITCH.

I SUCK AT PHOTOSHOP.
I WISH I COULD AFFORD TO TAKE A CS CLASS.
KLIK KLIK

NEEDLES + PINS - RAMONES 2-21-14

THANK GOD ITS FRIDAY.
CAN YOU COME IN AND WORK TOMORROW!

I STARTED DRINKING AS SOON AS I GOT HOME.
YES!

OOPS.
NOO!

THE REASON YOUNG PEOPLE USE DRUGS- ABNER JAY
2-22-14
TODAY I HAD TO GO IN TO WORK.
AFTERWARD I PICKED UP MY NEW SNAKEPIT KOOZIES FROM JAMES!
AWESOME!!
JUDGE PRINT
I ATE TACOS WITH KAREN.
AWESOME!
SEVENTEEN-SEX PISTOLS
2-23-14
TODAY KAREN + I DROVE OUT TO MANOR TO SEE ABOUT HOUSES THERE.
LEAVING AUSTIN
WE LOVED IT!! IT HAS A MUCH MORE DIVERSE VIBE THAN CEDAR PARK
HOTEL
MARKET
WE CAME HOME AND WATCHED "WHATS EATING GILBERT GRAPE"
THIS WAS FILMED IN MANOR!
THE SHORTEST STRAW- METALLICA
2-24-14
I TALKED TO MY CO-WORKERS THAT LIVE IN MANOR TODAY.
I LOVE IT THERE!
ME TOO!
I LOOKED AT THE MORTGAGE INFORMATION FOR MANOR. ITS REALLY CHEAP.
WOW!
WE'RE GONNA HOLD OFF ON DECIDING ANYTHING FOR A WHILE, BUT I REALLY LIKE THE IDEA.
COUNTRY LIVIN'!
I THINK I LOVE YOU- THE PARTRIDGE FAMILY
2-25-14
WENT TO WORK TODAY.
STAPLED + FOLDED ALL OF MY SPLIT ZINES WITH MITCH FOR THIS WEEKEND.
THEN I HUNG OUT WITH KAREN.

DO IT TO ME TONIGHT- HASIL ADKINS

2-26-14

WORK WAS COOL TODAY.

I CAME HOME AND DID A GOOD WORKOUT.
I KNOW I'M GONNA MISS A LOT OF EXERCISE IN MARCH SO I GOTTA GET A LOT IN WHILE I CAN!

THEN I WENT OVER TO SPENT+WENDY'S. SPENT LET ME TRY SOME OF HIS NEW BEERZ!
THANKS DUDE!
SURE!

YOUTH OF AMERICA- WIPERS

2-27-14

TODAY I WENT TO WORK.

THE WEATHER IS WARMING UP NICELY. I TOOK PEEBER ON A LONG WALK.

THEN I GOT EVERYTHING READY FOR STAPLE THIS WEEKEND.

BOOKS, ZINES, SHIRTS, KOOZIES, BUTTONS+ SKATE DECKS.

I LIKE IT- THE REZILLOS

2-28-14

WORK WAS NICE TODAY.

I GOT HOME AND BOTTLED MY LATEST BATCH OF BEER
I THINK FOR MY NEXT ONE, I'M READY TO STOP USING EXTRACTS.

TOOK IT EASY FOR THE REST OF THE NIGHT. I HAVE A BIG DAY TOMORROW.

MR. MOONLIGHT- CLINIC

3-01-14 OOPS!

TODAY I WENT TO STAPLE AND SAT AT A TABLE WITH MITCH+ AMANDA.
BAND

AFTERWARD, I WENT WITH KAREN TO THE CROWN + ANCHOR.

THEN GHOST KNIFE PLAYED A FUN SHOW AT SPIDER HOUSE

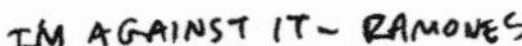
I'M AGAINST IT - RAMONES

3-2-14

THE SECOND DAY OF STAPLE WENT A LOT BETTER THAN THE FIRST.

I WAS SUPER TIRED WHEN IT WAS OVER.
IT'S SURPRISINGLY DRAINING JUST SITTING AT A TABLE FOR 8 HOURS.

I SPENT THE REST OF THE NIGHT RELAXING LIKE A MOTHERFUCKER.

NEVER AGAIN - DISCHARGE

3-3-14

BACK AT STUPID-ASS WORK.

I PUT THE SPLIT ZINE WITH MITCH FOR SALE ON THE INTERNET.
THREE CLICKS OF THE MOUSE AND WATCH THE CASH ROLL IN!

THEN I STARTED PREPARING FOR THIS WEEKEND.
GOTTA GET THIS SPEECH READY.

PICTURE OF HEALTH - PARQUET COURTS

3-4-14

WORK WASN'T TOO BAD, CONSIDERING IT WAS ALREADY HUMP-DAY.

I GOT HOME AND DID A TON OF DRAWING TO GET MY CHOPS UP FOR THIS WEEKEND.

DETROIT, HERE I COME!
DEAD OR ALIVE, YOU'RE COMING WITH ME!

SKIN DEEP - GUNS-N-WANKERS

3-5-14

I ONLY WORKED HALF A DAY TODAY. I HAD TOO MUCH TO DO!!

KAREN + I WENT OUT TO LUNCH.

THEN I SPENT THE REST OF THE EVENING PACKING AND GETTING MY SPEECH READY.

COCAINE BLUES - ABNER JAY

3-6-14

I GOT UP SUPER EARLY + FLEW TO DETROIT!

IVAN PICKED ME UP FROM THE AIRPORT AND TOOK ME TO LUNCH
IVAN!

WE DROVE AROUND TOWN LOOKING AT ALL THE RUINS. IT'S INSANE.

DEAD INDUSTRIAL ATMOSPHERE - LEATHERFACE

3-7-14

THIS MORNING I WENT TO THE LIBRARY WITH IVAN
WHOA!

THEN I MET UP WITH BRIAN AND HE TOOK ME TO A KILLER BEER STORE
WHOA!

THEN WE HUNG OUT AND IT WAS COOL.
SICKO
BRIAN!

BLACK ICE - MUNICIPAL WASTE

3-8-14

THIS MORNING I WALKED DOWNTOWN TO GET A REAL-DEAL DETROIT CONEY.
THIS IS JUST A DUMB-ASS CHILI DOG. ITS NOT VERY IMPRESSIVE.

THEN I DID MY SPEECH AT THE MUSEUM. I WAS A LITTLE NERVOUS BUT I THINK IT WENT WELL.

BLAH BLAH BLAH I'M SO AWESOME

AFTERWARDS I HAD A GREAT DINNER WITH DAN AND KATIE FROM GREEN BRAIN COMICS!

DAN + KATIE!

SURFIN' BIRD - THE TRASHMEN

3-9-14

GOT UP EARLY THIS MORNING AND FLEW BACK TO AUSTIN.

ALL THE BEERS I BROUGHT BACK WITH ME MADE IT HOME SAFE!

KAREN AND I SNUGGLED ON THE COUCH.

SO NICE TO BE BACK HOME!

LET THE GOOD TIMES ROLL - JIMI HENDRIX

3-10-14

BACK TO WORK TODAY.

I DID A GOOD WORKOUT TO TRY AND MAKE UP FOR ALL THE DAYS I'VE MISSED LATELY.
GUH!

THEN KAREN + I WATCHED THE FINALE OF TRUE DETECTIVE WHILE WE DRANK FANCY BEERS FROM MICHIGAN!
MCCONAGHEY + HARRELSON ARE MY GENERATION'S LEMMON + MATTHAU.

OSCILLATIONS - SILVER APPLES

3-11-14

TODAY I WENT TO WORK.

THEN I PLAYED MUSIC WITH BRANDON + MIKE. MIKE'S ONLY IN TOWN FOR SXSW SO WE'RE GONNA TRY TO WRITE + RECORD A QUICK 7"

THEN I TOOK KAREN OUT TO DINNER.

(ANESTHESIA) PULLING TEETH - METALLICA

3-12-14

WORK WAS PRETTY BUSY TODAY.

GHOST KNIFE PLAYED A SHOW FOR SXSW.

AFTERWARD I HUNG OUT WITH FRIENDS AT THE YELLOW JACKET.

GREYHOUND BUS - BENT OUTTA SHAPE

3-13-14

I SAW ON THE NEWS THIS MORNING THAT A CAR DROVE INTO A SXSW CROWD LAST NIGHT, KILLING 2 PEOPLE.
HOLY SHIT! I WAS IN THAT VERY INTERSECTION JUST A FEW MINUTES BEFORE IT HAPPENED!

AFTER WORK I WENT AND BORROWED AN ACOUSTIC GUITAR FROM BRAD.

TO GET READY FOR MY BROOKLYN SHOW.

THEN I WENT OUT TO DINNER WITH KAREN.
I'M SO WIPED OUT BY SXSW!

STARVING TO DEATH ON MY GOVERNMENT CLAIM - ABNER JAY
3-14-14

GLAD IT'S FRIDAY, THIS HAS BEEN A LONG WEEK
I CAME HOME AND DID A SMALL WORKOUT. I'M SLIPPING!
GOTTA GET BACK UP ON IT!

WENT TO BED SUPER EARLY. I NEED TO CATCH UP ON SLEEP.

DESPERATION STREET - HARD SKIN

3-15-14

GOT TO RELAX A BIT TODAY.

THEN I HUNG OUT WITH BRANDON + JULIAN.

AFTER THAT I WENT TO A SHOW AT THE GRAND + GOT WAY TOO DRUNK!

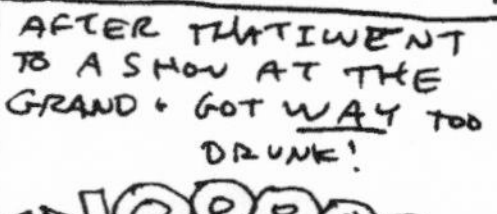
NNOOOOOOO

PINEAPPLE FACE - LARD

3-16-14

OH SHIT WHAT A HANGOVER.

I MANAGED TO SCRAPE MYSELF UP TO DO THE LANDRY.

BUT THAT'S ABOUT IT.
I JUST CAN'T PARTY LIKE I COULD 15 YEARS AGO.

HUMAN CANNONBALL - BUTTHOLE SURFERS

3-17-14

BACK AT WORK WITH A VENGEANCE. I WAS THERE FOR ELEVEN HOURS!
GOOD GRIEF!

I'M GLAD ITS A SHORT WEEK.
NEW YORK THIS WEEKEND!!!

TONIGHT I WATCHED COSMOS WITH KAREN.

SO GOOD!

CARRY ON MY WAYWARD SON - GWAR

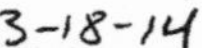
3-18-14

I WOKE UP TODAY WITH A SORE THROAT.
OH SHIT! PLEASE NO! DON'T LET ME GET SICK NOW!

I TRIED TO TAKE IT EASY AND DRINK TEA ALL DAY.

I ALSO PRACTICED MY SET FOR THE WEEKEND.
I CANNOT BE STOPPED!!

TWO BLOCKS AWAY - ISOCRACY

3-19-14

I LEFT WORK EARLY TODAY
SMELL YA LATER!

PICKED UP KAREN FROM SCHOOL AND WE WENT TO LUNCH.
NOODLE

THEN I GOT PACKED AND READY FOR MY TRIP!
READY FOR NYC!

OUT ON AN ISLAND - COCK SPARRER

3-20-14

GOT UP EARLY AND FLEW TO NEW YORK!
AIRPLANE!

SHELLSHAG PICKED ME UP AND WE ATE SOME PIZZA.
GREAT! LET'S DIG IN!
I WANT SOME!
SHEL
SHAG

THEIR PLACE HERE IS INCREDIBLE!!
I SUCK AT DRAWING. THIS PLACE IS A HUGE FULLY-FUNCTIONING TV STUDIO. SORRY I CAN'T DRAW IT VERY WELL
WHOA!

SUZY IS A HEADBANGER - RAMONES

3-21-14

THIS MORNING SHELL TOOK ME INTO MANHATTAN TO A HUGE AWESOME BEER STORE!

I PAINTED A GIANT MURAL FOR THE SET OF THE TV SHOW

THEN I WENT AND PLAYED MY SOLO SHOW. IT WAS WEIRD BUT I SAW A BUNCH OF OLD FRIENDS, WHICH WAS AWESOME.
ULP

MECHANICAL - SUPERNOVA

3-22-14

LAST NIGHT AFTER THE SHOW WE PARTIED SUPER HARD LONG INTO THE NIGHT.

TODAY WE WORKED ALL DAY FILMING THE SHOW

WE GOT EVERYTHING DONE IN TIME AND SPENT THE EVENING PARTYING (AGAIN!)
WHOA!

I CAN'T STOP FARTING - THE QUEERS

3-23-14

THIS MORNING BEFORE I LEFT SHELLSHAG TOOK ME ON THE BROOKLYN BREWERY TOUR!

THEN I FLEW BACK TO AUSTIN
MAN I CAN'T STOP FARTING ON THIS PLANE. SORRY EVERYONE!

IT WAS SO GOOD TO SEE KAREN + PEEBER AGAIN!!

CRY OF THE WEREWOLF - SCIENTIST

3-24-14

BOY DID I FEEL LIKE HELL AT WORK TODAY.

I LEFT EARLY, CAME HOME AND TOOK A FOUR HOUR NAP.
ZZZ

BUT THEN I WOKE UP FEELING GREAT!

SHOVE THAT WARRANT UP YOUR ASS - GG ALLIN

3-25-14

WORK WAS MUCH MORE DO-ABLE TODAY.

CAME HOME AND DID A HARDCORE WORKOUT. I'VE LET MYSELF GO SO BAD THIS MONTH.
WOW THIS DRAWING CAME OUT REALLY GOOD.

THEN KAREN + I DRANK ALL OF THE BEERS I BROUGHT BACK FROM NY.
CHEERS!
CHEERS!

DEATH IS PSYCHOSOMATIC - WORLD BURNS TO DEATH

3-26-14

WORK WAS STRAIGHT-UP CHILL TODAY.

KAREN AND I WATCHED STAR TREK

AND WENT TO BED EARLY.
ZZZ

WHITE PUNKS ON HOPE - CRASS

3-27-14

ANOTHER RELAXING DAY AT WORK.

AFTERWARDS I BOUGHT SOME SUPPLIES FOR HOMEBREWING.

THEN I WENT TO GHOST KNIFE PRACTICE.

DON'T STOP - STONE ROSES

3-28-14

WORK WAS ALMOST NON-EXISTENT TODAY.

WE CLOSED UP THE SHOP EARLY AND HAD A COMPANY BBQ OUT IN THE PARKING LOT.
IT'S WEIRD DRINKING WITH MY CO-WORKERS.

KAREN MADE A CHEESE-CAKE WHILE I PLAYED VIDEO GAMES.
GIMME DAT CHEEZ CAYKE!
P.U.!

MONSTER - L7

3-29-14

FINALLY! A DAY ALL TO MYSELF WITH NOTHING TO DO!
THIS IS ALMOST THE EXACT SAME PICTURE I DREW FIVE DAYS AGO. OOPS.

I TOOK PEEBER ON A NICE LONG WALK

AND DID A HEARTY WORKOUT.

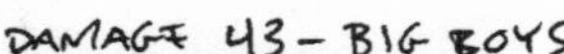
DAMAGE 43 - BIG BOYS

3-30-14

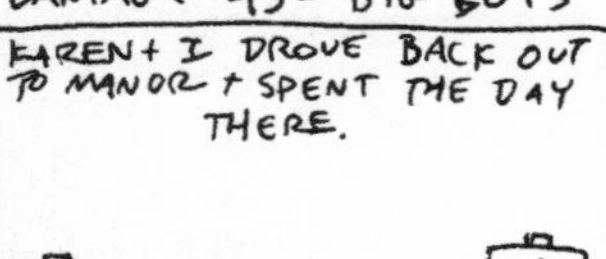
KAREN + I DROVE BACK OUT TO MANOR + SPENT THE DAY THERE.
← BIG CITY
→ SMALL TOWN

WE WENT TO THE GHOST TOWN WHICH WAS A LOT OF FUN.
BANK
JAIL

WE DECIDED 100% THAT WE'RE GONNA BUY A HOUSE THERE!
MANO

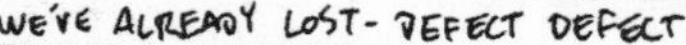
WE'VE ALREADY LOST - DEFECT DEFECT

3-31-14

WORK WAS REALLY SLOW TODAY.

I LEFT EARLY AND PICKED KAREN UP FROM SCHOOL.
SKOOL

SHE MADE BBQ RIBS FOR DINNER!

SURPRISE! YOU'RE DEAD - FAITH NO MORE

4-1-14

TODAY I DIED. I TOTALLY FUCKING DIED.

HERE LIES BEN. HE TOTALLY FUCKING DIED

AND I FOUND OUT I AM PREGNANT.
OH SHIT!

AND THEN I DIED AGAIN.

SOMETHING'S GONE WRONG AGAIN - BUZZCOCKS

4-2-14

WORK GOT MUCH BUSIER TODAY.

I CAME HOME AND DID A GNARLY WORKOUT.
78... 79... 80!

THEN I DRANK SOME BEER.
81... 82... 83... 84
RAUCH BIER
SCOTCH ALE

BEETHOVEN'S 9th SYMPHONY

4-3-14

ANOTHER DING DONG DAY AT DING DONG WORK.

I TOOK KAREN OUT TO DINNER.

WE CAME HOME AND GOT DRUNK AND LISTENED TO CLASSICAL MUSIC TOGETHER

PROMISE- SHELLSHAG

4-4-14

WORK WAS NICE AND EASY TODAY.

ON THE WAY HOME I STOPPED AT THE HOME-BREW STORE AND GOT ALL THE INGREDIENTS FOR MY FIRST REAL ALL-GRAIN BATCH!

AUSTIN HOMEBREW SUPPLY
THIS PLACE IS KINDA INTIMIDATING

THEN I GOT TO SEE MY FINISHED EPISODE OF SHELLSHONIC SHAG-O-VISION!!!

MY DADDY RIDES THAT SHIP IN THE SKY...

HA HA! AWESOME!

SLIDING DOWN A STREAM- CHELSEA

4-5-14

TODAY I BREWED MY BEER! EVERYTHING WENT OFF WITH-OUT A HITCH.

THEN GHOST KNIFE DROVE DOWN TO SAN ANTONIO TO PLAY AT MARCO+JEN'S WEDDING!

SAN ANTO →

IT WAS A LOT OF FUN!

4AM- THE BANANAS

4-6-14

DIDN'T GET HOME FROM SAN ANTONIO LAST NIGHT TIL 4AM.

SLEPT IN SUPER LATE, WOKE UP AND STARTED DRINKING.

THIS IS A GREAT IDEA.

PASSED OUT KINDA EARLY. I WAS ONLY AWAKE FOR 11 HOURS ALL DAY.

A GREAT IDEA.

NEVERMIND- NIRVANA

4-7-14

BACK TO WORK. I GOT THE MONDAYS.

I DRANK A BUNCH OF THE FANCY BEER I PICKED UP IN SAN ANTONIO.
OOOH YEH.

I THINK MAYBE I NEED TO DIAL BACK THE DRINKING JUST A TAD.
OOOH NO.

THE FRAYED ENDS OF SANITY- METALLICA

4-8-14

ANOTHER DAY AT WORK.

I PINCHED A NERVE WHILE WORKING OUT.

OW!

KAREN BOUGHT ME TACOS.

MY HEART'S TONIGHT IN TEXAS- CARTER FAMILY

4-9-14

TODAY WE GOT OFFICIALLY PRE-APPROVED FOR A MORTGAGE LOAN!

NEW MESSAGE
CONGRATULATIONS BEN! YOU'VE BEEN PRE-APPROVED. YOU CAN START SHOPPING FOR HOUSES NOW.

FUCK YES!

I GOT IN TOUCH WITH A REALTOR.

MY OLD FRIEND JULIE CAN PROBABLY HELP US.

THIS SHIT IS REALLY HAPPENING!

I'VE WANTED TO OWN A HOUSE EVER SINCE I WAS A LITTLE KID!

DOGS IN HEADLOCKS- PINK RAZORS

4-10-14

TODAY I GOT AN EMAIL FROM MY FRIEND JULIE. SHE'S OUR NEW REALTOR!

SHE SENT ME A LIST OF 18 DIFFERENT HOUSES FOR SALE IN MANOR.

YOUR LISTINGS

KAREN + I SPENT THE EVENING PORING OVER THE DETAILS OF EACH ONE.

THIS ONE HAS HARDWOOD FLOORS BUT THE KITCHEN IS TOO SMALL.
THIS ONE HAS A GOOD KITCHEN BUT NO FENCED YARD.
THIS ONE IS NICE BUT IN A CRUMMY NEIGHBORHOOD.

ZERO - THE DONNAS

4-11-14

MY BOSS IS ON VACATION, SO WORK WAS SUPER CHILL TODAY.

I GOT ANOTHER EMAIL FROM JULIE. WE'RE GOING TO LOOK AT HOUSES ON SUNDAY!
AWESOME!

KAREN + I DRANK BEER AND WATCHED EPISODES OF "MY FIRST HOME" ON NETFLIX.
SO PUMPED!
ME TOO!

BOAT RACE- SHELLSHAG

4-12-14

THIS MORNING I DID A SUPER GNARLY WORKOUT

THEN I DID A PHONE INTERVIEW WITH GARY FOR HIS PODCAST.
BLAH BLAH BLAH I'M PRETTY AWESOME

THEN I WATCHED STAR TREK WITH KAREN.
BLAH BLAH BLAH
YOU'RE PRETTY AWESOME

MARIA BARTIROMO- JOEY RAMONE

4-13-14

TODAY KAREN + I MET UP WITH JULIE AND TOURED HOUSES!

WE LOOKED AT SIX DIFFERENT ONES IN MANOR.
THIS ONE HAS NICE FLOORS BUT THE YARD ISN'T VERY PRIVATE

ONE OF THEM WE REALLY LIKED A LOT!
THIS ONE!
YEAH THIS ONE!

COULD YOU BE THE ONE- HÜSKER DÜ

4-14-14

KAREN + I TALKED A LOT ABOUT THE HOUSE LAST NIGHT
MOVING TO MANOR WILL PRESENT A LOT OF CHALLENGES. SO WILL STAYING IN AUSTIN + RENTING.

WE MADE AN APPOINTMENT WITH JULIE TO GO LOOK AT IT AGAIN TOMORROW.
6:30 TOMORROW GOOD FOR YOU?
YEAH!

THIS COULD BE THE ONE!

DON'T COME BACK KNOCKIN' - BUDDY HOLLY

4-15-14

TODAY WE WENT AND SAW THE HOUSE AGAIN. WE LOVE IT!
WE WANNA PUT IN AN OFFER!
OKAY COOL!

JULIE CALLED THE SELLER'S AGENT RIGHT THEN AND THERE.
HI THIS IS JULIE AT THE GILL AGENCY...

SORRY GUYS, THEY ALREADY HAVE A SIGNED OFFER.
DOES THAT MEAN THERE'S NO HOPE?
YEAH.

THE NIGHT OF THE HOLOCAUST - SHITLICKERS

4-16-14

TODAY I WAS PRETTY DISCOURAGED ABOUT EVERYTHING
SIGH

BUT I'M SURE THIS WILL HAPPEN A FEW TIMES BEFORE WE FIND A HOUSE.
NOTHING WORTHWHILE IS EVER EASY.

IN OTHER NEWS, I BOUGHT A HYDROMETER TODAY!
IT MEASURES ABV!

DOWN WITH THE OLD CANOE - THE DIXON BROTHERS

4-17-14

ANOTHER HOUSE CAME UP ON THE MARKET TODAY.
OOOH!

WE DROVE OUT AND LOOKED AT IT, IT'S SO AWESOME!
OH WOW!

WE IMMEDIATELY PUT AN OFFER IN ON IT!
WE REALLY REALLY WANT IT!!
OKAY!

THE WAITING - TOM PETTY

4-18-14

WORK WAS PRETTY SLOW TODAY.

I TALKED TO JULIE, THERE'S ANOTHER OFFER ON THE HOUSE, BUT WE GOT OURS IN FIRST. WE'LL JUST HAVE TO WAIT + SEE.
JUST GOTTA WAIT AND SEE.

I BOTTLED MY NEWEST BATCH OF BEER.
THE BEST BATCH YET!

ZYKLON-B-MOVIE - SUBHUMANS

4-19-14

THIS MORNING I WENT TO THE HOME BREW STORE AND PICKED UP STUFF TO BREW ANOTHER BATCH.
GOTTA STAY BUSY THIS WEEKEND SO I DON'T GO CRAZY.
GRAIN

PEEBER AND I WENT TO OUR FAVORITE TACO SPOT.
TACO DOG!

KAREN + I BOUGHT GROCERIES.
TOMORROW WE WILL BAKE A PIE AND BREW BEER. ANYTHING TO KEEP OUR MINDS OCCUPIED.

I'M SO DEPRESSED - ABNER JAY

4-20-14

WE DIDN'T HAVE TO KEEP OUR MINDS OCCUPIED LONG

OH SHIT!

NEW TEXT FROM JULIE

THE OTHER PEOPLE OUT-BID US. WE DIDN'T GET THE HOUSE.
AH SHIT.

WE BREWED OUR BEER ANYWAY.
LET'S CALL THIS RECIPE "BROKEN HEARTED STOUT."

METAL STORM/FACE THE SLAYER - SLAYER

4-21-14

BACK AT WORK TODAY, I WAS STILL PRETTY BUMMED OUT.
KAREN GOT ME A PRESENT TO CHEER ME UP.
A GROWLER OF PECAN PORTER AND A NEW PAIR OF TULIP GLASSES TO REPLACE THE ONE I BROKE! AWESOME!

SHE IS SERIOUSLY THE SWEETEST MOST THOUGHTFUL WOMAN IN THE WHOLE WORLD!
I LOVE YOU SO MUCH!

NO DICE - FU MANCHU

4-22-14

THIS MORNING A NEW HOUSE POPPED UP ON THE MARKET.
HMM. THIS LOOKS INTERESTING.

WE MET UP WITH JULIE TO CHECK IT OUT.
HEY GUYS!

IT WAS KINDA CRAPPY.
WHAT DO YOU THINK?
YEAH.
MEH.

WE GO SO GOOD TOGETHER - GROOVIE GHOULIES

4-23-14

SAW ANOTHER ONE COME ON THE MARKET TODAY. JULIE MADE ARRANGEMENTS TO SEE IT ON FRIDAY.

AFTER WORK I WENT TO GHOST KNIFE PRACTICE.
HOW'S THE HOUSE HUNT GOING?
SHITTY.

I ATE A SALAD FOR DINNER
CRUNCH CRUNCH

NICE NEW OUTFIT - FUGAZI

4-24-14

A NORMAL DAY AT WORK TODAY.

IT WAS NICE TO HAVE A WHOLE DAY WITH NO EMOTIONAL DRAMA.

KAREN WORKED LATE SO I STAYED UP AND PLAYED VIDEO GAMES.

ANCHORED IN LOVE - CARTER FAMILY

4-25-14

WORK WAS PRETTY CHILL TODAY

KAREN + I WENT TO SEE A COUPLE OF HOUSES.
MANOR

WE REALLY LIKED THE SECOND ONE A LOT!
LET'S MAKE AN OFFER!
OKAY!

I'M HAPPY - HASIL ADKINS

4-26-14

GOT A TEXT FROM JULIE THIS MORNING...
BUZZ BUZZ

OFFER ACCEPTED! WE GOT THE HOUSE!
WOW, THERE WERE FIVE OFFERS ON IT THE VERY FIRST DAY!

KAREN AND I WENT OUT TO CELEBRATE

BOHEMIAN RHAPSODY- QUEEN
4-27-14
WE CELEBRATED A BIT TOO HARD LAST NIGHT.
OW HANGOVER
WE GOT IT TOGETHER IN TIME TO GO SEE WRESTLING.
ONE! TWO! THREE!
THEN WE ATE PIZZA.
MUNCH MUNCH
BE REAL- GANGSTA BOO
4-28-14
AT WORK TODAY I MADE AN APPOINTMENT TO GET THE HOUSE INSPECTED TOMORROW.
KAREN + I WENT GROCERY SHOPPING.
THEN WE ATE TACOS AND WATCHED STAR TREK.
SUBURBAN HOME-DESCENDENTS
4-29-14
I LEFT WORK EARLY TODAY...
MET UP AT THE HOUSE WITH THE INSPECTOR.
HE SAYS THE HOUSE IS IN PRETTY GOOD SHAPE!
MR. PRESIDENT-PRINCE FAR I
4-30-14
WORK WAS A LITTLE SLOW TODAY.
ZZZ
AFTERWARDS I MET UP WITH MITCH AT BILLY'S.
SORRY MITCH, I TRIED TO DRAW YOU IN YOUR STYLE FROM MEMORY.
BAND
WE HUNG OUT AND DRANK BEERS AND HAD A GOOD TIME.
HA HA
HA HA
BAND

PICK THAT CHICKEN - HASIL ADKINS

5-1-14

I MADE A PROMISE TO MYSELF FOR THE MONTH OF MAY.
1. NO DRINKING.
2. WORKOUT EVERY DAY.
3. GO BACK ON DIET!

I REALLY WANT TO BE IN THE BEST SHAPE OF MY LIFE ON MY 40TH BIRTHDAY.
I'M PRETTY HAPPY WITH WHERE I AM NOW. BUT I JUST WANNA TIGHTEN UP HERE AT THE END.

I ALSO NEED TO NOT SPEND A BUNCH OF MONEY ON BEER + EATING OUT.
WE CLOSE ON THE HOUSE ON JUNE 10TH, AND I'M SURE WE WILL NEED A LOT OF MONEY.

I HATE MY FUCKING JOB - M.O.T.O.

5-2-14

WORK SUPER SUCKED TODAY. MY BOSS YELLED AT ME FOR SOMETHING I DIDN'T DO.
*#@!!

BUT WHEN I GOT HOME I SAW THAT MY SPLIT COMIC WITH MITCH IS LISTED ON THE USA TODAY WEBSITE.
HOLY SHIT!

SOMETIMES I WISH I COULD TELL MY CO-WORKERS ABOUT MY LIFE, BUT IT'S TOO RISKY

FUCK YOU YOU STUPID LITTLE TURD! I HAVE SIX BOOKS PUBLISHED, I'VE TRAVELED THE WORLD, WON AN AWARD AND SPOKE AT A MUSEUM. ALL YOU'VE EVER DONE IS WORK HERE!

I REMEMBER YOU - RAMONES

5-3-14

TODAY WAS A NICE, LEAN, SOBER SATURDAY.
83.. 84.. 85!

PEEBER AND I WENT ON A NICE WALK.

THEN KAREN + I WENT OUT TO DINNER. I GOT A VERY SENSIBLE MEAL + NO DRINK.

DICK ON A DOG - RFTC

5-4-14

WOKE UP AND DID SOME SUNDAY STUFF.

THEN WE CLEANED THE APARTMENT SUPER DEEP.

THEN WE WATCHED STAR TREK.

I FELT LIKE A GRINGO - MINUTEMEN

5-5-14

BACK AT WORK TODAY. IT WAS CHILL

I HAD TO LEAVE EARLY TO GIVE KAREN A RIDE TO RUN AN ERRAND.

THEN I CAVED AND DRANK SOME BEERS.
OOPS

LOOKIN' OUT MY BACK DOOR - CCR

5-6-14

TODAY KAREN + I HAD TO READ + SIGN OVER 200 PAGES OF SHIT FOR OUR MORTGAGE.

THIS IS GONNA SUCK.

THEN WE HAD TO TAKE A STUPID ONLINE CLASS.

TRUE OR FALSE: A DEED MEANS THAT YOU HAVE DONE A GOOD DEED IN BUYING A HOUSE.

FOR REAL?

BUYING A HOUSE IS A PAIN IN THE ASS.
LOOKS LIKE I PICKED THE WRONG MONTH TO QUIT DRINKING.

ABUSEMENT PARK - MUNICIPAL WASTE

5-7-14

ANOTHER EASY-ASS WORK DAY.

KAREN WORKED LATE SO I WATCHED A MOVIE AND ATE A PIZZA.

THE WILD LIFE

AND PLAYED WITH PEEBER.

LOWER EAST SIDE - DAVID PEEL + THE LOWER EAST SIDE

5-8-14

WORK WAS SUPER CHILL TODAY.

AFTERWARDS I WORKED ON A RECORDING WITH BRANDON + MAX

THEN I WENT TO BEERLAND AND GOT WASTED.
I FEEL LIKE I'M 27 AGAIN. THROWBACK THURSDAY!

TO LIVE AND LEARN - UNSEEN TERROR

5-9-14

I CALLED IN SICK TO WORK TODAY.
OH, HELL NO.

I WALKED AND GOT SOME BREAKFAST TACOS.

IT WAS A NICE DAY OFF.

DON'T MESS WITH MY TOOT TOOT - DENISE LASALLE

5-10-14

TODAY I RAN A BUNCH OF ERRANDS.
SOUTH AUSTIN

THEN KAREN + I WENT OUT TO DINNER.

AFTER THAT WE DRANK BEERS ON THE PORCH.

AGAIN + AGAIN - COCK SPARRER

5-11-14

GOT GROCERIES THIS MORNING.
ENCHILADITOS "THEY MAKE YA WANNA EAT EM!"
CHIPS

DID A BUNCH OF DRAWING.

PLAYED WITH PEEBER.

SHE'LL BE COMIN' ROUND THE MOUNTAIN WHEN SHE COMES

5-12-14

BACK AT WORK. ANOTHER STUPID-ASS MONDAY.
PRETTY GOOD GARFIELD FROM MEMORY, HUH?

I CAME HOME AND DID SOME WORK ON THE GHOST KNIFE RECORD COVER
PHOTOSHOP IS SO FUCKING TEDIOUS!

KAREN MADE CHICKEN N DUMPLINGS FOR DINNER.

MONEY- EMBRACE

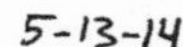
5-13-14

GOT AN EMAIL FROM OUR MORTGAGE LENDER TODAY.
YOUR HOUSE WAS APPRAISED BELOW SALE PRICE. YOU MUST NOW NEGOTIATE WITH THE SELLER.
UHH...

SO I TALKED TO JULIE.
BASICALLY, YOU'RE GOING TO HAVE TO COME UP WITH AN EXTRA $2000. OR LOSE THE HOUSE AND THE $1500 YOU'VE ALREADY PAID INTO IT.
ERR...

FUCK.
WHAT A FUCKING STUPID BACKWARDS FUCKED UP SYSTEM.
STRESS HIVES

SKIN CANCER- BOBBY JOE EBOLA + THE CHILDREN MACNUGGITS

5-14-14

SUPER STRESSED ALL DAY AT WORK.

THEN, A MIRACLE!!
MY DAD IS GONNA LEND US THE MONEY WE NEED!!

RELIEVED, KAREN + I WENT OUT FOR BURGERS.
WE'LL BE HOME-OWNERS IN LESS THAN A MONTH!!
CLINK

JOHN HARDY- LEADBELLY

5-15-14

BY PURE CHANCE TODAY, A JOB OPPORTUNITY FELL INTO MY LAP.
HMM. THIS COMPANY IS ASKING FOR A RESUME...

THEY CALLED AND ASKED ME FOR AN INTERVIEW TOMORROW.
CAN YOU COME BY AT 10:30 TOMORROW?
SURE!

EVERYTHING'S COMING UP SNAKEPIT!!!
ALL THIS GOOD NEWS HAS GOT ME WORRIED THAT I'M GONNA DIE IN A CAR ACCIDENT OR SOMETHING.

HALF LIFE- FUTURE VIRGINS

5-16-14

THIS MORNING I WENT TO MY JOB INTERVIEW. I THINK I ACED IT!!!
WE'LL LET YOU KNOW ON MONDAY.
THANKS!

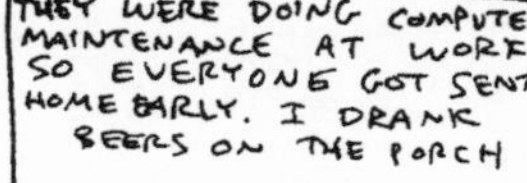
THEY WERE DOING COMPUTER MAINTENANCE AT WORK SO EVERYONE GOT SENT HOME EARLY. I DRANK BEERS ON THE PORCH

KAREN CAME HOME WITH A BUCKET OF CHICKEN AND WE WATCHED A MOVIE.
WHAT A GREAT DAY!

WAR ENSEMBLE - SLAYER
5-17-14
TODAY I TOOK PEEBER TO THE PARK.
THEN I CLEANED THE APARTMENT A LITTLE BIT.
409
THEN I PLAYED VIDEO GAMES.
ON HIGH-ACTION PATROL
5-18-14
TODAY I STARTED TO PACK UP STUFF FOR THE MOVE.
I CAN CERTAINLY PACK UP THESE BOOKS + ZINES THAT I NEVER READ.
I BANGED MY TOE SUPER-HARD ON A PIECE OF FURNITURE.
YEOW!
BAM!
I'M PRETTY SURE I BROKE IT.
UHH...
DENHAM TOWN - WINSTON + GEORGE
5-19-14
I TAPED UP MY TOE AND LIMPED THROUGH WORK TODAY.
IT ACTUALLY DOESN'T HURT MUCH AT ALL
I WAS HOPING TO GET A CALL BACK ABOUT MY JOB INTERVIEW, BUT NO LUCK
HMPH
MY TOE LOOKS SUPER BRUISED + GROSS
FIELD OF GERBILS - HORNY MORMONS
5-20-14
WORK WAS FINE TODAY.
I CAME HOME AND DID SOME DRAWINGS.
FOR EXAMPLE, MY NOSE. WHAT A GREAT JOB I'VE DONE.
KAREN MADE AWESOME NACHOS FOR DINNER AND WE WATCHED A DOC. ABOUT MAKING NIGHT OF THE LIVING DEAD.

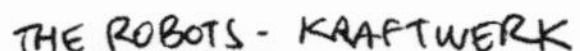
THE ROBOTS - KRAFTWERK

5-21-14

TODAY SEEMED LIKE IT WAS JUST GOING TO BE ANOTHER NORMAL DAY...

THEN MY PHONE RANG...
I GOT THE JOB!

I TOOK KAREN OUT TO CELEBRATE!
NO MORE SHITTY LITTLE NAPOLEAN BOSS! NO MORE GROSS BALONEY LADY! WOOHOO!

SULLY MY NAME- MARKED MEN

5-22-14

I BARELY GOT ANY SLEEP LAST NIGHT I WAS SO EXCITED ABOUT THE FUTURE.

WORK WAS EXTRA HARD TODAY. I'M SURE IT WILL BE FOR A WHILE.
I SO DON'T CARE!

I HAVE JUST COMPLETELY GIVEN UP ON WORKING OUT ALTOGETHER.
I SO DON'T CARE!

I'M DANGEROUS TONIGHT- POISON 13

5-23-14

WORK HAS GOTTEN SUPER BUSY ALL OF A SUDDEN.
CAN YOU COME IN ON SATURDAY?
YEAH

ON THE WAY HOME FROM WORK I STOPPED AT THE HOMEBREW STORE.

MY LAST TWO BATCHES CAME OUT UNDER-CARBONATED. I THINK I KNOW WHAT WENT WRONG AND I CAN FIX IT. HOMEBREWING SURE IS AN EXPENSIVE HOBBY.

YEASTS

I CAME HOME AND MADE A BATCH OF SCOTCH ALE.

HEAD ON- PIXIES

5-24-14

IT'S SATURDAY, I WENT IN TO WORK.
SO MUCH FOR A 3-DAY WEEKEND.

IT WASN'T SO BAD, AND I TREATED MYSELF TO LUNCH AT MY FAVORITE TACO PLACE.

¡MUCHOS TACOS POR FAVOR!

THEN I TOOK PEEBER ON A SUPER-LONG WALK.
IN JUST A FEW MORE WEEKS, YOU'RE GONNA HAVE YOUR OWN YARD!

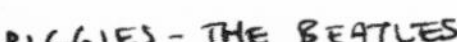
PIGGIES - THE BEATLES
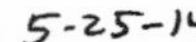
5-25-14

TODAY WE CLEANED UP THE APARTMENT
A POTENTIAL SUBLETTER IS COMING TO SEE IT TOMORROW.

THEN I DID LAUNDRY WHILE KAREN BAKED A CAKE.
WHAT IS THIS? A CORN DOG?
ITS A WHISK!

AFTER THAT WE WENT TO WRESTLING.

LOST IN THE SUPERMARKET - THE CLASH

5-26-14

TODAY WAS SUPER RAINY AND COLD.

I PLAYED VIDEO GAMES AND DRANK BEER ALL DAY.
BUURP!

IT WAS AWESOME.
MEMORIAL DAY!

THE THING THAT ONLY EATS HIPPIES - DEAD MILKMEN

5-27-14

BACK AT WORK, IT'S SUPER BUSY. IT'S HARD TO PRETEND TO GIVE A SHIT.

I CAME HOME AND TOOK A NAP.
Z Z Z

THEN I WATCHED A MOVIE WITH KAREN.
THIS MOVIE SUCKS.
YEAH.
MAXIMUM OVERDRIVE

SWEET LEAF - BLACK SABBATH

5-28-14

I WORKED ALMOST TEN HOURS TODAY.

I CAME HOME AND DID SOME DRAWING.

I'M SO SICK OF JUST WAITING.
WAITING TO MOVE WAITING TO START MY NEW JOB.

VISION CONQUEST – NAPALM DEATH

5-29-14

ANOTHER DING-DONG ASS WORK DAY.

I'VE PRETTY MUCH TOTALLY GIVEN UP ON WORKING OUT.
I DUNNO WHAT HAPPENED. ONE DAY I JUST STOPPED CARING.

I TOOK A GRAVITY READING ON MY NEW BATCH OF BEER. IT'S GONNA BE 7.5%!!
WHOA!

IT FOLLOWS – MINOR THREAT

5-30-14

TODAY WAS PAYDAY. THE LAST ONE I'LL EVER HAVE AS A NON-HOMEOWNER!

I TREATED KAREN TO INDIAN FOOD

ALSO I GOT A HAIRCUT

A CRESCENDO OF PASSION BLEEDING – CRADLE OF FILTH

5-31-14

TODAY I MADE MYSELF DO A WORKOUT
23... 24... 25...

I BOTTLED MY SCOTCH ALE.

THEN I WATCHED STAR TREK WITH KAREN.

LOVE ME – POISON 13

6-1-14

THIS MORNING I PLAYED VIDEO GAMES.

THEN I WENT TO GHOST KNIFE PRACTICE.
STILL GOT IT

THEN KAREN + I WATCHED COSMOS
THERE IS NO GOD!

THE DRUG IS FOOTBALL- VANILLA MUFFINS 6-2-14

BACK AT WORK TODAY, PRETENDING TO GIVE A SHIT.

CAME HOME AND HELPED KAREN PACK.

WE GOT ALL THE UTILITIES STRAIGHTENED OUT!

WATER AND ELECTRICITY ON THE 10TH!

INTERNET AND GAS ON THE 16TH!

JACK THE RIPPER- LINK WRAY 6-3-14

ANOTHER DINGDONG/ASS DAY AT WORK.

A QUICK BAND PRACTICE BEFORE OUR SHOW TOMORROW..

THEN NACHOS WITH KAREN!

HURDY GURDY MAN- BUTTHOLE SURFERS 6-4-14

WORK WAS ALL WHATEVER TODAY.
I WENT TO BEERLAND AND PLAYED A SHOW WITH GHOST KNIFE.
IT WAS FUN.

TREADING ON HEELS- AVAIL 6-5-14

I FELT AWFUL TODAY. I WENT HOME FROM WORK EARLY
I SPENT MOST OF THE DAY LYING ON THE COUCH, FEELING SHITTY.

I DON'T THINK I'M EVER GOING OUT TO A SHOW ON A WEEKNIGHT AGAIN. EVER.
THIS IS 40.

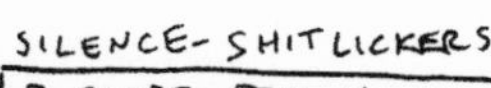
SILENCE- SHITLICKERS

6-6-14

I SLEPT TEN HOURS LAST NIGHT.
I FEEL GREAT!

TODAY KAREN TOLD ME HER SISTER HAD HER BABY LAST NIGHT!
THEY NAMED HIM WYATT STERLING.
I HAVE A NEPHEW!

WE RELAXED AND ENJOYED EACH OTHER'S COMPANY.
IT'S OUR LAST WEEKEND IN THIS APARTMENT.

IN TIME - UNIFORM CHOICE

6-7-14

IT'S OUR LAST WEEKEND IN THIS APARTMENT. I WENT AND GOT TACOS AT MY FAVORITE SPOT.
THESE ARE FAR FROM THE BEST TACOS IN TOWN, BUT THEY'RE MY FAVORITE ONES IN THIS NEIGHBORHOOD.

I SPENT THE AFTER-NOON PACKING STUFF

AND I SPENT THE EVENING PLAYING VIDEO GAMES + BEING LAZY.
NEXT WEEK IS GONNA BE ONE OF THE BIGGEST OF MY LIFE!

SIX FEET UNDER - KING DIAMOND

6-8-14

THIS MORNING KAREN+PEEBER AND I WENT TO THE PARK.

I DID LAUNDRY AND GOT GROCERIES.

THEN I WATCHED NIGHTMARE ON ELM STREET 2.
WHOA I NEVER REALIZED HOW GAY THIS MOVIE IS!

CAN THIS BE? - THE WIPERS

6-9-14

BACK AT WORK, STILL PRETENDING TO GIVE A FUCK.

KAREN + I DROVE OUT TO THE HOUSE AND DID A FINAL WALK-THROUGH WITH JULIE.

I CAN'T WAIT TO MOVE IN!!!

USELESS EATER- VOMIT PIGS
6-10-14
WORK WENT BY PRETTY FAST TODAY.
I CAME HOME AND HELPED KAREN DO SOME PACKING.
THE WALL OF BOXES IS GROWING!
THEN I WENT TO BED.
ZZZ
TALK SHIT GET SHOT - BODY COUNT
6-11-14
WORK IS GETTING SUPER BUSY. THEY'RE GONNA BE SO BUMMED WHEN I QUIT.
KAREN+I ORDERED A PIZZA + DID MORE PACKING.
THE WAITING IS KILLING ME!!!
TEN TIMES SWEETER- WINSTON FRANCIS
6-12-14
LAST DAY OF WORK OF MY THIRTIES!
COMPLETELY FINISHED PACKING EVERYTHING.
WE HAD A CRAZY ALMOST-TORNADO TONIGHT!
WHOOSH
YEEK!
BLIMBO- HORACE ANDY
6-13-14
TODAY WE WENT AND SIGNED A BUNCH OF PAPERS.
ULP!
THEN WE GOT THE KEYS TO OUR HOUSE!!!!
WE TOOK PEEBER WITH US AND ATE DINNER IN IT!
THIS IS OUR HOUSE!
HOLY SHIT!
TAKE OUT

PAPPY - F.Y.P.

6-14-14

HOLY SHIT I'M FUCKING 40 YEARS OLD!
GET THE HELL OFF OF MY PROPERTY YOU SON-OF-A-BITCHES!

I SPENT THE DAY MOVING STUFF INTO THE NEW HOUSE.
U-HAUL

THEN KAREN TOOK ME OUT TO DINNER AT BILLY'S!
MAX+MEL CAME TOO!

RIPPING CORPSE - KREATOR

6-15-14

ANOTHER DAY SPENT MOVING.

WE GOT MOST EVERYTHING. JUST A FEW RANDOM THINGS LEFT TO GET.

OUR FIRST NIGHT SLEEPING IN THE NEW HOUSE WAS AMAZING!
IT'S PITCH BLACK AND THERE ARE A MILLION CRICKETS.

NIGHT OF THE LONG KNIVES - AC&DC

6-16-14

TODAY I FINALLY PUT IN MY TWO-WEEKS NOTICE AT WORK!
THE BOSS

AFTERWARD, I LOADED UP THE VAN WITH A HUGE AMOUNT OF STUFF.
UGH!

KAREN + I SPENT THE EVENING UNPACKING.
HOW DID WE HAVE THIS MUCH SHIT IN THAT TINY APARTMENT?

BAD REPETATION - WOODY GUTHRIE

6-17-14

WORK WAS CHILL TODAY.

I DROVE ANOTHER LOAD OF STUFF FROM THE APARTMENT TO THE HOUSE.

MORE UNPACKING AND ENJOYING OUR NEW PLACE.
IT'S REALLY COMIN' TOGETHER.

ALL TOMORROW'S PARTIES - VELVET UNDERGROUND
6-18-14
AT WORK TODAY, I THINK THEY HIRED A GUY TO TAKE MY PLACE.
YOU'RE GONNA HATE IT
GOT THE VERY LAST LOAD OF STUFF FROM THE APARTMENT.
KAREN + I WATCHED OUR FIRST EPISODE OF STAR TREK IN THE NEW HOUSE!
IF YOU KNOW WHAT I MEAN.
MIXED BLESSING - SQUIRREL BAIT
6-19-14
I'M SUPER PHONING IT IN AT WORK NOW.
I GOT AN EMAIL ABOUT THE CRAIGSLIST AD I PUT UP. SOMEBODY WANTS TO SUBLET OUR APT!
WHEW. I WAS STARTING TO STRESS.
DID A LOT OF UNPACKING TONIGHT.
WAH! I DONT WANNA DO ALL THIS.
LAUNDROMAT SONG - DEAD MILKMEN
6-20-14
SO GLAD TODAY IS FRIDAY.
KAREN + I WENT TO THE LAUNDROMAT.
HOPEFULLY WE WON'T HAVE TO DO THIS FOR VERY LONG!
YEAH
THEN WE WENT TO THE OPENING PARTY FOR SPENT'S BREWERY!
CONGRATULATIONS DUDE!
THANKS!
IN THE BEGINNING - HICKEY
6-21-14
MY FIRST SATURDAY IN THE NEW HOUSE! I MOWED THE LAWN.
FINISHED UNPACKING AND SET UP MY OFFICE.
VIOLA!
KAREN CAME HOME AND WE TOOK PEEBER FOR A WALK.
PEEBER LIKES OUR NEW NEIGHBORHOOD.
SO DO I!

SHE FLOATED AWAY_ HUSKER DU

THIS MORNING I BOUGHT A GRILL.
BBQ GRILL
BBQ GRILL

WE HAD OUR FIRST PROPER COOK OUT.

6-22-14
I LOVE BEING A HOME-OWNER!

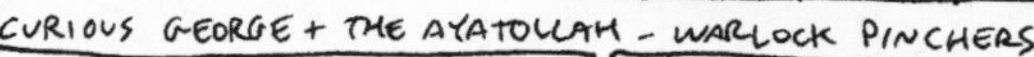
CURIOUS GEORGE + THE AYATOLLAH - WARLOCK PINCHERS.

BACK AT WORK TODAY.

I WENT + SHOWED OUR APARTMENT TO A POTENTIAL SUBLETTER.
HERE IT IS..
OKAY.

6-23-14
WHEN I GOT HOME, I FOUND OUT...
THE STOVE STILL ISN'T GONNA BE FIXED FOR ANOTHER WEEK.
SIGH.

13 CANDLES - UNCLE ACID + THE DEADBEATS

6-24-14

ANOTHER PHONED-IN DAY AT WORK...

I CAME HOME AND FIXED THE REFRIGERATOR.

THEN WE GOT A CALL FROM OUR APARTMENT MANAGER.
YOUR SUBLETTER'S APPLICATION WAS NOT APPROVED.
FUCK! ITS ALMOST JULY 1!

THE PILL - LORETTA LYNN

6-25-14

I GOT A CALL TODAY AT WORK.
HEY BEN, IT'S YOUR NEW BOSS. YOUR SHITTY BOSS AT YOUR OLD JOB CALLED YOUR NEW CO-WORKER AND TOLD HER SHES BEING REPLACED. SHE GOT MAD AND WALKED OUT. CAN YOU COME IN AND WORK TODAY?

SO I WENT AND WORKED HALF A DAY AT MY NEW JOB.
HOLY FUCK, THIS SOFTWARE IS TOTALLY ALIEN TO ME. I HAVE NO IDEA WHAT I'M DOING. I'M TOTALLY IN OVER MY HEAD!

I COULDN'T SLEEP ALL NIGHT I WAS PANICKING SO HARD.

WHAT IF MY NEW BOSS FIRES ME? HOW AM I GONNA LEARN THIS COMPLICATED SOFTWARE WITH NOBODY TO TRAIN ME? WHAT AM I GONNA DO?

MUD - UNIVERSAL ORDER OF ARMAGEDDON
6-26-14
ONLY ONE MORE DAY AT WORK!
ULP!
I FOUND A COPY OF THE SOFTWARE I'LL BE USING AT MY NEW JOB.
HOPEFULLY I CAN FIGURE THIS OUT.
CLICK CLICK
STILL NO NEWS ON THE SUBLETTING FRONT.
FUCK! IT LOOKS LIKE WE'RE GONNA HAVE TO PAY RENT ON OUR VACANT APARTMENT FOR JULY.
CLICK CLICK
HAPPY IS... - DEAD MILKMEN
6-27-14
MY LAST DAY AT MY JOB WAS SURPRISINGLY EMOTIONAL.
I'M ACTUALLY GONNA MISS THIS HORRIBLE PLACE AND THESE HORRIBLE PEOPLE.
TING + MAILIN
KAREN + I WENT OUT TO OUR NEW MEXICAN LOCAL SPOT.
RAMOS RESTAURANT
MANOR I MOTEL
I STAYED UP LATE, GOOFING OFF.
I DOUBT I'LL HAVE ANOTHER STRESS-FREE NIGHT IN A WHILE.
NETFLIX
THE GAMES PEOPLE PLAY - BOB ANDY
6-28-14
TODAY WAS A NICE SATURDAY. I ORGANIZED THE GARAGE.
I GOT AN EMAIL FROM A PROSPECTIVE SUBLETTER! I'M GONNA SHOW HIM THE APARTMENT TOMORROW.
FUCK YES!
KAREN CAME HOME FROM WORK AND WE GRILLED A CHICKEN IN THE BACK YARD.
WHERE WERE YOU ON THE NIGHT OF MAY 23RD?
OINK OINK - DAVID PEEL + THE LOWER EAST SIDE
6-29-14
THIS MORNING I SHOWED THE APARTMENT TO A NICE COUPLE THAT SEEMED VERY INTERESTED.
HERE'S THE KITCHEN...
LATER TODAY THEY SENT ME A TEXT.
FUCK!
SORRY. NOT INTERESTD. - COUPLE
KAREN MADE DINNER ON THE GRILL AGAIN.
WHEN DOES THE FUCKING STOVE GET FIXED!?!
TOMORROW?

UP FRONT- WIPERS

6-30-14

TODAY I STARTED AT MY NEW JOB.

THE LEARNING CURVE ON THIS NEW SOFTWARE IS PRETTY INSANE...
ULP!

BUT I STILL LIKE IT MORE THAN MY LAST JOB!
AT LEAST I DON'T HAVE A SHITTY, PISSY LITTLE-MAN BOSS WITH A NAPOLEAN COMPLEX!

BEERSHIT- BLACK RANDY + THE METRO SQUAD

7-1-14

WELL, WE ENDED UP HAVING TO PAY JULY'S RENT ON OUR VACANT APARTMENT.
GRRR
RENT

WRESTLING WITH THE SOFTWARE AT WORK ALL DAY WAS STRESSFUL.
GRR
UR DUM

I CAME HOME AND RELAXED WITH SOME STAR TREK WITH KAREN.
IS THAT A WARP PLASMA CONDUIT IN YOUR POCKET OR ARE YOU JUST HAPPY TO SEE ME?

PURPLE RAIN- PRINCE

7-2-14

WORK WAS BETTER TODAY. I'M NOT REALLY GETTING THE HANG OF THE NEW SOFTWARE BUT I'M LEARNING HOW TO FAKE IT.

GRUMMMBLE

KAREN + PEEBER + I WENT ON A SUPER LONG WALK THROUGH OUR NEW NEIGHBORHOOD.

WHEN WE GOT HOME, WE WERE ALL SUPER-POOPED!
Z Z Z Z Z Z Z Z Z Z

SPLIT MYSELF IN TWO - MEAT PUPPETS

7-3-14

THIS MORNING MY BOSS GAVE ME A BREAKFAST TACO!
RAD!

THEN MY OTHER BOSS TOOK ME OUT TO LUNCH!
RADDER!

THEN KAREN TOOK ME OUT TO DINNER!
RADDEST!

NIGHTMARE ON MY STREET - DJ JAZZY JEFF + FRESH PRINCE

7-4-14

SPENT THE DAY FRUSTRATEDLY SHOWING THE APARTMENT TO PEOPLE. STILL NOBODY'S RENTED IT YET.
HERE'S THE FUCKING KITCHEN.

I CAME HOME HOT + SWEATY + EXHAUSTED + PISSED OFF.

THEN WE WENT OUT AND SAW ALL THE FIREWORKS IN OUR NEIGHBORHOOD AND MY MOOD DID A TOTAL 180!
I LOVE LIVING HERE!

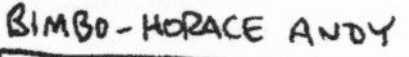

BIMBO - HORACE ANDY

7-5-14

THIS MORNING I MOWED THE LAWN.
RRRRRRR

THEN I DID A BUNCH OF DRAWING.

AND STAYED UP LATE PLAYING VIDEO GAMES.

SKATE + DESTROY - THE FACTION

7-6-14

TODAY WAS WEIRD. I WAS IN A SUNDAY FUNK.

THERE'S JUST SO MUCH BIG CHANGE IN MY LIFE RIGHT NOW.
NEW JOB
NEW HOUSE

I HAD CRAZY, UNSETTLING DREAMS.

LEAVE MY SOUL ALONE - MERCYFUL FATE

7-7-14

BACK AT WORK TODAY, I'M STARTING TO GET MORE USED TO IT.

AFTERWARDS I SHOWED THE APARTMENT TO TWO MORE PEOPLE.
HERE IS THE KITCHEN

I REALLY FUCKING HOPE SOMEBODY RENTS IT.
I REALLY DONT NEED THE EXTRA STRESS RIGHT NOW.

WORRIED MAN BLUES- WOODY GUTHRIE

7-8-14

ANOTHER VERY SLOW DAY AT WORK. THEY KEEP TELLING ME ITS GONNA GET BUSY.
HMPH

I DRANK A COUPLE TOO MANY BEERS TONIGHT AND GOT DEPRESSED.

THERE'S JUST A LOT OF CHANGE IN MY LIFE AND ITS STRESSFUL TO DEAL WITH.

SORRY. I KNOW YOU'RE SICK OF HEARING ME BITCH AND COMPLAIN ABOUT CHANGES I BROUGHT ON MYSELF. I'LL SHUT UP NOW.

BABY COME BACK- THE EQUALS

7-9-14

WORK WAS MUCH BETTER TODAY.
I'M STARTING TO GET THIS.

AS WAS COMING HOME.
MAN, I DUNNO WHY I'M SO DOWN ON EVERYTHING. IT'S FUCKING GORGEOUS OUT HERE!

IT'S AMAZING WHAT YOU CAN ACCOMPLISH WHEN YOU CHANGE YOUR OWN ATTITUDE.

I HAVE A LOVING WIFE, A HIGH-PAYING JOB (FOR ME) AND I FINALLY OWN MY OWN HOUSE! WHAT DO I HAVE TO BE BUMMED ABOUT?

RADIO RADIO RADIO- RANCID

7-10-14

MY JOB IS STILL TRICKY BUT GETTING WAY MORE COMFORTABLE.

KAREN + I SHOWED THE APARTMENT TO SOME PEOPLE...
HERE'S THE KITCHEN

THEN WE CAME HOME AND WATCHED STAR TREK
WHOA!

I DON'T WANNA GO DOWN TO THE BASEMENT- RAMONES (R.I.P. TOMMY!) 7-11-14

FRIDAY AT WORK WAS TIGHT. I GOT THE LAST CHECK FROM MY OLD JOB.
I HOPE I NEVER HAVE TO COME BACK HERE AGAIN

KAREN + I SHOWED THE FUCKING APARTMENT AGAIN.
HERE IS THE GODDAMN MOTHERFUCKING KITCHEN.

I GOT SOME OLD WOODEN PALLETS FROM WORK. I'M GONNA TRY TO BUILD A DOG HOUSE.
I DON'T REALLY KNOW WHAT I'M DOING.

THE CALL OF KTULU - METALLICA

7-12-14

TODAY I DECIDED TO WALK TO THE CLOSEST STORE TO MY HOUSE (A GAS STATION)
THIS LOOKS DO-ABLE.
GOOGLE MAPS
4MI

IT TOOK OVER AN HOUR!
WHOA. FOR THE LAST 20 YEARS I'VE ALWAYS LIVED IN A WALKABLE CITY. THIS IS GONNA TAKE SOME GETTING USED TO!

TODAY I GOT INTERVIEWED ON THE PHONE FOR A MAGAZINE.
WHY YES AS A MATTER OF FACT I AM QUITE AWESOME.

STRUGGLE LIKE NO OTHER - EPOXIES

7-13-14

THIS MORNING KAREN + I TOOK A WALK AROUND DOWNTOWN MANOR.

THEN WE DROVE TO ELGIN AND HAD THEIR FAMOUS BBQ FOR LUNCH.

WHAT A NICE DAY OUT.

NO TOMORROW - THE DICTATORS

7-14-14

BACK AT WORK TODAY, IT WAS COOL. I'M GETTING MORE USED TO IT.

I CAME BACK TO THE APARTMENT AND SHOWED IT TO ANOTHER GUY.
IT'S DIRTY IN HERE. IT SMELLS BAD.
OKAY.

KAREN MADE ME A DELICIOUS DINNER.
FUCK THAT GUY.

ATTIC - CRUSADES

7-15-14

I KICKED ASS AT WORK TODAY.
YEAH! SUCK MY DICK, B.C.C. MAIL MANAGER!

CAME HOME TO A WONDERFUL MEAL MADE BY KAREN.

MY LIFE IS GREAT. I HAVE NO REASON TO COMPLAIN.

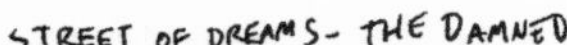
STREET OF DREAMS- THE DAMNED

7-16-14

WORK IS GETTING COOLER AND COOLER.
MAN, I'M GETTING SO MUCH BETTER AT THIS!

SHOWED THE APARTMENT TO A COUPLE PEOPLE.
HERE'S THE KITCHEN

CAME HOME AND KAREN MADE A PIZZA.
I LOVE YOU!

CHICKEN SCRATCH- YOUNG MEN

7-17-14

I KICKED WORK'S ASS TODAY!
IN CASE YOU WERE CURIOUS, I DO STILL USE ONE OF THESE BIG MACHINES AT MY JOB JUST NOT AS MUCH.

I CAME HOME AND WORKED ON PEEBER'S DOG HOUSE WHILE KAREN DID HOMEWORK.
I HAVE NO IDEA WHAT I'M DOING.

THERE WAS A CRAZY AND COOL THUNDER-STORM

BRA-CYMANDE

7-18-14

TODAY WAS MY FIRST REAL PAYDAY AT MY NEW JOB.
HOLY SHIT!

I TOOK KAREN OUT TO DINNER.

WHILE THERE, I GOT AN AWESOME PHONE CALL
SOMEBODY RENTED YOUR APARTMENT!

PARANOID- THE DICKIES

7-19-14

THIS MORNING WE SIGNED THE SUBLEASE AGREEMENT.

I DID A BUNCH OF ERRANDS IN AUSTIN.

PEEBER AND I GOT ATTACKED BY FIRE ANTS!

ME, I DISCONNECT FROM YOU - GARY NUMAN

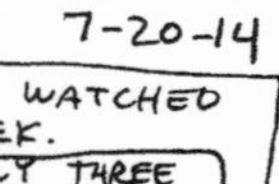
7-20-14

A NICE DAY OFF. MY ANKLE WAS SWOLLEN UP LIKE A WATERMELON.
FUCK A FIRE ANT.

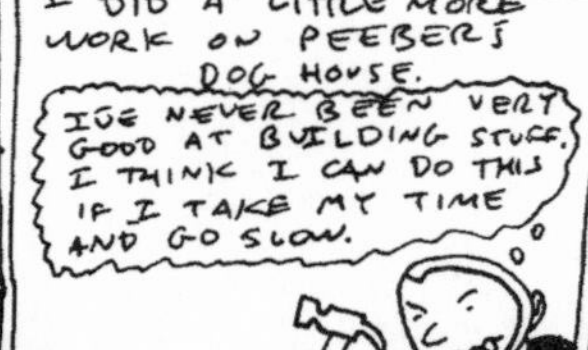
I DID A LITTLE MORE WORK ON PEEBER'S DOG HOUSE.
I'VE NEVER BEEN VERY GOOD AT BUILDING STUFF. I THINK I CAN DO THIS IF I TAKE MY TIME AND GO SLOW.

KAREN AND I WATCHED STAR TREK.
THERE ARE ONLY THREE EPISODES OF VOYAGER LEFT!!!!
BYE, NEELIX

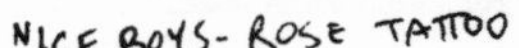
NICE BOYS - ROSE TATTOO

7-21-14

BACK TO WORK TODAY.

KAREN + I GOT SOME GROCERIES
THESE 75 CENT BAGS OF PEANUTS ARE MY JAM!
PEANUTS
PEANUTS
PEANUTS

THEN WE WATCHED THE DOCUMENTARY ABOUT DIVINE.

FACE TO FACE - SHELLSHAG

7-22-14

WORK SUCKED TODAY. I FUCKED UP A JOB.
SHIT!

WHEN I GOT HOME, THE EVAPORATER FAN MOTOR I ORDERED FOR THE FRIDGE HAD ARRIVED.
HMM... CAN I DO THIS?

I REPLACED IT AND IT ACTUALLY WORKS!
I DID IT! I'M SO PROUD OF MYSELF!

FORM ANOTHER STONE - CAMPER VAN BEETHOVEN

7-23-14

WORK WAS PRETTY STRESSFUL TODAY.

I CAME HOME AND GOT DRUNK.
GLUG GLUG

STRESSFUL OR NOT, MY LIFE IS PRETTY GOOD.

CENOTAPH- BOLT THROWER

7-24-14

TODAY MY BOSS TOOK ME OUT TO LUNCH.
THINGS ARE GOING TO GET REALLY CRAZY IN A FEW MONTHS.

THEN I WENT TO DO SOME TRAINING AT A FANCY DOWNTOWN OFFICE.
BLAH BLAH BLAH BLAH BLAH BLAH BLAH BLAH

I HOPE I'M NOT IN OVER MY HEAD WITH THIS NEW JOB.
HOLY FUCK. I DON'T REALLY KNOW WHAT I'M DOING AT ALL.

NOTHIN' TO LOSE- KISS

7-25-14

WORK WAS VERY STRESSFUL TODAY.

I CAME HOME AND MOWED THE LAWN.
RRRR RRRRR

KAREN AND I GOT IN AN ARGUEMENT.
I SHOULDN'T BE TAKING OUT MY WORK STRESS ON KAREN. SHE'S THE ONLY ALLY I HAVE.

LIGHT THAT FUSE! - TIGHT BROS FROM WAY BACK WHEN

7-26-14

A MUCH-NEEDED LAZY SATURDAY. I SPENT MOST OF THE DAY RE-ORGANIZING THE MUSIC ON MY COMPUTER.

I RODE MY BIKE TO THE STORE.
I HAVEN'T RIDDEN MY BIKE IN YEARS!

AND I GAVE PEEBER A BATH.

GARY'S NOTE- SHELLSHAG

7-27-14

THIS MORNING KAREN + I WENT TO THE LAUNDROMAT

AFTER THAT I WENT AND HUNG OUT WITH MY NEIGHBORS. THEY ARE NICE!
THEY HAVE A COOL RECORDING STUDIO IN THEIR GARAGE!
CECELIA
GARY

THEN KAREN + I STARTED WATCHING STAR TREK: ENTERPRISE.
I HAVEN'T HEARD A LOT OF GOOD STUFF ABOUT THIS SHOW...
ITS GONNA BE HARD TO TOP VOYAGER!

WE WON'T CHANGE - DEAD MOON

7-28-14

A SUPER CRAZY DAY AT WORK. I HAD TO DRIVE A BIG-ASS TRUCK.
BACKING INTO THE LOADING DOCK!

IT WAS A STRESSFUL DAY, BUT I LEARNED A LOT OF STUFF.
I HAVE SO MUCH MORE RESPONSIBILITY HERE!

I CAME HOME AND RELAXED.
I'M LETTING MYSELF GET FAT AGAIN.

PROUD MARY - CCR

7-29-14

WORK WAS A LOT MORE CHILL TODAY

I TRIED TO FIX MY CAR STEREO BUT ENDED UP BREAKING IT.
OOPS.

KAREN AND I STARTED WATCHING HALT + CATCH FIRE. IT'S SILLY BUT PRETTY GOOD.
IT REMINDS ME OF THE "BUSINESS PORN" FROM MAD MEN.
THE WHAT?

LIKE DYING - FUNERAL ORATION

7-30-14

TODAY MY OLD JOB CALLED AND ASKED ME TO COME IN AND HELP OUT.

SURE!

IT WAS NICE TO GO BACK FOR A MINUTE.

ALSO MAKES ME REALLY GLAD I LEFT!

KAREN ORDERED A PIZZA.
PIZZA
A PIZZA
WITH STUFF ON IT!

ALL NIGHT VIVARIN JAG - MOTO

7-31-14

WORK WAS MUCH MORE CHILL TODAY.

I GOT THE BIGGEST PAYCHECK I'VE EVER GOTTEN IN MY LIFE.
WHOA

I RODE THE BUS TO THE AIRPORT AFTER WORK AND RENTED A CAR.

PATTERNS OF EVIL - ELECTRIC WIZARD

8-1-14

THIS MORNING I TOOK A WRONG TURN AND ENDED UP GETTING TO SAN ANTONIO LATE!
FUCK!

IT WAS OKAY THOUGH. I SAT AT MY TABLE FOR WIZARD WORLD ALL DAY.
I'VE SOLD ONE BOOK ALL DAY.
FUCK.

WHEN IT WAS OVER I HUNG OUT WITH MITCH AND AMANDA.
BAN
MILO!

GIVE ME THE CURE - FUGAZI

8-2-14

DAY 2 OF THE COMIC CON WAS NOT VERY LUCRATIVE FOR ME.
SO THESE ARE SELF-PUBLISHED?

I HUNG OUT WITH MITCH + MARCO AFTER. WE GOT TACOS.
BAND

THEN WE ALL WENT BACK TO MITCH'S PLACE AND DRANK BEEEERZ.
BAND

JIGGY JIG - ROCKET FROM THE CRYPT

8-3-14

I DECIDED TO DITCH THE COMIC CON AND GO HOME EARLY.
FUCK THIS!

KAREN AND I RAN A BUNCH OF ERRANDS.

I KINDA WISH I'D JUST STAYED HOME ALL WEEKEND.
ONCE UPON A TIME I WOULD'VE GIVEN ANYTHING TO DO SOMETHING LIKE THAT.
FUNNY HOW TIME CHANGES SO MUCH.

METAL GODS - JUDAS PRIEST

8-4-14

BACK AT WORK TODAY. I DON'T MIND IT ONE BIT.

KAREN MADE FRIED CHICKEN FOR DINNER!
THIS IS WHAT HAPPENS WHEN I TRY TO DRAW KAREN AS COLONEL SANDERS, WHICH IS A BAD IDEA TO BEGIN WITH.
I'M SORRY KAREN. ♡

WATCHED SOME MORE HALT + CATCH FIRE
THIS SHOW IS CHEESY BUT KINDA GOOD!

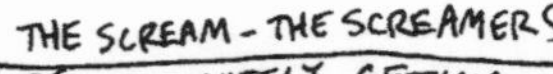
THE SCREAM - THE SCREAMERS

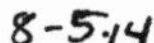
8-5-14

I'M DEFINITELY GETTING MORE USED TO MY JOB.

KAREN + I RELAXED AND ENJOYED THE MANY BEERS I BROUGHT BACK FROM SAN ANTONIO.

THEN I WENT TO BED EARLY. FUCK, I'M TIRED.
ZZZ

REPROVISIONAL - FUGAZI

8-6-14

WORK WAS OKAY TODAY.

I CAME HOME AND DID SOME DRAWING.

THEN I WATCHED TV.

PHARMAKON - NOMOS

8-7-14

WORK GOT PRETTY STRESSFUL TODAY.

I WAS SUPER EXHAUSTED WHEN I GOT HOME.

WE'RE STILL TRUDGING THROUGH STAR TREK: ENTERPRISE BUT IT SUCKS SO BAD.
OH GOD, THIS THEME SONG.
MAYBE IT WILL GET BETTER.

777 - DANZIG

8-8-14

WORK WAS KINDA NUTS TODAY, BUT I GOT THROUGH IT.

I MET UP WITH KAREN AND AMY AT "CAFE MUELLER" WHICH IS JUST A GROCERY STORE.

LATER I GOT DRUNK AND BOUGHT A WEED EATER AT WAL-MART.
WEED EATER

I WANNA BE ME - SEX PISTOLS
8-9-14
THIS MORNING I MOWED THE LAWN AND USED MY NEW WEED EATER!
WOW, I'VE MANGED TO DRAW THE WORST WEED EATER EVER DRAWN!
RRRR
I HAD A VERY RELAXING DAY OFF...
ZZZ
SHIT MAY BE CRAZY AND STRESSFUL AT WORK, BUT I'M OKAY WITH THAT.
MY LIFE IS REALLY FUCKING AWESOME.
ANTI-CIMEX - ANTI-CIMEX
8-10-14
TODAY KAREN + I HAD TO RUN A BUNCH OF ERRANDS "IN TOWN"
AUSTIN
I WENT TO GHOST KNIFE PRACTICE.
I HAVEN'T PLAYED IN SO LONG!
I BOUGHT A NEW STEREO FOR MY VAN. THE OLD ONE BROKE A WHILE AGO.
HMM
MANIC DEPRESSION - JIMI HENDRIX
8-11-14
BACK AT WORK. IT'S EITHER CRAZY STRESSFUL OR TOTALLY BORING.
WHEN I GOT HOME, I INSTALLED MY NEW CAR STEREO BY MYSELF.
ONE OF THE MOST IMPORTANT THINGS I'VE LEARNED SINCE BECOMING A HOMEOWNER:
YOU CAN FIX ANYTHING YOU SET YOUR MIND TO. IT WAS MADE BY A PERSON JUST LIKE YOU, AND YOU ARE CAPABLE OF FIXING IT!
THE SNAKE PIT - THE CURE
8-12-14
WORK WAS PRETTY OKAY TODAY.
I HAD A NICE DINNER WITH KAREN.
SNAKE PIT

DESTINATION - HEROIN

8-13-14

WORK WAS OKAY TODAY.

I CAME HOME AND HUNG OUT IN MY GARAGE.

SOMETIMES THE DAYS ARE TOO SHORT.

PLAN 9 CHANNEL 7 - THE DAMNED

8-14-14

WORK WAS WEIRD TODAY. A DUDE QUIT, AND SUPPOSEDLY THERE'S A NEW BOSS STARTING ON MONDAY.
NICE WORKIN' WITH YOU.
UH, OKAY.

I WAS TIRED WHEN I GOT HOME.

KAREN + I DECIDED TO GO TO IKEA THIS WEEK-END.
WE NEED SOME BOOK SHELVES.
OKAY
IKEA
2014

RAM IT DOWN - JUDAS PRIEST

8-15-14

GOT OUT OF WORK EARLY WITH A BIG-ASS PAYCHECK!
UH, OKAY!

I BOUGHT A WASHER AND DRYER FROM PENNY + SHAWN.
RAD!

TOOK KAREN OUT FOR PIZZA.
NOT BAD!

UNCERTAINTY BLURS THE VISION - NAPALM DEATH

8-16-14

TODAY I BREWED A BATCH OF BEER. IT FEELS GOOD TO GET BACK UP ON IT!

THE REST OF MY DAY WAS PRETTY LAZY.
ZZZ

KAREN AND I SHOPPED FOR CARS ON THE INTERNET.
NOW THAT MY VAN IS PAID OFF...

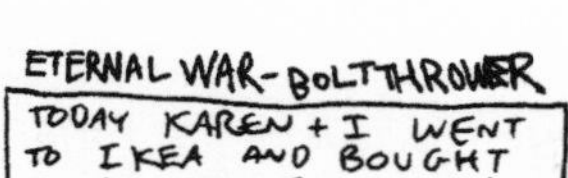
ETERNAL WAR - BOLTTHROWER
TODAY KAREN + I WENT TO IKEA AND BOUGHT STUFF FOR THE LIVING ROOM.

IKEA

8-17-14
I YELLED + CUSSED + MADE A RUCKUS, BUT I MANAGED TO PUT IT ALL TOGETHER.
@*#!!
THE LIVING ROOM LOOKS AWESOME!

DECIDE - CHELSEA

8-18-14

BACK TO WORK. I MET MY NEW BOSS. HE SEEMS FINE.

I CAME HOME AND ENJOYED SOME BEERS WITH MY WIFE.

LIFE'S NOT SO BAD. IN FACT, ITS FUCKING GREAT.
AMAZING HOW SUCH A SIMPLE LIFE..
...CAN BE SO SATISFYING.

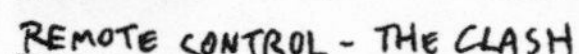
REMOTE CONTROL - THE CLASH

8-19-14

TODAY THEY MOVED ME INTO A NEW OFFICE AT WORK.

KAREN + I ORDERED A PIZZA FOR DINNER.
WHAT A SHITTY LOOKING PIZZA.
WHY DO I SUCK AT DRAWING SO BAD?

WE SAT OUT ON THE BACK PORCH.

SENIORITIS - FU MANCHU

8-20-14

NEW OFFICE ISN'T BAD.

I CLEANED MY ROOM AT HOME.

AND HUNG OUT IN THE GARAGE

TIME TO GET ILL - BEASTIE BOYS

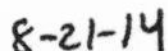

TODAY I WENT TO WORK

THEN I WENT TO BAND PRACTICE

THEN I WENT TO HOME.

MANOR→

PARALLEL WOMAN. SHONEN KNIFE

8-22-14

I GOT OUT OF WORK SUPER EARLY TODAY.

I GOT A HAIRCUT AND BOUGHT GROCERIES.

SPENT THE EVENING SITTING OUTSIDE, LOOKING AT THE STARS

BORN BACKWARDS - ASSUCK

8-23-14

TODAY I WENT TO A BBQ AT ALISON + BRYAN'S HOUSE.

THEN GHOST KNIFE PLAYED A SHOW AT TRAILER SPACE.

I HAD FUN AND THE DRIVE BACK TO MANOR WASN'T SO BAD.

MANOR→

SWEAT LOAF - BUTTHOLE SURFERS

8-24-14

BEST, LAZIEST DAY OFF EVER.

I BREWED SOME BEER.

AND WATCHED A MOVIE.

Z Z Z

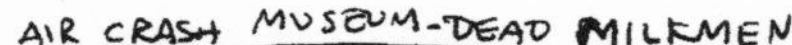
AIR CRASH MUSEUM-DEAD MILKMEN

8-25-14

BACK AT WORK WAS NO SWEAT TODAY.

KAREN + I GOT APPROVED TO BUY A NEW CAR!
WHOA!!

BEING A GROWN-UP IS WEIRD.
? ? ? ? ?

WAYNE THE DEAD BATTERY GUY- WARLOCK PINCHERS

8-26-14

WORK WAS COOL TODAY, I'M GETTING INTO THE SWING OF IT.

I CAME HOME AND HUNG OUT IN THE GARAGE.

LOOKED ONLINE AT CARS.
MAZDA

I CAN'T FEEL NOTHIN', PT. 1- CAPTAIN BEYOND

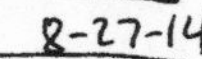
8-27-14

THINGS GOT A LITTLE BIT BUSY AT WORK TODAY.

KAREN + I HAVE STARTED WATCHING "BEAUTY AND THE BEAST," THE SHOW FROM 1987 WITH RON PERLMAN.
IT'S KINDA AWESOME.

WENT TO BED EARLY.
Z Z Z

SPLINTERED IN HER HEAD- THE CURE

8-28-14

WORK WAS SUPER BUSY TODAY BUT I ROLLED WITH IT.

AFTER WORK I WENT TO BAND PRACTICE.

WE GOT A LETTER ABOUT OUR CAR LOAN. WE HAVE TO COME UP WITH A BIGGER DOWN PAYMENT.

URGH.

WE CARE A LOT - FAITH NO MORE

8-29-14

WORK WAS BUSY BUT NICE TODAY.

I GOT PAID AND GOT TO LEAVE EARLY!

I BOUGHT A PAIR OF SHOES ON THE INTERNET
IT'S A WILD LIFE, I TELL YA.

AMERICAS PREMIERE FAITH BASED INITIATIVE - DILLINGER FOUR

8-30-14

TODAY I INSTALLED LINUX ON AN OLD COMPUTER.
JUST TO SEE WHAT ITS LIKE.

THEN GHOST KNIFE PLAYED A SHOW.

IT WAS FUN BUT I DUCKED OUT EARLY.
MANOR

PUNGENT EXCRUCIATION - CARCASS

8-31-14

AWESOME LAZY SUNDAY. KAREN + I GOOFED OFF.

WE GRILLED STEAKS AND DRANK BEERS ON THE BACK PATIO.

I STAYED UP LATE WATCHING STUPID STUFF ON YOUTUBE
HUH HUH

NEW LEAF - BAD RELIGION

9-1-14

I'VE LET MYSELF GET TOO FAT.
SIGH.

STARTING TOMORROW, I AM GONNA GET BACK IN SHAPE.

I'VE DONE IT BEFORE...
I CAN DO IT AGAIN!

TOMORROW.
OINK
ICE CREAM
POP CORN
PIZZA

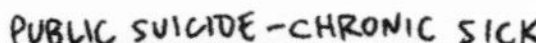
PUBLIC SUICIDE - CHRONIC SICK

9-2-14

TODAY IS THE FIRST DAY OF THE REST OF MY LIFE.

CAME HOME AND DID A WORKOUT WITH KAREN.
1..2..3..4..

DIDN'T DRINK ANY BEERS AND WENT TO BED AT A REASONABLE HOUR.

USSA - BUTTHOLE SURFERS

9-3-14

TODAY WORK WAS REALLY CRAZY AND STRESSFUL.

I DID AN EVENING WORKOUT WITH KAREN

THEN I DROVE BACK TO AUSTIN AND PLAYED A GHOST KNIFE SHOW.

HOPE - DESCENDENTS

9-4-14

EVERYTHING FROM WORK YESTERDAY ENDED UP BEING OKAY.
WHEW!

I HURT MY ARM YESTERDAY FROM THE WORKOUT, SO I DIDN'T EXERCISE TONIGHT.

BUT I'M STILL ON IT!

BOY AM I FUCKIN TIRED.
PANT PANT

THE LUNG - DINOSAUR JR

9-5-14

I ONLY WORKED HALF A DAY TODAY.

I WENT AND DID SOME STUPID BULLSHIT.
*#@!!

THEN I WORKED OUT WITH KAREN.
HA HA HA

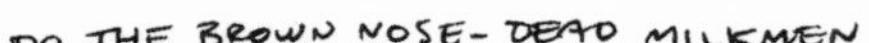
DO THE BROWN NOSE - DEAD MILKMEN

9-6-14

THIS MORNING I BOTTLED SOME MORE BEER.

I WAS A LAME PIECE OF SHIT AND DIDN'T WORK OUT.

BUT I DID DRIVE OUT TO THE LIQUOR STORE IN ELGIN.
SPEC'S

I DON'T CARE - BLACK FLAG

9-7-14

KAREN + I WENT TO THE LAKE TODAY...
COWABUNGA!

...BUT IT WAS MUGGY AND OVERCAST AND NOT REALLY MUCH FUN.
I'M COLD!
I KEEP GETTING BIT BY MOSQUITOES.

I DID A PRETTY HALFASS WORKOUT.
PSH. I JUST DON'T CARE ABOUT EXERCISING LIKE I USED TO.
OR DRAWING.
OR PLAYING MUSIC
OR ANYTHING

THREE NIGHTS - BLACK FLAG

9-8-14

BACK AT WORK TODAY, IT WAS FINE.

DID A WORKOUT WITH KAREN.

ATE INDIAN FOOD AND WATCHED STAR TREK.

FOCUS POCUS - BIG BUSINESS

9-9-14

WORK KINDA SUCKED TODAY.

I BROKE EDGE AND DRANK SOME BEER.

SHH

THAT PART WAS NICE.

LEATHER LEATHER - VIDEO

9-10-14

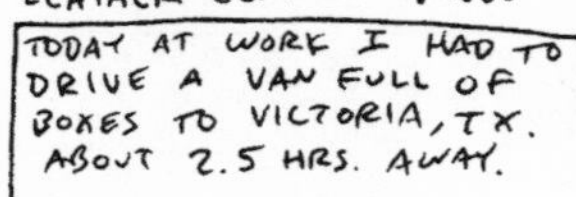
TODAY AT WORK I HAD TO DRIVE A VAN FULL OF BOXES TO VICTORIA, TX. ABOUT 2.5 HRS. AWAY.

WORK VAN

IT WAS A PRETTY DRIVE BUT IT MADE MY NECK HURT.

LATER I DRANK A BIG CAN OF GROSS BEER.
BLEAH! WHY DID I BUY THIS?
GROSS BEER

EVIL HOODOO - THE SEEDS

9-11-14

WORK WAS PRETTY SLOW TODAY. I WENT HOME EARLY.
CAPITAL METRO

KAREN ORDERED A PIZZA. SHE SOMEHOW MANAGED TO PICK THE GROSSEST COMBINATION OF TOPPINGS KNOWN TO MAN
THIS TASTES LIKE A GYM SOCK.
OOPS

LATER WE WATCHED STAR TREK.

STYROFOAM - FUGAZI

9-12-14

AWESOME PAYDAY AT WORK.
YEAH!

I WANTED TO TREAT KAREN TO A NICE DINNER BUT THERE WAS A CRAZY RAINSTORM.

SO WE STAYED HOME AND ATE LEFTOVERS.
NOW THIS TASTES LIKE A GYM SOCK.
HA HA.

ITS SO HARD TO FALL IN LOVE - SUPERCHUNK

9-13-14

I HAD A NICE SATURDAY OFF WITH KAREN. WE WATCHED A MOVIE.
THIS WAS FILMED IN MANOR!
COOL!

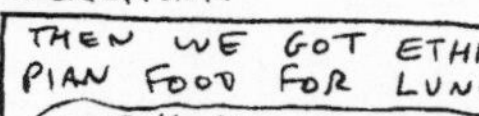
THEN WE GOT ETHIOPIAN FOOD FOR LUNCH.

LATELY ALL YOU DRAW IS PICTURES OF US EATING.
IT SEEMS LIKE THE ONLY SLIGHTLY INTERESTING THING WE DO.

AFTER THAT WE BOUGHT A BIRD FEEDER.
SEE? THIS IS INTERESTING!
YEAH I GUESS SO.

ARMOURED ASSAULT - EVILE
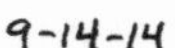
9-14-14

TODAY I BREWED SOME BEER WITH RAIN WATER!

I ALSO SPENT A LOT OF TIME DRAWING.

LATER I BOUGHT A BAG OF SALT FOR THE WATER SOFTENER.
I DON'T EVEN REALLY KNOW WHAT A WATER SOFTENER DOES, BUT ACCORDING TO GOOGLE, MY WATER PRESSURE WILL INCREASE IF I ADD MORE SALT*
*NOT TRUE

I'M SORRY I GOT FAT - WESLEY WILLIS

9-15-14

IT'S TIME TO COME TO GRIPS WITH A HARD TRUTH.
I JUST DON'T CARE ABOUT WORKING OUT ANYMORE
ICE CREAM

IF I LEARNED ANYTHING FROM THE LAST TIME I LOST WEIGHT, ITS THAT IF YOU DON'T REALLY WANT IT, YOU CAN'T DO IT.
AND I DON'T REALLY WANT IT.

SORRY KAREN.
PLEASE DON'T DIVORCE ME!
ICE CREAM

I'M THE ONE WHO LOVES YOU - CORNELL CAMPBELL

9-16-14

WORK WAS COOL TODAY.

I CAME HOME AND CAUGHT UP ON SOME DRAWING.

ALSO I TOOK PEEBER FOR A WALK.

SIEGE OF POWER - NAPALM DEATH

9-17-14

WORK IS STARTING TO PICK UP.

KAREN + I DROVE TO ELGIN THIS EVENING. WE SAW A RAINBOW ON THE DRIVE!
COOL!

CAME HOME AND DRANK A COUPLE OF BEERS.

BORN ON THE BAYOU - CCR
9-18-14
WORK WAS PRETTY BUSY TODAY.
I CAME HOME AND TOOK A SHOWER.
AND WENT TO BED.
MY LIFE IS SO EXCITING.
DARK ROOM - THE FACTION
9-19-14
THIS MORNING THE CAR WOULDN'T START!
OH SHIT
CLICK CLICK
THE AAA GOT IT GOING AND I TOOK IT TO THE MECHANIC.
YOST AUTOMOTIVE
PUTT PUTT
THEY SAID THEY COULD NOT FIND ANYTHING WRONG WITH IT.
IT STARTED FINE FOR US A BUNCH OF TIMES.
HMM
DEATH WISH KIDS - POISON IDEA
9-20-14
I HAD A GREAT DAY TODAY!
I MADE SOME BEER.
I LOVE MY WIFE!
SORRY. KINDA DRUNK!
HAY - BUTTHOLE SURFERS
9-21-14
TODAY I RAN ERRANDS WITH K-DAWG.
I WISH YOU WOULDN'T CALL ME "K-DAWG"!
WHY NOT, K-DAWG?
THEN WE CLEANED UP THE HOUSE TO PREPARE FOR NEXT WEEK'S PARTY.
AND I MOWED THE LAWN.

9-22-14

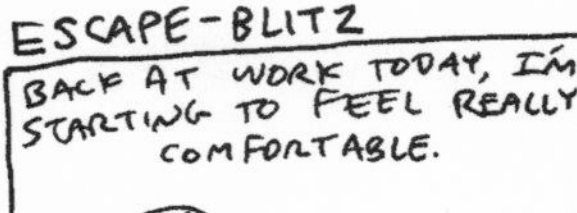
ESCAPE-BLITZ
BACK AT WORK TODAY, I'M STARTING TO FEEL REALLY COMFORTABLE.

WE'RE HAVING ISSUES WITH THE WATER PRESSURE IN THE HOUSE.
ANW MAN

I GUESS WE'RE GONNA HAVE TO CALL A PLUMBER.
ANW MAN

HELP- THE DAMNED

9-23-14

WORK WAS COOL. I WENT TO IT.

KAREN AND I WATCHED "COOL RUNNINGS."
FINISH

IT WAS SURPRISINGLY GOOD!

AFTERLIFE- BOLT THROWER

9-24-14

WORK WAS BUSY TODAY.

I CAME HOME AND TRIED SOME OF MY HOMEBREWS. THE BATCH DIDN'T CARBONATE.
DAMMIT!

KAREN + I ATE A PIZZA.

LUNACY- THE ESTRANGED

9-25-14

ANOTHER SUPER-BUSY DAY AT WORK.

I PUT MORE SALT IN THE WATER SOFTENER AND THE PRESSURE WENT BACK UP TO NORMAL.
I HAVE NO IDEA WHY THIS WORKS
SALT
40lbs

KAREN + I DID SOME PLANNING FOR OUR BBQ ON SUNDAY.
I'LL GET THE BEER!
I BET YOU WILL.

CHARITY HILARITY - FLUX OF PINK INDIANS
9-26-14
GOT OUT OF WORK EARLY.
KAREN + I BOUGHT A BUNCH OF SUPPLIES FOR THE PARTY.
BEER
BEER
BE
BEER
WE CAME HOME AND WATCHED T.V.
FALL ON YOUR SWORD - WORLD BURNS TO DEATH
9-27-14
TODAY I BOTTLED THE RAIN-WATER BEER I MADE A COUPLE WEEKS AGO. IT WAS BAD.
UGH. THIS SMELLS AWFUL.
SPENT THE REST OF THE DAY CLEANING THE HOUSE AND GETTING READY.
I MOWED THE LAWN, TOO.
MRRR
UP YOUR IRONS - VANILLA MUFFINS
9-28-14
TODAY WE HAD OUR LITTLE HOUSEWARMING/KAREN'S BIRTHDAY PARTY!
A BUNCH OF FRIENDS SHOWED UP
THANKS FOR DRIVING ALL THE WAY OUT HERE!
IT WAS A GREAT DAY.
DIAMONDS + WOOD - UGK
9-29-14
TERRIBLE HANGOVER AT WORK TODAY.
TO MAKE MATTERS WORSE, WE WERE SUPER BUSY.
GET TO WORK!
I WENT HOME AND TOOK A HOT BATH.

9-30-14

FORENSIC SCENE- FUGAZI

TODAY WAS STRAIGHT-UP THE WORST DAY AT WORK.
YOU FUCKED THIS UP!

I CAME HOME AND WAS TOO TIRED TO DO ANY-THING.

I HAD HORRIBLE NIGHTMARES ABOUT WORK.
BLEEARGH!

I CAN SEE AN ANGEL- PATSY CLINE

10-1-14

WORK WAS BETTER TODAY. EVERY TIME SOMETHING GOES WRONG, I LEARN FROM IT.
WHEW

KAREN TOOK ME OUT TO DINNER AT THE DOG AND DUCK.
I LOVE IT HERE

I CAME HOME AND DID SOME DRAWING.

HENRIETTA- THE TRASHMEN

10-2-14

I'M FEELING A LOT MORE CONFIDENT AT WORK.
ALRIGHT! I GOT THIS! (AT LEAST I THINK I GOT THIS)

CAME HOME AND WATCHED STAR TREK

WE HAD A CRAZY RAIN STORM TONIGHT!

BRAINSTORM- MORBID ANGEL

10-3-14

FRIDAYS AT WORK ARE PRETTY CHILL.
FREE DONUTS!

I WENT TO THE HOMEBREW STORE.
GRAIN
YEAST
HOPS

THEN I ATE CHICKEN WINGS WITH KAREN.
OH GOD THESE ARE SOOOO HOT!

MURDERS IN THE RUE MORGUE - IRON MAIDEN
10-4-14
TODAY MATT CAME OVER AND FILMED ME BREWING BEER FOR A VIDEO HE'S MAKING.
KAREN + I WATCHED THE MOVIE "OBVIOUS CHILD." IT WAS REALLY GOOD.
*#!@!
THIS IS THE SWEETEST MOVIE ABOUT ABORTION I'VE EVER SEEN.
WE ATE QUESO FOR DINNER
FIRE IN THE WESTERN WORLD - DEAD MOON
10-5-14
NICE LAZY SUNDAY MORNING.
8:00
I TRIED DOING YOGA WITH KAREN. I ACTUALLY REALLY LIKED IT!
WHEW!
LATER WE WENT TO SEE WRESTLING.
DASHER HATFIELD!
UGLATTO - DEVO
10-6-14
WORK WAS GOOD TODAY.
KAREN CALLED THE PLUMBER TO FIX OUR WATER HEATER.
WENT TO BED EARLY, I WAS SUPER TIRED.
DO YOU LIKE READING COMICS ABOUT ME SLEEPING?
HALLOW'S VICTIM - ST. VITUS
10-7-14
OUT OF NOWHERE, WORK GOT COMPLETELY INSANE.
I CAME HOME AND CRACKED OPEN ONE OF MY RAINWATER HOMEBREWS. IT WAS SURPRISINGLY AWESOME!
HEY!
I'M GLAD I'M NOT A TOTAL FAILURE AT MAKING BEER.
IT'S LIKE THE ONLY THING I ENJOY DOING ANYMORE.
MALT
YEAST
HOPS

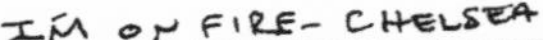
I'M ON FIRE- CHELSEA

10-8-14

ANOTHER BALLS-OUT CRAZY FUCKING WORKDAY.

I CAME HOME AND PLAYED CANDY CRUSH ON MY PHONE UNTIL BEDTIME.
I ONLY NEED 3 MORE JELLIES!

MY LIFE IS SO FUCKING BORING.

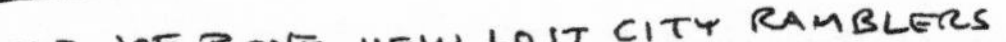
OLD JOE BONE- NEW LOST CITY RAMBLERS

10-9-14

WORKED ABOUT 10 HOURS TODAY.

NOTHING COULD HAVE PREPARED ME FOR THIS INSANITY.

THIS IS NOT WORTH $14.50 AN HOUR!

I HAD NIGHTMARES ABOUT WORK.
FUCK!

FINAL MASSAGE- THE GOBLINS

10-10-14

GLAD IT'S FRIDAY/PAYDAY, BUT I STILL HAD TO WORK ALMOST 10 HOURS.
MAN, FUCK THIS.

I TOOK KAREN OUT TO DINNER.

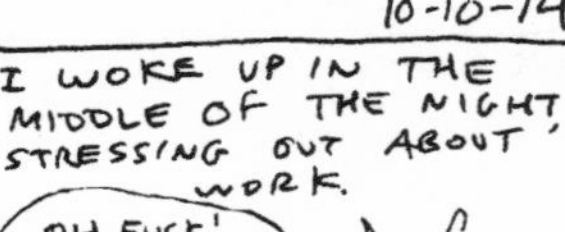

I WOKE UP IN THE MIDDLE OF THE NIGHT STRESSING OUT ABOUT WORK.
OH FUCK! DID I FORGET TO RUN THAT AS CARRIER ROUTE?

OI POWER- DISCOCKS

10-11-14

TODAY I HAD A TOTAL MAN-PERIOD DAY. I PLAYED GUITAR,

I PLAYED VIDEO GAMES,

AND I ATE A PINT OF ICE CREAM.
BLUE BELL

METAL STORM/FACE THE SLAYER - SLAYER
10-12-14
TODAY KAREN + I WENT TO THE HALLOWEEN STORE.
WE ALSO GOT GROCERIES.
LOOK, A TINY DRONE!
WE CAME HOME AND I MOWED THE LAWN.
VINE POUND HAMMER - THE MONROE BROTHERS
10-13-14
BACK INTO THE IMPOSSIBLE RUINFUCK OF WORK.
I CAME HOME AND WAS SUPER GRUMPY.
CAN I GET YOU ANYTHING?
A CYANIDE PILL.
I HUNG OUT IN THE GARAGE.
I HATE MY FUCKING JOB - M.O.T.O.
10-14-14
WORK IS FUCKING OUT OF CONTROL.
I THINK I'M GOING TO START LOOKING FOR ANOTHER JOB.
A LADY ON THE PHONE AT THE POST OFFICE MADE ME CRY TODAY. FOR REAL.
KAREN ORDERED A PIZZA.
I HOPE IT HAS CYANIDE ON IT!
I HATE MY FUCKING JOB - M.O.T.O.
10-15-14
WORK WORK WORK WORK
WORK WORK WORK WORK
WORK WORK WORK WORK

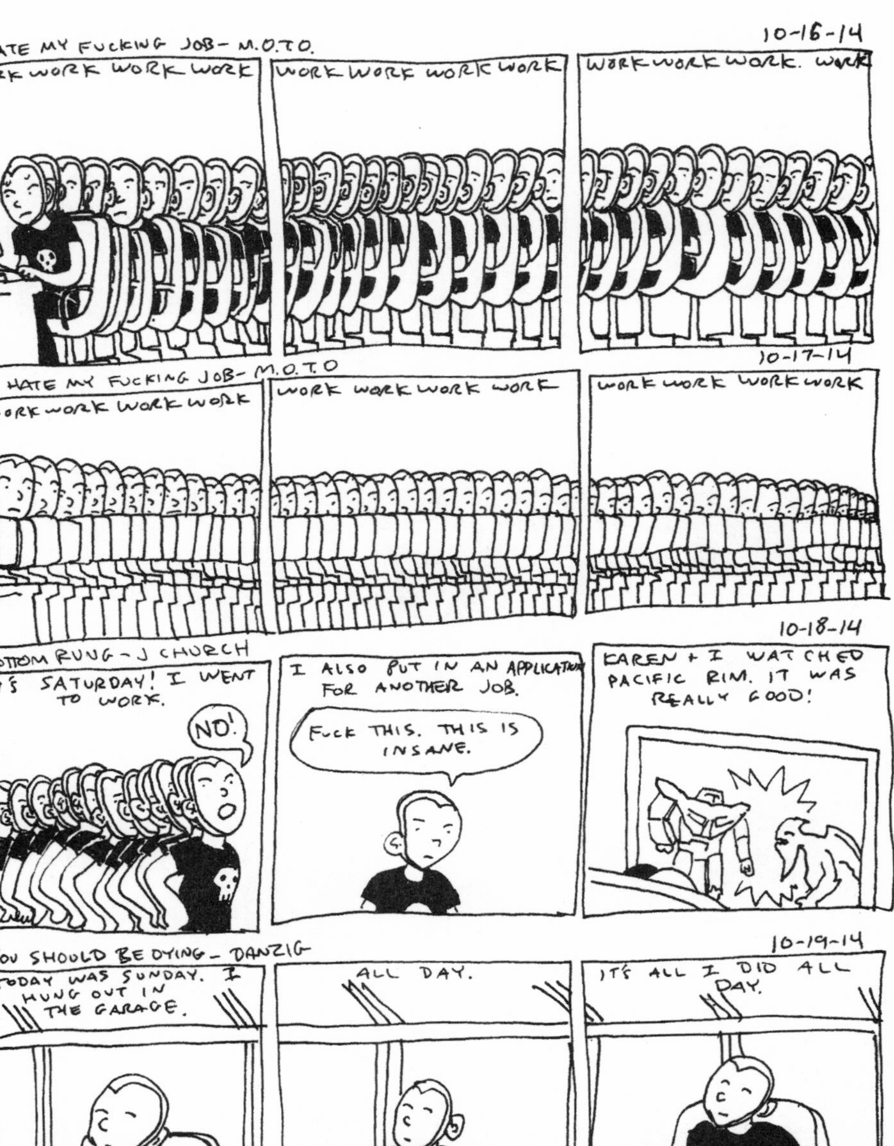
I HATE MY FUCKING JOB - M.O.T.O.
10-16-14
WORK WORK WORK WORK
WORK WORK WORK WORK
WORK WORK WORK. WORK
I HATE MY FUCKING JOB - M.O.T.O
10-17-14
WORK WORK WORK WORK
WORK WORK WORK WORK
WORK WORK WORK WORK
BOTTOM RUNG - J CHURCH
10-18-14
IT'S SATURDAY! I WENT TO WORK.
NO!
I ALSO PUT IN AN APPLICATION FOR ANOTHER JOB.
FUCK THIS. THIS IS INSANE.
KAREN + I WATCHED PACIFIC RIM. IT WAS REALLY GOOD!
YOU SHOULD BE DYING - DANZIG
10-19-14
TODAY WAS SUNDAY. I HUNG OUT IN THE GARAGE.
ALL DAY.
IT'S ALL I DID ALL DAY.

I HATE MY FUCKING JOB - M.O.T.O.
10-20-14
OH GOD HERE IT COMES AGAIN
WORKWORKWORK WORK WORKWORK
WORK WORK WORK WORK
WORK WORK WORK WORK
I HATE MY FUCKING JOB - M.O.T.O.
10-21-14
WORKWORK WORK WORK
WORKWORKWORKWORK
THIS IS GONNA END, RIGHT?
WORKWORK WORK WORK
I HATE MY FUCKING JOB - M.O.T.O.
10-22-14
WORKWORK WORK WORK WORK
WORKWORKWORKWORKWORK
WORK WORK WORK WORK WORK
I HATE MY FUCKING JOB - M.O.T.O.
10-23-14
WORKWORKWORK WORK WORK
WORKWORK WORKWORKWORK
WORKWORKWORKWORK WORK

I HATE MY FUCKING JOB- M.O.T.O.
10-24-14
IT'S STILL GOING HOLY SHIT!
WORK WORK WORK WORK WORK WORK
WORK WORK WORK WORK
I'VE CRIED TWICE AT THE POST OFFICE THIS WEEK.
WORK WORK WORK WORK
10-25-14
I HATE MY FUCKING JOB- M.O.T.O.
WORK WORK WORK WORK WORK
WORK WORK WORK WORK WORK
WORK WORK WORK WORK WORK
10-26-14
MY ONLY DAY OFF THIS WEEK.
I SPENT IT RECOVERING. HOLY SHIT.
I THINK THERE'S STILL A WEEK LEFT.
10-27-14
I HATE MY FUCKING JOB- M.O.T.O.
WORK WORK WORK WORK
WORK WORK WORK WORK WORK
WORK WORK WORK WORK WORK

I HATE MY FUCKING JOB - M.O.T.O.

10-28-14

WORK WORK WORK WORK WORK

WORK WORK WORK WORK WORK

USPS FORM 3602

WORK WORK WORK WORK WORK

USPS FORM 8125

I HATE MY FUCKING JOB - M.O.T.O.

10-29-14

WORK WORK WORK WORK WORK

WORK WORK WORK WORK

WORK WORK WORK WORK

10-30-14

ANOTHER GODDAMNED INSANE-ASS WORK DAY.

THEN, ALL OF A SUDDEN, THE LAST POLITICAL JOB WENT OUT THE DOOR.

THAT'S IT. IT'S FINALLY OVER.

THE DEAD - KING DIAMOND

10-31-14

TODAY WAS TOTALLY CHILL AND NORMAL.

KAREN + I WATCHED BEETLEJUICE AND HANDED OUT CANDY TO TRICK-OR-TREATERS.

WE GOT SO MANY OF THEM!!

I LIKE LIVING IN THIS NEIGHBORHOOD.

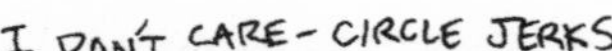
I DON'T CARE - CIRCLE JERKS
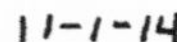
11-1-14

A FUCKING DAY OFF. HOLY CRAP.

I DREW ALL THOSE CRAZY PANELS FROM 2 PAGES AGO.

SPENT A LOT OF TIME IN THE GARAGE.
FINAL REVELATION - BOLT THROWER
11-2-14

A NICE LAZY SUNDAY MORNING.
9:30

KAREN+I WENT INTO AUSTIN AND GOT HAIR CUTS.
BZZZZZ
MINE GOT KINDA FUCKED UP

THEN WE WENT OUT TO DINNER.
STARLADY - PENTAGRAM
11-3-14

BACK AT WORK TODAY, THINGS WERE SO CHILL.

I STILL WANT TO FIND A DIFFERENT JOB, THOUGH.
THIS PLACE IS SUPER-DISORGANIZED

I KEEP LOOKING EVERY DAY.
CRAIGS LIST
FLIPPING YOU OFF WITH EVERY FINGER ON MY HAND - M.O.T.O.
11-4-14

WORK WAS REALLY SLOW. I LEFT EARLY.

I TOOK THE BUS TO MEET KAREN.
CAPITAL METRO

I KIND OF LIKE THE COMMUTE HOME TO MANOR.

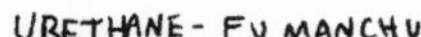
URETHANE- FU MANCHU

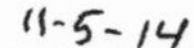
11-5-14

IT WAS ANOTHER SLOW DAY AT WORK.

THE WEATHER HAS BEEN COLD AND RAINY LATELY. I REALLY LIKE IT.

GOING TO BED WITH THE WINDOW OPEN.
ZZZ

DIE WITH YOUR BOOTS ON-IRON MAIDEN

11-6-14

WORK HAS BEEN NEARLY DEAD ALL WEEK.
I HAVE TO KEEP LOOKING BUSY.

I CAME HOME AND PLAYED VIDEO GAMES AND DIDN'T DO MUCH ELSE.

I'M CERTAINLY NOT COMPLAINING!
STRESS

THE HELLION/ELECTRIC EYE-JUDAS PRIEST

11-7-14

NICE GIGANTIC PAYDAY!

I WENT TO THE FANCY BEER STORE AND TREATED MYSELF.
50.00

AND I TOOK KAREN OUT TO DINNER.

MURDER THE SONS OF BITCHES- BORN AGAINST.

11-8-14

SATURDAY. I SLEPT IN LATE.
ZZZ

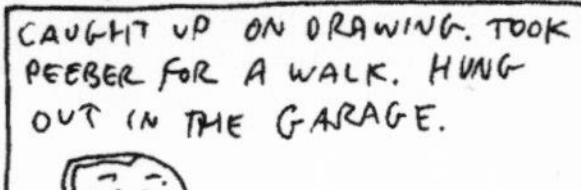
CAUGHT UP ON DRAWING. TOOK PEEBER FOR A WALK. HUNG OUT IN THE GARAGE.

KAREN + I WENT TO THE MANOR WALMART.
IT'S OUR MANOR DATE!

NEW YORK LOOP- SECOND STORY WINDOW

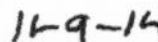
11-9-14

TODAY I CHANGED THE OIL IN MY CAR.
THEN I TOOK KAREN TO GET A NEW PHONE.
WAITING AT THE PHONE STORE FOR 3 HOURS.
THEN WE ATE AT BILLYS!!

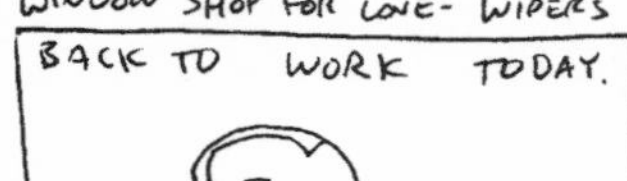
WINDOW SHOP FOR LOVE- WIPERS
BACK TO WORK TODAY.

AFTER WORK MY BOSS TOOK ME OUT FOR A BEER. IT WAS ANKWARD.

11-10-14
WENT HOME AND LOVED ALL OVER KAREN.

SCAPES OF TRAGEDY- FRAMTID
ANOTHER DAY AT WORK. I HATE MY JOB.

I CAME HOME AND ATE DINNER WITH KAREN.

11-11-14
THEN I HUNG OUT IN THE GARAGE.

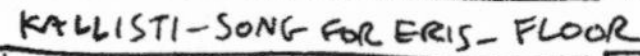
KALLISTI-SONG FOR ERIS- FLOOR

11-12-14

TODAY IS WEDNESDAY.

I CAME HOME FROM WORK.

PRODUCTS OF A COLD WAR - TRAGEDY
11-13-14
ANOTHER DUMBASS DAY AT WORK.
AFTERWARD I HUNG OUT IN THE GARAGE.
THEN I WATCHED A MOVIE WITH KAREN.
DECENT + CLEAN - DICKS
11-14-14
THIS MORNING I DROPPED KAREN OFF AT WORK...
THEN I PICKED MY MOM UP AT THE AIRPORT.
HI MOM
WE TOOK HER OUT TO A SUPER-FANCY DINNER.
IF IT KILLS YOU - DRIVE LIKE JEHU
11-15-14
TODAY MY MOM AND I WENT TO IKEA.
IKEA
SHE BOUGHT US SOME FURNITURE FOR OUR LIVING ROOM.
WE HAD DINNER AT BLACK STAR CO-OP.
11-16-14
TODAY WE WENT OUT FOR BRUNCH.
THEN WE PUT UP THE CHRISTMAS TREE WITH MY MOM.
WE WENT TO BED EARLY. I HAVE TO TAKE MY MOM TO THE AIRPORT AT 6:00 AM.
ZZZ

INSTANT HIT- THE SLITS
11-17-14
DROPPED OFF MOM SUPER EARLY THIS MORNING.
THEN I WENT TO WORK.
CAME HOME AND DID SOME WIFESNUGGLING.
EFFORTLESS-ATHLETICO SPIZZ 80
11-18-14
THINGS ARE BACK TO NORMAL. I WENT TO WORK THIS MORNING.
THEN I DROVE HOME.
MANOR
HUNG OUT IN THE GARAGE.
COMING DOWN TO EARTH-PIERCED ARROWS
11-19-14
HEY DO YOU WANT TO DO YOGA WITH ME?
NAH.
COME ON.
IS THAT A HINT?
UH...
I MEAN, YOU HAVE PUT ON SOME WEIGHT.
UH...
YOU SHOULD TRY OUT THE DIET I'M ON.
FIRE SPIRIT- GUN CLUB
11-20-14
WORK WAS PRETTY COOL TODAY.
KAREN AND I WATCHED STAR TREK.
TOOK PEEBER FOR A LIL WALK.

ULTRA FINE DAY - VANILLA MUFFINS

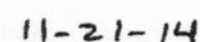
11-21-14

TODAY WAS PAYDAY. I WENT HOME EARLY.

KAREN + I HAD A NICE DINNER WITH FINE BEERS.

I'M EXCITED TO HAVE A DAY OFF TOMORROW!
I'M STAYING UP UNTIL 10:40!

SURFIN' DEAD - THE CRAMPS

11-22-14

AWESOME DAY OFF!!!

I GOT A LOT OF DRAWING DONE.

I EVEN HUNG OUT IN THE GARAGE.

BELIEVE - FORCED VENGEANCE

11-23-14

HAD A NICE BREAKFAST WITH KAREN.

THEN I WENT TO GHOST KNIFE PRACTICE. SHAKIN' OFF THE RUST.
DOOBLY DOOP

AFTER THAT I TRIED OUT PLAYING SOME NEW SONGS WITH CHRIS + IAN.

THE REVENGE OF ANUS PRESLEY - BUTTHOLE SURFERS

11-24-14

BACK AT WORK TODAY. IT'S BEEN PRETTY SLOW.

CAME HOME AND HAD DINNER.

WE STARTED GETTING READY FOR OUR TRIP TO TULSA.
I'VE BEEN READING ABOUT THIS PODCAST "SERIAL". LET'S LISTEN TO IT ON THE TRIP.
COOL!

HERE THEY COME AGAIN - COCKNEY REJECTS
11-25-14
WORK WAS REAL EASY TODAY.
GOT HOME AND HAD DINNER.
WATCHED TV AND WENT TO BED.
ZZZ
GUITAR BREAKDOWN - WOODY GUTHRIE
11-26-14
LEFT WORK EARLY TODAY AND TOOK THE BUS TO THE AIRPORT
PICKED UP THE RENTAL CAR TO DRIVE TO TULSA.
THEN WE GOT ALL PACKED + READY.
LORD OF ALL FEVERS + PLAGUE - MORBID ANGEL
11-27-14
HIT THE ROAD THIS MORNING.
DO YOU LIKE MY AWESOME DRAWING OF TEXAS? ITS PRETTY GOOD ISN'T IT?
WE GOT TO TULSA IN TIME FOR DINNER WITH KAREN'S PARENTS.
IT WAS A LONG DAY.
ZZZ
PUPPET ON A STRING - LYN TAITT + THE JETS
11-28-14
TODAY WE HAD THANKSGIVING DINNER WITH KAREN'S FAMILY.
I GOT TO MEET MY NEPHEW, WYATT.
AFTER DINNER WE VISITED THE PRAIRIE ARTISAN BREWERY!
COOL!

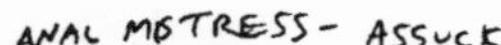
ANAL MISTRESS - ASSUCK

11-29-14

THIS MORNING I WENT TO THE FLEA MARKET WITH KAREN'S DAD + UNCLE ROY.

THEN WE WENT OUT FOR BRUNCH.

ZAC TOOK ME RAPPELLING BUT I WAS TOO CHICKEN TO TRY IT.
COME ON, IT'S FUN!
NOPE.

BLAME IT ON BUD - CANNABIS CORPSE

11-30-14

UP AND ON THE ROAD BACK TO MANOR BY 5:30 AM!

I WAS SO GLAD TO SEE PEEBER! (OUR NEIGHBOR GARY WATCHED HIM FOR US)
SNORT
SNORT
SNORT

I HAD TO MOW THE LAWN.

UNREQUITED - J CHURCH

12-1-14

WORK WAS SLOW SO I ONLY WORKED A HALF DAY.

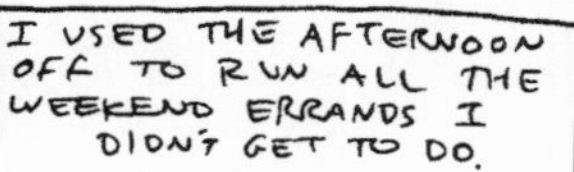
I USED THE AFTERNOON OFF TO RUN ALL THE WEEKEND ERRANDS I DIDN'T GET TO DO.

TOWN ←
ACROSS TOWN →

THEN I FINALLY HAD SOME TIME TO MYSELF.

QUIT - SEPTIC DEATH

12-2-14

WORK PICKED UP A BIT TODAY.

I TOOK PEEBER FOR A WALK
GOOD DRAWING, BEN!

AND I HUNG OUT IN THE GARAGE
WHOA! PEEBER JUST TALKED!

AT MY JOB - DEAD KENNEDYS

12-3-14

ANOTHER DAY WORKING AT MY JOB

I MADE A BUNCH OF NEW SNAKEPIT STICKERS.
SNAKE PIT
CLUB

I'M GOING TO A ZINE FEST IN A COUPLE OF WEEKS.
HOPEFULLY I CAN SELL OFF SOME OF THESE BOOKS

CHAPEL OF GHOULS - MORBID ANGEL

12-4-14

WENT TO WORK TODAY.

I TOOK PEEBER FOR A WALK.

I PLAYED VIDEO GAMES TIL BED.

PULL THE PLUG - DEATH

12-5-14

SLOW PAYDAY = LEAVE EARLY.
WOO HOO!

I BOUGHT A LADDER.
HOME OWNER SHIT

AND I TOOK KAREN OUT TO DINNER.
HUSBAND SHIT

CAN'T STOP THE WORLD - GOGOS

12-6-14

TODAY I TALKED TO MY DAD.

I'M COMING TO VISIT.
COOL! WHEN?
NEXT WEEK, MONDAY TIL WEDNESDAY
UH, I HOPE I CAN GET OFF WORK.
ANOTHER FANTASTIC DRAWING BY BEN SNAKEPIT →

I SPENT THE DAY JUST GOOFING OFF AND HANGING OUT IN THE GARAGE.

I THINK MAYBE I SHOULD STOP HANGING OUT IN THE GARAGE SO MUCH.

LATER I WENT TO WAL MART AND BOUGHT A STAPLE GUN.

CHA CHUNK!

IN THE GARAGE- WEEZER
12-7-14
TODAY I DECIDED THAT I NEED TO STOP HANGING OUT IN THE GARAGE.
IN CASE YOU HAVEN'T FIGURED IT OUT, "HANGING OUT IN THE GARAGE" IS CODE FOR SMOKING WEED.
I REALLY HAD QUIT THIS YEAR, BUT THE WORK STRESS OF OCTOBER CAUSED ME TO START UP AGAIN.
BUT NOW IT'S TIME TO QUIT. AGAIN.
I'M NOT LOOKING FORWARD TO THIS.
WHETHER YOU BELIEVE IT OR NOT, I KNOW FIRST-HAND THAT WEED WITHDRAWAL IS VERY REAL.
ALL HELL BREAKS LOOSE- MISFITS
12-8-14
BACK AT WORK TODAY.
CAME HOME AND WATCHED BLACK MIRROR ON NETFLIX. WHAT A RAD SHOW!
WHOA!
I ALSO STARTED READING A BOOK ABOUT THE MISFITS.
THIS BOOK IS WRITTEN LIKE SHIT BUT STILL PRETTY INTERESTING.
THIS MUSIC LEAVES STAINS
EN MORK HORISONT- MORTIIS
12-9-14
WORK WAS SLOW TODAY.
I DID A BUNCH OF DRAWING WHEN I GOT HOME.
THEN I PLAYED WITH THE DOG.
ARF! ARF!
BAPTISM BY FIRE- MARDUK
12-10-14
WORK PICKED UP A BIT. I DON'T MIND IT.
I CAME HOME AND WRAPPED KAREN'S CHRISTMAS GIFTS.
XMAS GIFT
SHE GRILLED STEAKS FOR DINNER.

O COME ALL YE FAITHFUL- BAD RELIGION

12-11-14

WORK WAS COOL TODAY.

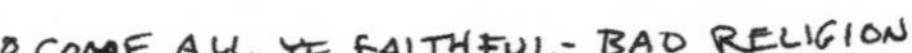

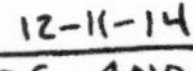

KAREN IS FINALLY DONE WITH HER SEMESTER OF SCHOOL, SO WE CAN HANG OUT!

WE DRANK BEERS AND LISTENED TO FUNNY CHRISTMAS SONGS
I THINK THE BAD RELIGION CHRISTMAS RECORD IS GOOD!
YEAH KINDA

DOOMSDAY CELEBRATION-MORBID ANGEL

12-12-14

I ONLY WORKED HALF A DAY TODAY
YOU'RE ABOUT TO GO INTO OVERTIME. GO HOME AT NOON.
OK!

I TOOK PEEBER FOR A WALK

THEN I TOOK KAREN OUT FOR WINGS
I'M NOT GOOD ENOUGH OF AN ARTIST TO PROPERLY CONVEY THIS JOKE.

12-13-14

CURE FOR HICCUPS-BANANAS

DID A SHITLOAD OF YARD WORK TODAY.
WRRRRRR

GHOST KNIFE PLAYED A SHOW AT RED 7

I CLIMBED UP ON THE ROOF OF MY GARAGE TO WATCH A METEOR SHOWER.

OINK OINK- DAVID PEEL + THE LOWER EAST SIDE

12-14-14

TODAY I HAD A TABLE AT THE AUSTIN ZINE FEST.
KAREN WENT WITH ME!

IT WAS AWESOME AND I MADE A TON OF MONEY!
RAD!

CAME HOME AND GOT THE HOUSE CLEAN AND READY FOR MY DAD'S VISIT TOMORROW.

GUILTY OF BEING TIGHT - MUNICIPAL WASTE

12-15-14

THIS MORNING I PICKED UP MY DAD AT THE AIRPORT.
(MY DAD AND I LOOK ALIKE)

I TOOK HIM OUT TO LUNCH AND SHOWED HIM AROUND MANOR.
RESTAURANT
MOTEL

KAREN MADE A FANCY DINNER AND WE HAD A NICE EVENING SITTING AROUND AND TALKING.

BLOODLUST - VENOM

12-16-14

TODAY MY DAD + I WENT TO IKEA. HE BOUGHT US A NEW COUCH.
THANKS DAD!
MERRY CHRISTMAS!
IKE

THEN WE WENT OUT TO A FANCY RESTAURANT.

AFTER THAT WE DROVE AROUND OUR NEIGHBORHOOD AND LOOKED AT CHRISTMAS LIGHTS.

SCORCHED EARTH - MARDUK

12-17-14

THIS MORNING I DROPPED MY DAD OFF AT THE AIR PORT.
GOOD VISIT, SON!

I AM SICK. I THINK I CAUGHT SOMETHING AT THE ZINE FEST.
KOFF
KOFF

I TOOK NYQUIL AND WENT TO BED EARLY.
6:00

MASTER OF DISHARMONY - DIMMU BORGIR

12-18-14

I FELT LIKE SHIT TODAY.
BLEAH

I ONLY WENT INTO WORK FOR A COUPLE HOURS TO CATCH UP.

I'VE ALREADY MISSED THREE DAYS THIS WEEK. MY CHECK IS GONNA SUCK.

THEN I WENT HOME AND SLEPT FOR 16 HOURS.
SNAKEPIT
1974
TO
2014

SKALD AV SATANS SOL - DARKTHRONE

12-19-14

I WAS ABLE TO WORK A WHOLE DAY TODAY.
SNIF
SNIP

KAREN + I GOT SOUP FOR DINNER.
YOU HATE SOUP.
NOT WHEN I'M SICK!

I'LL LICK THIS COLD IF IT'S THE LAST THING I DO!
AND IT MIGHT BE!
KOFF
KOFF

GRIM + FROSTBITTEN KINGDOMS - IMMORTAL

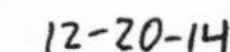
12-20-14

I WOKE UP FEELING BETTER TODAY! 95%
YES!

I CLEANED THE SHIT OUT OF THE HOUSE
THERE'S GROSS SNOTTY TISSUES EVERYWHERE!

KAREN + I STAYED UP LATE AND HAD A GREAT CONVERSATION.

AFTER THE BOMB - WARLOCK

12-21-14

HAD A GREAT DAY TODAY. KAREN + I WENT TO THRIFT STORES.
THESE CREEPY CLOWN DOLLS WILL BE A PERFECT WHITE ELEPHANT GIFT!

WE ATE LUNCH AT SUPER BURRITO!

THEN WE WENT TO HER WORK XMAS PARTY.
AHH! WHO BROUGHT THE CREEPY CLOWN DOLLS?
HEE HEE

GHETTO MECHANIC - NAKED RAYGUN

12-22-14

BACK TO WORK TODAY.

I CAME HOME AND WATCHED STAR TREK WITH KAREN...

... TWICE

THE DESOLATE ONE- BLASPHEMY

12-23-14

TODAY WAS OUR WORK XMAS PARTY.

MY SECRET SANTA GOT ME A STAR TREK LUNCHBOX AND A SIX-PACK OF BEER!
RAD!
COLD BEERZ
STAR TREK

KAREN MADE A CHEESECAKE WHILE I WATCHED.

ANGEL DUST- VENOM

12-24-14

I HAD TO GO IN TO WORK FOR TWO HOURS TODAY.
WHY EVEN BOTHER?

I DROVE ACROSS TOWN AND PICKED UP ONE MORE PRESENT FOR KAREN.
BOOK STORE

WE WATCHED SCROOGED AND DRANK MANY DRINKS.

THE NUCLEAR VICTIMS- DISCLOSE

12-25-14

IT'S CHRISTMAS! KAREN GOT ME A NEW CAMERA.
COOL!
NIKON

I GOT HER A NEW COFFEE MAKER.
COOL!
COFFEE TIME

WE HAD FUN GOOFIN' OFF ALL DAY.

ÇA PLANE POUR MOI- PLASTIC BERTRAND

12-26-14

WOW, A WHOLE DAY TO MYSELF!

I DID SOME DRAWING AND CLEANED THE HOUSE.

IT WAS A NICE, BORING DAY.
ZZZ

DISORDER- JOY DIVISION

12-27-14

ANOTHER DAY OFF. SOMETIMES IT CAN GET PRETTY LONELY WAY OUT IN MANOR.
SIGH

I PLAYED VIDEO GAMES AND GOOFED OFF ALL DAY.

BOY WAS I GLAD WHEN KAREN GOT HOME!
I MISSED YOU SO MUCH!
I WAS ONLY GONE A FEW HOURS.

TOMORROW + TONIGHT - KISS

12-28-14

TODAY KAREN AND I HAD A NICE LAZY DAY OFF TOGETHER.

SORRY I DREW YOUR HAIR SO BIG!

ME TOO!

WE WENT TO THE ART SUPPLY STORE SO I COULD GET A SKETCH BOOK FOR 2015
THIS WILL WORK!
SKETCH BOOK

THEN WE ATE DINNER AND WATCHED A MOVIE.
BOYHOOD

I JUST CAN'T GET ENOUGH - DEPECHE MODE

12-29-14

BACK AT WORK TODAY, THERE WAS NOTHING TO DO.
ZZZ

KAREN + I GOT TACOS FOR DINNER.

THEN WE DRANK SOME BEERS AND GOOFED OFF.
I LOVE YOU!
I LOVE YOU!

IT'S NOT PECULIAR - HUSKER DU

12-30-14

WORK WAS TOTALLY NORMAL TODAY.

NOW THAT WE'VE FINISHED ALL OF THE STAR TREK SERIES, WE'RE AT A LOSS FOR WHAT TO WATCH.
WHAT WILL BE OUR DOUBLE ENTENDRE NOW?

LOOKING BACK, 2014 WAS A PRETTY AWESOME YEAR!
WENT TO DETROIT, WENT TO NYC, GOT A NEW JOB, BOUGHT A HOUSE!

BRAND NEW YEAR- STUN GUNS
12-31-14
HAPPY NEW YEAR!
18304
FROM MANOR, TX

2015

DEAD MOON NIGHT - DEAD MOON

1-1-15

TODAY WAS A NICE START TO A NEW YEAR. WE SLEPT IN LATE.
ZZZ
ZZZ

I WENT TO BAND PRACTICE.

THEN OUR WASHING MACHINE BROKE.
AH CRAP. OH WELL, WE ONLY PAID $25 FOR IT.

BLOODY CHUNKS - CANNIBAL CORPSE

1-2-15

BACK TO WORK TODAY. (IT'S FRIDAY, THOUGH)

GHOST KNIFE PLAYED A SHOW TONIGHT.
BEING IN A BAND IS FUN WHEN YOU ONLY DO IT LIKE THREE TIMES A YEAR!

I HAD A LOT OF FUN!
DRIVING INTO AUSTIN FROM MANOR FOR A SHOW DOWNTOWN IS FUN WHEN YOU ONLY DO IT LIKE THREE TIMES A YEAR!
ONLY 2 BEERS ALL NIGHT

PHANTOM LORD - METALLICA

1-3-15

TODAY I TOOK DOWN ALL OF OUR CHRISTMAS DECORATIONS.
XMAS STUFF

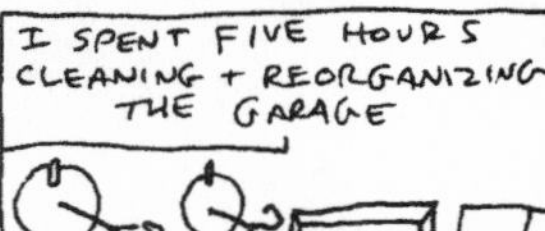
I SPENT FIVE HOURS CLEANING + REORGANIZING THE GARAGE

VIOLA!

KAREN MADE SCOTCH EGGS FOR DINNER.
DELICIOUS!
THANKS!

CARS - GARY NUMAN

1-4-15

TODAY I TOOK MY CAR TO GET INSPECTED. IT DIDN'T PASS.
THE "CHECK ENGINE" LIGHT IS ON.
A CHECK ENGINE LIGHT IS AN AUTOMATIC FAIL.
BUT THAT'S JUST A MALFUNCTIONING SENSOR! I'VE HAD IT LOOKED AT.

OH WELL. THE MECHANIC TOLD ME IT'LL BE $500 TO FIX THE SENSOR.
FUCK THAT. I'M JUST GONNA DRIVE IT WITH AN EXPIRED STICKER UNTIL I GET CAUGHT.

KAREN+I BOUGHT A NEW WASHER FROM CRAIGSLIST.
AT LEAST ONE THING WENT RIGHT TODAY.

1-5-15

TODAY I HAD TO TAKE A DELIVERY TO SAN ANTONIO FOR WORK.

I ATE LUNCH AT TACO PALENQUE.

I CAME HOME AND WATCHED SERENITY WITH KAREN.

WHY DID FIREFLY GET CANCELED?

BECAUSE LIFE SUCKS.

BABY WON'T YOU COME OUT TONIGHT- BUDDY HOLLY

1-6-15

GOD DAMMIT I THINK I'M GETTING SICK AGAIN.

KOFF KOFF

WORK FELT PRETTY ROTTEN.

I DRANK NYQUIL AND WENT TO BED EARLY.

YOU'RE NOT GONNA GET IT- EPICYCLE

1-7-15

I FELT COMPLETELY AWFUL TODAY.

WENT TO BED EARLY AGAIN.

UUUG

KEPT WAKING UP IN THE MIDDLE OF THE NIGHT, VOMITING BOOGERS

KA-HACK!

CARRY NO BANNERS- MENACE

1-8-15

STILL FEEL LIKE SHIT. I BARELY MADE IT THROUGH WORK.

I REALLY CAN'T AFFORD TO MISS ANY MORE DAYS.

KAREN MADE ME A HOT TODDY.

THANKS HONEY

I'M SORRY YOU FEEL SO BAD.

I BARELY GOT ANY SLEEP.

TOSS

TURN

KOFF KOFF

ONLY ONE - SCARED OF CHAKA

1-9-15

STILL NO END IN SIGHT.
BLARF

KAREN TOOK ME OUT TO DINNER, I BROKE MY TOOTH ON A PEANUT.
JESUS CHRIST. I'M FALLING APART!
CRUNCH

I WAS COUGHING SO MUCH SHE MADE ME SLEEP ON THE COUCH.
KOFF KOFF

SUFFERING QUOTA - ASSUCK

1-10-15

TODAY I DID SOME GOOGLE SEARCHING AND I'M PRETTY SURE I HAVE BRONCHITIS.

"SYMPTOMS USUALLY LAST 2-3 WEEKS." FUCK.

I SPENT MOST OF MY DAY ON THE COUCH, WATCHING TV AND HACKING UP PHLEGM.
GOD WHAT A WASTE

KAREN MADE ME SLEEP ON THE COUCH AGAIN TONIGHT.
KOFF KOFF

FOUR MEASURE START - UNIVERSAL ORDER OF ARMAGEDDON

1-11-15

ANOTHER GODDAMNED DAY OF SITTING AROUND JUST WATCHING TV AND COUGHING UP GROSS SHIT.
PHLEGM PAIL

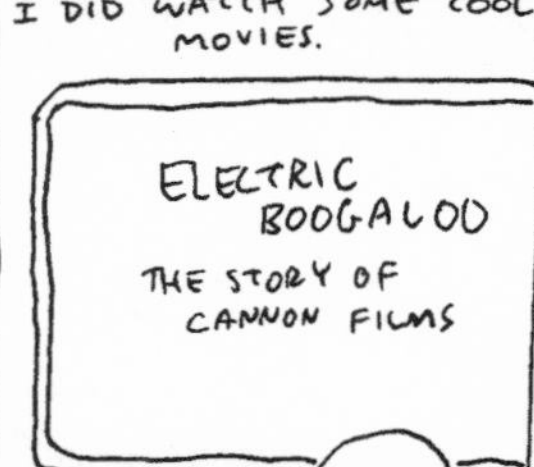

I DID WATCH SOME COOL MOVIES.
ELECTRIC BOOGALOO
THE STORY OF CANNON FILMS

AND I ATE ICE CREAM WITH KAREN.

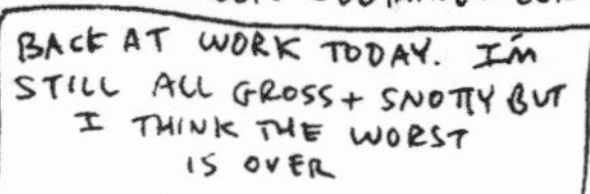

WOLF IN SHEEP'S CLOTHING - CORNELL CAMPBELL

1-12-15

BACK AT WORK TODAY. I'M STILL ALL GROSS + SNOTTY BUT I THINK THE WORST IS OVER
SNIF SNIF

I GOT THIS THING CALLED KODI FOR MY COMPUTER. WITH THE RIGHT PLUG-IN I CAN WATCH ALL KINDS OF COOL STUFF.

EVERY TV SHOW AND MOVIE EVER. EVER.

WHOA!

KAREN + I STARTED WATCHING THE SOPRANOS.
I'VE ALWAYS WANTED TO SEE THIS.
IT'S SO GOOD!
YOU PRICK!

SOMEDAY IN THE FUTURE- BAD SPORTS

1-13-15

WORK HAS BEEN ACTUALLY KINDA REWARDING THE PAST FEW DAYS.

AND I'M DEFINETLEY ON THE MEND WITH MY BROCHITIS.
KOFF KOFF

LIFE AINT SO BAD.
I STILL GOTTA FIGURE OUT WHAT TO DO ABOUT MY CAR INSPECTION, THOUGH.

FABULEY- HOLY ROLLERS

1-14-15

WORK WAS COOL. I ONLY BLEW MY NOSE ABOUT 500 TIMES INSTEAD OF 2000.

HONK

KAREN + I ATE FRIED CHICKEN + WATCHED THE SOPRANOS.
MOTHER FUCKER!

WE WATCHED THE MOVIE WHIPLASH. HOLY SHIT IT WAS GOOD.

ONE WAY TICKET TO PLUTO- DEAD KENNEDYS

1-15-15

WORK HAS BEEN COOL THIS WEEK.

I'VE GOTTEN SO MUCH BETTER AT MY JOB!

KAREN MADE TACOS AND WE WATCHED A MOVIE.

I'M NOT 100% BETTER BUT I'M 90% BETTER.
SNIF

CRUISE- CONFLICT

1-16-15

TODAY WAS PAYDAY.

I TOOK KAREN OUT TO A NICE DINNER.

WE CAME HOME AND GOOFED OFF.

STAR TREK

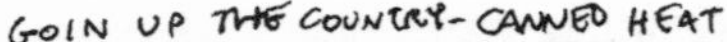
GOIN UP THE COUNTRY - CANNED HEAT

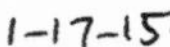
1-17-15

THIS MORNING KAREN + I BOUGHT A CAR!
2012 HONDA CIVIC

THEN I WENT TO BAND PRACTICE

AFTER THAT I TOOK THE NEW CAR FOR A RIDE OUT IN THE COUNTRY!
WOO HOO!

DEAN'S DREAM - DEAD MILKMEN

1-18-15

TODAY I MOWED THE LAWN.
RRRRRRR

I CHANGED THE OIL IN MY VAN

AND I PAINTED THE FRONT DOOR.

HEAVEN ON MY MIND - TROUBLE

1-19-15

BACK AT WORK TODAY.

I CAME HOME AND WATCHED TV WITH KAREN.

SHE RE-PAINTED THE DOOR BECAUSE SHE DIDN'T LIKE THE FIRST COLOR.

OSCAR - DUB SPECIALIST

1-20-15

WORK WAS OKAY TODAY.

KAREN + I WENT TO THE MANOR SPORTS BAR. IT WAS FUN.

WE WATCHED PEOPLE RIDE THE MECHANICAL BULL.

HAVE YOU EVER SEEN THE RAIN - MINUTEMEN

1-21-15

I SCREWED UP A BIG JOB AT WORK TODAY.
DAMMIT! JUST WHEN I WAS ABOUT TO ASK FOR A RAISE.

CAME HOME AND WATCHED TV WITH KAREN.

THAT'S ABOUT IT.

SATURDAY SAINTS - FLESHIES

1-22-15

WORK WAS BETTER TODAY.

I WENT TO GHOST KNIFE PRACTICE.

THEN I ATE A PIZZA.
THIS DRAWING LOOKED A LOT BETTER IN MY MIND THAN IT DOES ON PAPER.

FRIEND, YOU'VE GOT TO FALL - HUSKER DU

1-23-15

LEFT WORK EARLY TODAY.

I PUT NEW WHEELS ON MY BASS AMP.

GHOST KNIFE PLAYED A REALLY FUN SHOW.
I CAN'T WAIT TO EAT TACOS AFTER THIS

AS HE CREATES SO HE DESTROYS - NILE

1-24-15

I TOOK PEEBER TO THE PARK TODAY.

KAREN + I WENT OUT TO DINNER

I TRIED TO WATCH INHERENT VICE BUT IT SUCKED TOO BAD.
WHAT'S GOING ON?
WHO CARES?

GRAVEYARD - BUTTHOLE SURFERS
1-25-15
EVER SINCE WE MOVED INTO OUR HOUSE, WE'VE NOTICED A MYSTERIOUS IRON CAGE JUST ON THE OTHER SIDE OF OUR BACKYARD FENCE.
WHAT IS THAT?
TODAY MY CURIOSITY GOT THE BEST OF ME AND I CLIMBED OVER TO INVESTIGATE IT.
IT'S A TINY CEMETERY! CONTAINING TWO GRAVES FROM THE 1870'S!
HOLY SHIT!!
BIG IRON DOOR - CHARLES MANSON
1-26-15
BACK TO WORK TODAY!
CRACK!
OW
I TOOK A SHOWER AND GAVE MYSELF A "MANNY PEDI!"
ITS WHERE YOU SORTA HALF-ASSEDLY CUT YOUR TOENAILS A LITTLE.
THEN I PLAYED SKYRIM.
1-27-15
HITCH A RIDE - BOSTON
WORK WAS OKAY TODAY.
I WENT TO WALMART AND BOUGHT SOME MORE MELATONIN.
THIS STUFF TOTALLY RULES.
MELATONIN 10MG
THEN I PLAYED ON MY COMPUTER ALL NIGHT.
DUURRP
GOAT SODOMY - IMPALED NAZARENE
1-28-15
TODAY MY BOSS GAVE ME A TALKING-TO.
DAMN! I THOUGHT I WAS DOING REALLY GOOD.
WHEN I GOT HOME I SAW THAT MY SHITTY REDNECK NEIGHBORS ARE MOVING OUT!
YES! THOSE GUYS SUCKED SO BAD!
U-HAUL
KAREN + I WATCHED THE NEW PATTON OSWALT SPECIAL.
I DUNNO. THIS IS OKAY BUT NOT NEARLY AS FUNNY AS HE USED TO BE.

SAFE IN THE LOVE OF MY MAN - JEAN SHEPARD
1-29-15
TODAY I FOUND OUT THAT THE BOSS GAVE EVERYONE A TALKING-TO YESTERDAY, SO I DON'T FEEL SO BAD.
WHEW
HOWEVER, JUST FOR THE HELL OF IT, I APPLIED FOR A JOB AT THE POST OFFICE TODAY.
I DON'T REALLY WANT TO WORK THERE, BUT I'M CURIOUS TO SEE WHAT THE DEAL IS.
APPLY ONLINE
I ALSO TOOK KAREN OUT FOR TACOS.
TIME TO GET ILL - BEASTIE BOYS.
1-30-15
WORK WAS COOL TODAY. IT WAS PAYDAY, TOO.
WHEN I GOT HOME, MY NEIGHBOR JASON + I HAD FUN TALKING SHIT ABOUT THE REDNECKS THAT MOVED OUT.
GOD THEY SUCKED.
HA HA TOTALLY
LATER I GOT SUPER DRUNK
CHURNING THE MAELSTROM - NILE
1-31-15
TODAY WAS COOL. I BOUGHT AN ANNIVERSARY GIFT FOR KAREN.
HEH HEH
SECRET PLACE
SECRET THING
THEN I REPLACED A BROKEN LIGHT FIXTURE IN OUR HALLWAY.
HOME OWNER!
AFTER THAT I PLAYED SOME MORE SKYRIM
I'M A TURD WITH A SWORD!
WHAT WE HATE - SCREECHING WEASEL
2-1-15
TODAY KAREN + I WENT TO THE STORE + GOT LOTS OF SNACKS.
CHICKEN WINGS
THE WE WATCHED THE *GASP* SUPER BOWL!
WHAT HAS BECOME OF ME?
WHATEVER. THIS IS FUN!
25
THE BUDWEISER AD TALKING SHIT ABOUT CRAFT BEER PISSED ME OFF SUPER BAD.
BULLSHIT!

CHARIOT CHOOGLE - T REX
2-2-15
TODAY I WENT TO WORK.
WHOA. DRAWING WORK FROM THE OTHER DIRECTION FEELS WEIRD. LIKE WIPING YOUR BUTT WITH YOUR LEFT HAND.
I CAME HOME AND GOOFED OFF
KAREN + I DID OUR TAXES. WE'RE ACTUALLY GETTING A LOT OF MONEY BACK!
I'M SO GLAD WE GOT THE MORTGAGE CREDIT CERTIFICATE WHEN WE BOUGHT OUR HOUSE!
SPIRITS IN THE MATERIAL WORLD - THE POLICE
2-3-15
WORK WAS PRETTY CHILL TODAY.
I WENT AND TOOK A TEST FOR MY POST OFFICE JOB APPLICATION.
WOW THIS IS ACTUALLY KINDA HARD.
THEN I FOUND OUT AN UGLY TRUTH.
THE JOB I'M APPLYING FOR IS PART-TIME WITH NO BENEFITS. NEVER MIND.
SHE'S LIKE HEROIN TO ME - GUNCLUB
2-4-15
BUSINESS IS REALLY PICKING UP AT WORK.
I CAME HOME AND WATCHED TV.
IS MY LIFE FUCKING EXCITING OR WHAT?
YOU FUCKING LOVE READING THIS SHIT, DON'T YOU?
SHREDDED HUMANS - CANNIBAL CORPSE
2-5-15
WORK WAS BUSY TODAY.
UH OH!
KAREN + I WENT OUT FOR MARGARITAS AND TEX-MEX.
I GOT LOCKED OUT OF MY FACEBOOK ACCOUNT BECAUSE OF MY "FAKE" NAME.
BUT BEN SNAKEPIT IS MY NAME!

NUCLEAR WINTER - SODOM

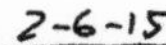
2-6-15

MAN, WHEN MY JOB GETS BUSY, IT GETS REALLY BUSY.

I USED PHOTOSHOP TO MAKE A FAKE I.D. TO GET BACK INTO MY FACEBOOK ACCOUNT.
TEXAS
HEH HEH

KAREN + I DRANK BEERS AND WATCHED EXCALIBUR
THIS MOVIE KINDA SUCKS.
YEAH.

SEE THAT MY GRAVE IS KEPT CLEAN - BOB DYLAN

2-7-15

TODAY I CLEANED UP THE LITTLE GRAVEYARD BEHIND OUR HOUSE.

THERE ARE TWO GRAVES, A TEN-YEAR-OLD GIRL AND A STILLBORN BOY.

I LOOKED THROUGH THE SURVEYORS NOTES OF THE PROPERTY WE GOT WHEN WE BOUGHT THE HOUSE, BUT FOUND NO MENTION OF THE GRAVES.

PETER BAZOOKA - DEAD MILKMEN

2-8-15

TODAY WAS FUN. KAREN AND I CLEANED THE HOUSE.
WAIT, THIS IS FUN?
SURE!

THEN I WENT TO GHOST KNIFE PRACTICE. WE EVEN WROTE A NEW SONG!

LATER I GRILLED SOME BURGERS IN THE BACK YARD.

THE WAITING IS OVER - TEMPLARS

2-9-15

BACK AT WORK TODAY. IT'S BUSY BUT I HAVE IT UNDER CONTROL.

YEAH I HAVE IT UNDER CONTROL!

CAME HOME AND HAD FUN WITH KAREN.

WE ATE A PIZZA.

MISIRLOU- DICK DALE

2-10-15

THERE'S A LOCAL ELECTION IN SAN ANTONIO NEXT WEEK. MY JOB GETS REALLY BUSY DURING ELECTIONS.

I WON'T LIE, IT'S AFFECTING MY LIFE OUTSIDE OF WORK.
HEY!

I'VE BEEN HAVING AWFUL DREAMS LATELY.

DOWN THE LINE- BUDDY HOLLY

2-11-15

MORE OF THIS CRAZY-ASS WORK WEEK.

I'VE BEEN TAKING MELOTONIN TO FIGHT MY INSOMNIA.
GOTTA BE AWAKE + ALERT FOR MY STUPID FUCKING JOB.

IT WORKS, BUT AT A PRICE. MY DREAMS ARE SOOOOOO WEIRD!

CREEP IN THE CELLAR- BUTTHOLE SURFERS

2-12-15

WORK WAS STUPID BUSY AGAIN TODAY.
NOOOOOO

KAREN + I WENT OUT FOR SUSHI. IT'S OUR ANNIVERSARY!

AFTER THAT WE WENT TO A BAR
CHEERS TO THREE YEARS!

BIG EYES- CHEAP TRICK

2-13-15

TODAY IS FRIDAY THE 13TH

TRUE TO FORM, TONS OF SHIT WENT WRONG AT WORK TODAY.
FUCK!

BOY DID I GET DRUNK WHEN I GOT HOME.
RUSSIAN IMPERIAL STOUT, TAKE ME AWAY!

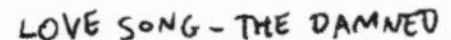
LOVE SONG - THE DAMNED

I GOT TONS OF STUFF DONE AROUND THE HOUSE TODAY.

I PLANTED A PEACH TREE IN THE FRONT YARD.

2-14-15
KAREN MADE US A SPECIAL VALENTINE'S DINNER.

LOVE WILL TEAR US APART - JOY DIVISION

2-15-15

TWAS A KINDA GLOOMY, COLD SUNDAY.

I WANTED TO DO A BUNCH OF STUFF OUTSIDE, BUT IT WAS TOO COLD.
SIGH

SO I CLEANED MY ROOM

ARCHANGEL - SAMHAIN

2-16-15

REALLY GLAD THE SAN ANTONIO ELECTION IS TOMORROW. WORK HAS FINALLY CHILLED OUT.
WHEW

I TOOK MY VAN TO THE SHOP SO IT WILL FINALLY PASS INSPECTION
I'M SICK OF FREAKING OUT EVERY TIME I SEE A COP.
YES I KNOW I DREW MYSELF IN THE WRONG SEAT.

KAREN + I HAD A FANCY DINNER THAT WE COULDN'T AFFORD.
YOU REALIZE IT MIGHT BE LIKE A THOUSAND DOLLARS TO FIX THE VAN?
YEAH.

HOW MUCH MORE - GO GO'S

2-17-15

WORK WAS CHILL TODAY.

I GOT THE BEST NEWS EVER FROM THE MECHANIC.
YOUR VAN IS READY. IT'S $266.00
FUCK YEAH!

ON THE WAY HOME, THE CHECK ENGINE LIGHT CAME BACK ON.
FUCK. OH WELL, IT'S GOT A PASSING STICKER ON IT.

2-17-15
SPILL THE BLOOD - SLAYER
ANOTHER DAY AT WORK.
I CAME HOME AND GOOFED OFF
PLAYED WITH PEEBER.
2-18-15
THE ENEMY - D.O.A.
WORK WAS JUST FINE TODAY.
KAREN + I WENT OUT FOR MEXICAN FOOD.
THEN WE WATCHED THE SATURDAY NIGHT LIVE 40TH ANNIVERSARY SPECIAL.
WHAT'S UP WITH EDDIE MURPHY?
I DUNNO. DID YOU DRAW THIS WITH YOUR LEFT HAND?
2-19-15
WHIRLING HALL OF KNIVES - BUTTHOLE SURFERS
IT WAS A FRUSTRATING DAY AT WORK TODAY.
BUSTED ASS TO GET A JOB READY, AND THE CLIENT DOESN'T HAVE ANY MONEY TO MAIL IT.
KAREN HAD A LOT OF SCHOOLWORK TONIGHT SO I PLAYED VIDEO GAMES.
AND WATCHED A MOVIE
ALIEN OUTPOST
THIS MOVIE SUCKS
2-20-15
GREAT EXPECTATIONS - KISS
TODAY I GOT A PHONE CALL FROM MY OLD JOB.
WE WANT YOU TO COME BACK. WE'LL PAY YOU MORE MONEY.
HMM
I TOLD THEM I'D THINK ABOUT IT.
I HATED THAT JOB, BUT I HATE THIS JOB TOO. BOTH OF THEM HAVE THEIR PROS + CONS.
HMM
I'M HOPING I CAN USE IT AS LEVEREGE TO GET A RAISE AT MY CURRENT JOB.
HMM

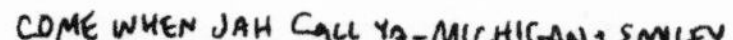
COME WHEN JAH CALL YA - MICHIGAN + SMILEY

2-21-15
TODAY KAREN + I WENT TO IKEA TO BLOW OUR TAX RETURN.
WE GOT A BUNCH OF STUFF FOR THE HOUSE.
HOW ARE WE GONNA FIT ALL THIS STUFF?
I SPENT ALL EVENING PUTTING EVERYTHING TOGETHER.
PUTTING THIS FURNITURE TOGETHER IS REALLY FUN.

FOREST RAY COLSON - HEX DISPENSERS

2-22-15

KAREN'S PARENTS CAME TO TOWN FOR A VISIT TODAY.

THEY BROUGHT ME A TON OF AWESOME PRAIRIE BEERS INCLUDING A GIANT 3LITER BOTTLE!
AWESOME!!!
WE HAD A NICE DINNER AND SPENT THE EVENING TALKING.

BUICK McKAYNE - T REX (OR HOWEVER THE FUCK YOU SPELL IT)

2-23-15

TODAY MY OLD BOSS WAS SUPPOSED TO CALL ME WITH A JOB OFFER, BUT HE NEVER DID.
FINE. FUCK THEM.
MY UN-RINGING PHONE

CAME HOME FROM WORK AND HAD ANOTHER NICE DINNER WITH MY IN-LAWS.

I'M REALLY HAPPY TO BE A PART OF THEIR FAMILY.

I GET ALONG WITH THEM BETTER THAN I DO WITH MY OWN PARENTS!

THIS GENERATION IS ON VACATION - SHOCK

2-24-15

WORK WAS COOL TODAY.

I CAME HOME AND WATCHED A BUNCH OF TV.

PRETTY BAD INSOMNIA TONIGHT.
ZZZ

I'D RATHER BE CLOGGING - KARP

2-25-15

MY PRESS BROKE AT WORK TODAY AND IT CAN'T BE FIXED YET.
MY BOSS HASN'T PAID HIS SERVICE CONTRACT BILL.

IT'S PRETTY FRUSTRATING, AND THE WORK IS PILING UP.
I BET I'M GONNA HAVE TO WORK THIS WEEKEND.
INBOX

I WISH THAT MY JOB DIDN'T TAKE UP SUCH A HUGE PERCENTAGE OF MY WAKING LIFE.
SIGH
NEGLECTED SKETCHBOOK

THE GRIM INFINITE - TRAGEDY

2-26-15

I FINALLY GOT A CALL FROM MY OLD BOSS TODAY ABOUT A JOB.
HOW MUCH MONEY DO YOU WANT?
EIGHTTEEN DOLLARS AN HOUR.
YEAH, PROBABLY NOT

AFTER WORK, KAREN AND I MET UP WITH SOME FRIENDS AT THE MANOR SPORTS BAR.

WE GOT SOME MORE BEERS ON THE WAY HOME.
NOT A GOOD IDEA!

VISIT TO A SAD PLANET - LEONARD NIMOY

2-27-15

LEONARD NIMOY
1931 - 2015

(APOLOGIES TO DAN HIGGS)

GHOSTS OF WAR - SLAYER

2-28-15

YEP, I HAD TO FUCKING WORK TODAY (IT'S SATURDAY)
GRR

I ONLY GOT ABOUT HALF OF MY WORK DONE BEFORE THE MACHINE BROKE AGAIN.
EITHER WE ARE RUNNING IT TOO HARD OR IT IS A PIECE OF SHIT.
FATAL ERROR

IT WAS A FRUSTRATING DAY. I STAYED UP LATE WATCHING STAR TREK MOVIES.

THE HIGHWAYMAN - GROOVIE GHOULIES
3-1-15
TODAY WAS THE LAZIEST. DAY. EVER.
ZZZ
I DID NOT PUT ON PANTS OR LEAVE THE HOUSE ALL DAY.
ZZZ
I DID, HOWEVER, WATCH STAR TREK MOVIES 1-5.
ZZZ
TAKE THE TIME - BIG EYES
3-2-15
BACK TO WORK TODAY. OH SHIT I'M SO GLAD.
I ATE VERY HEALTHY TODAY. I AM STARTING TO GET TOO FAT AGAIN.
SALAD
I DON'T WANNA LET MYSELF GET FAT AGAIN.
THE NIGHTMARE CONTINUES - DISCHARGE
3-3-15
THIS MORNING I GOT UP EARLY AND DID A WORKOUT TO START MY DAY.
TIME TO GET BACK ON IT!
WORK WAS COOL, I'M ABOUT TO GET REALLY REALLY BUSY.
I CAME HOME TO FIND MY COPIES OF THE SNAKEPIT GETS OLD REPRINTS WAITING FOR ME.
AT LAST! ALL OF MY BOOKS ARE BACK IN PRINT!
3-4-15
WORK GOT REALLY BUSY TODAY.
I WAS TOO TIRED TO DO ANYTHING WHEN I GOT HOME.
STUPID ASS JOB. MAYBE I WILL GO BACK TO MY OLD JOB.
OH YEAH, I DID ANOTHER WORKOUT THIS MORNING!
I HAD TO GO BACK TO THE LITTLE WIMPY BARBELLS

DR. FUNKENSTEIN - PARLIAMENT

3-5-15

I'M STAYING ON TOP OF MY MORNING WORKOUTS.
MAYBE I SHOULD PRACTICE DRAWING MORE.

WORK HAS BEEN SOOOOOOO BUSY!

I BOUGHT A NEW PAIR OF SHOES ON THE INTERNET
BEING 40 IS SOME EXCITING STUFF!

BITE THE BULLET - MOTÖRHEAD

3-6-15

WORK KICKED MY ASS TODAY.

KAREN + I GOT MARGARITAS AFTERWARD.

I GOT A BIG DAY TOMORROW.
ZZZ

CONDEMNED TO HELL - RIGOR MORTIS

3-7-15

TODAY I WENT TO STAPLE!
BUY SOME STUFF!

ONE OF THEIR PANELISTS CANCELED LAST-MINUTE AND THEY ASKED ME TO TAKE HIS PLACE!

AFTERWARDS I WENT TO BILLY'S WITH A BUNCH OF MY COMIC ARTIST FRIENDS!

PROWLER - IRON MAIDEN

3-8-15

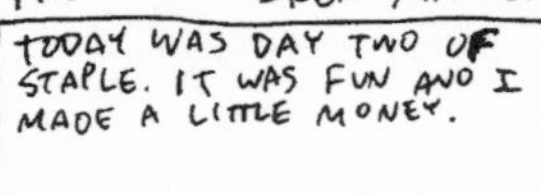

TODAY WAS DAY TWO OF STAPLE. IT WAS FUN AND I MADE A LITTLE MONEY.

KAREN + I ATE CHICKEN WINGS AND LISTENED TO MUSIC AND TALKED.

I'M NOT READY TO GO BACK TO BUSY-ASS WORK TOMORROW.
FUCK I'M SO TIRED.
10:30

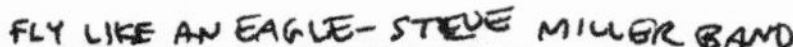
FLY LIKE AN EAGLE - STEVE MILLER BAND

3-9-15

WORK WAS SUCK-ASS BUSY AGAIN TODAY.

STAPLE WAS FUN + ALL, BUT I DIDN'T REALLY GET A WEEKEND.

ON THE WAY HOME, I GOT A NEW HEADLIGHT FOR MY VAN.

AH CRAP

I'M TOO LAZY TO PUT IT IN, THOUGH.

I'LL DO IT LATER.
LIGHT

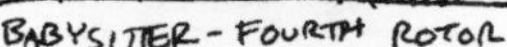
BABYSITTER - FOURTH ROTOR

3-10-15

FUCKING GODDAMN WORK

I GOT DRUNK AND PUT IN MY NEW HEADLIGHT

*@#!!!

IT PROBABLY WOULD'VE BEEN EASIER IF I WASN'T DRUNK. OR DOING IT AT NIGHT.

IT WORKS!

MY MANY SMELLS - DEAD MILKMEN

3-11-15

WORK CONTINUES TO KICK MY ASS

USPS
FORM 3602
OW!

I CAME HOME AND DID A WORKOUT (I'VE BEEN KEEPING UP WITH THEM ALL WEEK)

THEN I DRANK A BUNCH OF BEER AND UNDID THE WORKOUT.

I FIT CENTRAL HEATING - COCK SPARRER

3-12-15

WORK IS STILL TUFF, BUT I GOT IT UNDER CONTROL

USPS
FORM 3602
COME ON, BITCH

I GOT MY NEW SHOES IN THE MAIL.

KAREN + I WENT OUT FOR BURGERS

WE TRIED OUT A PLACE IN MANOR WE'D NEVER BEEN TO. IT WAS KINDA BROKE.

COVENANT OF DEATH- MORBID ANGEL

3-13-15

TODAY WAS A BIG DAY. MY OLD BOSS CALLED WITH A HUGE JOB OFFER.
WHOA! I'D ASKED FOR AN IMPOSSIBLY HIGH NUMBER JUST FOR THE HELL OF IT. I DIDN'T EXPECT TO ACTUALLY GET IT!

I TOLD MY NEW BOSS I WAS GOING TO QUIT IF HE DIDN'T MATCH IT. HE SAID OKAY AND MATCHED IT.
OKAY

SO BASICALLY, I GOT A GIGANTIC RAISE TODAY!
HAPPY FRIDAY THE 13TH!

SHOTGUN PETERSON- MACABRE

3-14-15

I HAD TO GO IN AND WORK OVERTIME TODAY.
I AM TOTES COOL WITH IT!

I CAME HOME AND MOWED THE LAWN.
RRRRRRR

THEN I BOUGHT A HAMMOCK!

SIX PACK- BLACK FLAG

3-15-15

TODAY RULED REALLY HARD.

THRIFT STORES

I GOT AN EMAIL ABOUT A JOB I APPLIED FOR LAST WEEK. THEY WANT TO INTERVIEW ME ON TUESDAY!
IT PAYS EVEN WAY MORE THAN THE HUGE RAISE I JUST GOT!
BEEP BEEP

I'M REALLY EXCITED. I HOPE I GET IT.
IT'S AT A PLACE I'VE WANTED TO WORK EVER SINCE I GOT INTO THIS INDUSTRY.

ALARMS + SIRENS- YOUNG PIONEERS

3-16-15

WENT BACK TO WORK TODAY.

HAD GHOST KNIFE PRACTICE AFTERWARDS.

ATE TACOS WITH KAREN.

TUNNEL VISION- FU MANCHU

3-17-15

TODAY I WENT TO MY JOB INTERVIEW.

HOLY SHIT, THE PLACE IS FUCKING AMAZING!

I WANT TO WORK THERE SO BAD!!!
SOMETIMES AT MY CURRENT JOB I WORK 70-HOUR WEEKS.
YOU WOULD NEVER HAVE TO DO THAT HERE.

CHRISTMAS ON MARS- GROOVIE GHOULIES

3-18-15

WENT TO WORK TODAY.

THEN I WENT DOWN TO SXSW.

GHOST KNIFE PLAYED A FUN SHOW.

FOREVER-SHELLSHAG

3-19-15

DAY OFF! I BOUGHT SOME CLOTHES.

I WENT TO THE DOCTOR FOR A CHECK-UP. FINALLY USING MY INSURANCE!
PROSTATE EXAM TIME!
EEP!

THEN I SAW SHELLSHAG PLAY A HOUSE SHOW!

TOSS THAT PIE- PERSONAL + THE PIZZAS

3-20-15

THIS MORNING I MOWED THE LAWN.

THEN I PLAYED A VIDEO GAME.

LATER I DROVE INTO AUSTIN + SAW SHELLSHAG AGAIN!
AUSTIN

RESILIANT BASTARD - SHELLSHAG

3-21-15

I WAS SUPER HUNGOVER THIS MORNING.

WHOA, I REALLY SHOULD NOT HAVE DRIVEN HOME.

THE SCREAMING FEMALES AND SHELLSHAG CAME OVER FOR DINNER.

MARISSA FINALLY GAVE ME THE TATTOO I'VE WANTED FOR A YEAR.

OPUS - HOLY ROLLERS

3-22-15

TODAY WAS AWESOME. I DIDN'T DO SHIT.

I PLAYED TROPICO 5 FOR A LONG TIME.

EL PRESIDENTE, THE PEASANTS ARE REVOLTING!

AND ATE BARBECUE AND SLEPT ON THE COUCH.

SLEEP - HOLY MOUNTAIN (OOPS I DID IT BACKWARDS. SORRY!)

3-23-15

BACK AT WORK TODAY.

I CAME HOME AND WATCHED TV WITH KAREN.

OH AND I GOT BACK ON THE WORKOUT TRAIN.

HIGGLE-DY PIGGLE-DY - THE MONKS

3-24-15

I GOT CALLED BACK IN FOR A SECOND INTERVIEW TODAY.

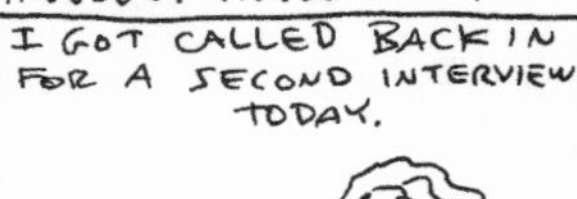

WHEN I WAS TALKING TO THE GUY, I NOTICED SOMETHING WRITTEN IN RED SHARPIE ON MY RESUME.

HIRE HIM!

THEY SAID THEY'D LET ME KNOW BY THE END OF THE WEEK!

OH PLEASE OH PLEASE OH PLEASE OH PLEASE OH PLEASE OH PLEASE OH PLEASE OH PLEASE OH PLEASE OH PLEASE OH PLEASE

BABY YOU'RE A RICH MAN - FAT BOYS

3-25-15

I WENT TO WORK TODAY.

KAREN + I WENT OUT FOR TACOS.

I CAME HOME AND WENT TO SLEEP.
ALL I CAN THINK ABOUT IS THIS NEW JOB

DUST MY BROOM - ROBERT JOHNSON

3-26-15

WORK WAS KINDA SLOW TODAY.
SIGH

AT THE END OF THE DAY, I GOT THE CALL!!!
WE'D LIKE TO OFFER YOU THE POSITION.

HOLY SHIT! I CAN'T BELIEVE I GOT THE JOB!!!

BURNING CAR - SCREAMING FEMALES

3-27-15

TODAY I GOT A CALL FROM THE DOCTOR
ALL OF YOUR TESTS CAME BACK NORMAL. YOU ARE IN PERFECT HEALTH!

I HAD TO GO TAKE A DRUG TEST FOR MY NEW JOB
SO GLAD I DIDN'T PARTY DURING SXSW!
TESTING FACILITY
PSSSS

DAVID CAME OVER AND STAYED IN OUR GUEST BEDROOM. HE'S GONNA BE STAYING WITH US FOR A FEW WEEKS.

GLASS SUN - SEA OF TOMBS

3-28-15

TODAY I SPENT THE DAY HANGING OUT WITH DAVID. HE'S LETTING ME HOLD ON TO HIS DRUM SET FOR AN INDEFINITE PERIOD.
THANKS DUDE!
NO SWEAT!

WE HUNG OUT AND DRANK BEERS AND TALKED ABOUT HIS FAMILY PROBLEMS.

KAREN CAME HOME FROM WORK AND WE ALL HAD TACOS.

VIOLENT DREAMS - OBITUARY

3-29-15

I HAD THE DAY TO MYSELF.

I PLAYED THE DRUMS FOR A WHILE.
WHOA! I AM REALLY OUT OF PRACTICE AND I SUCK

THEN I MADE HAMBURGERS FOR KAREN.

THE AXES OF EVIL - DUKES OF HILLSBOROUGH

3-30-15

TODAY I PUT IN MY 2 WEEKS NOTICE AT WORK.
BOSS MAN

I WOULD SAY "I'M GONNA MISS THIS PLACE" BUT IT WOULD BE A LIE.
FUCK THIS PLACE.

I WENT TO TARGET AND GOT A NEW BATHING SUIT.
WE'RE GOING TO THE BEACH THIS WEEKEND!
SWIM SUITS

IF WE CAN'T SIT AT THE TABLE (THEN LET'S KNOCK THE FUCKING LEGS OFF) - PINK RAZORS

3-31-15

MY BOSS HAS BEEN A SUPER DICK TO ME THE LAST TWO DAYS.
U MAD, BRO?

I CAME HOME FROM WORK AND WATCHED TV WITH DAVID.

IT'S COOL TO GET TO HANG OUT AND CATCH UP WITH HIM.
HA HA HA

RE-ENACT THE CRIME - UNWOUND

4-1-15

YAD DIPUTS REHTONA
GNINOHP YLLATOT FO
IKROW TA NI TI

I EMOH TOG I NEHW
OT DELLEPMOC SAW
EIVOM EHT HCTAW
"ANELES"
WHOA, HER DAD IS COMMANDER ADAMA!

WONK, UOY OS TSUJ #O,
GNIKROW NEEB EV'I
SIHT YAD YREVE TUO
KEEW

WHAT IT IS - DICTATORS
4-2-15
TODAY THE NEW GUY WHO'S REPLACING ME AT WORK STARTED.
HOWDY
TURNS OUT, HE'S ACTUALLY REALLY COOL AND WE HAVE A LOT IN COMMON.
YOU LIKE STAR TREK?
YEAH I HAVE A STAR TREK TATTOO
ME TOO!
KAREN AND I GOT READY FOR OUR LITTLE BEACH VACATION.
NO SPEED LIMIT FOR DESTRUCTION - INEPSY
4-3-15
I BLAZED THROUGH WORK AND LEFT EARLY TODAY.
KAREN + I DROVE TO OUR HOTEL IN GALVESTON.
WHOA!
WE HAD TACOS + BEER AT A SURFER BAR RIGHT ON THE BEACH.
BANZAI WASHOUT - DICK DALE
4-4-15
AFTER AN AWESOME BREAKFAST, WE TOOK A LONG WALK ON THE BEACH.
ATE A TON OF DELICIOUS CRAWFISH.
DRANK MARGARITAS IN THE POOL
I'VE ALWAYS WANTED TO DRINK AT A SWIM-UP BAR!
LET'S TAKE IT TO THE STAGE - FUNKADELIC
4-5-15
WE HAD ANOTHER NICE MORNING WALK ON THE BEACH.
GALVESTON RULES!
THEN ATE AN AMAZING EASTER BRUNCH AT OUR HOTEL.
WE DROVE BACK HOME FEELING REJUVINATED. (AND SUNBURNED!)
HOME →

CHERRY CHERRY - THE MUSIC MACHINE

4-6-15

BACK AT WORK TODAY, I WAS SUPER PHONING IT IN.
ZZZ

I LEFT EARLY AND WENT HOME TO DRINK BEER.
PSH. HAHAHA!

WATCHED THE ROOM WITH KAREN + DAVID.
YOU ARE TEARING ME APART LISA!

DOUBLE EDGED SWORD - NEUROSIS
4-7-15

"WENT" TO WORK TODAY.
ZZZ

MET UP WITH KAREN AT THE BANK. WE'RE REFINANCING OUR CAR FOR A LOT LESS.
CAME HOME AND DIDN'T DO MUCH.

ROMPING IN MY ROOM - STAGE LION

4-8-15

WORK WAS CHILL TODAY.

I'M STRESSING OUT A LITTLE BECAUSE I STILL HAVEN'T HEARD BACK FROM MY NEW JOB ABOUT MY BACKGROUND CHECK + DRUG TEST.
I'VE ONLY GOT 2 MORE DAYS OF WORK LEFT! ACK!
NO NEW EMAILS

KAREN FRIED A CHICKEN FOR DINNER.

SHE'S A DUMB - TEENGENERATE

4-9-15

I GOT NO SLEEP LAST NIGHT, STRESSING ABOUT THE JOB SITUATION.
SHIT

THEN TODAY I FINALLY GOT THE CONFIRMATION EMAIL. I OFFICIALLY GOT THE JOB!
I CAN'T BELIEVE IT! I PASSED A DRUG TEST!

DAVID MADE US TACOS FOR DINNER.

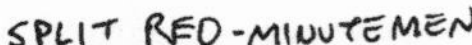
SPLIT RED-MINUTEMEN

4-10-15

TODAY WAS MY LAST DAY AT MY OLD JOB. I'M NOT GONNA MISS IT.
FUCK THIS PLACE
AMERICAN PRINTING

I CELEBRATED AT THE MANOR SPORTS BAR WITH KAREN + DAVID.

WE EVEN SANG KARAOKE!
GENERALS GATHERED IN THEIR MASSES
JUST LIKE WITCHES AT BLACK MASSES

DRUNKEN MARIA - THE MONKS

4-11-15

THIS MORNING I MOWED THE LAWN.
RRRRRR
I STARTED TO CHANGE THE OIL IN THE CAR, BUT IT FELL OFF OF THE JACK!
WHOA!
SCREEEK

LATER I WATCHED A MOVIE WITH KAREN + DAVID.
MIAMI CONNECTION

DESCENT INTO EMINENT SILENCE - IMMORTAL

4-12-15

TODAY I CHANGED THE OIL IN THE CAR.
GOTTA REMEMBER TO CHUCK THE WHEELS IN A FRONT-WHEEL DRIVE CAR!

I ALSO MET MY NEW NEIGHBOR. HE PLAYS IN A BAND.

KAREN BOUGHT A FIG TREE + I PLANTED IT IN THE BACK YARD.
VIOLA!

BODY POLITIC EQUATION - ASSUCK

4-13-15

TODAY WAS MY FIRST DAY AT MY NEW JOB.
I HAVE THREE COMPUTER MONITORS!

I THINK I'M REALLY GONNA LIKE IT THERE.
MY COWORKERS ALL SEEM COOL.

I DEFINITELY LIKE THE INSURANCE!
OH MY GOD IT'S SO MUCH CHEAPER!
BENEFITS

SPACE LAB - KRAFTWERK 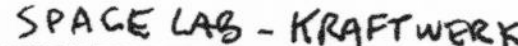

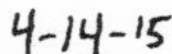

MY SECOND DAY OF WORK WENT GREAT!

DAVID MADE DINNER FOR ME + KAREN.

THEN WE ALL WATCHED A MOVIE
A MOVIE

MEAT FACTORY - F.O.D.

4-15-15

ANOTHER GREAT DAY AT MY NEW JOB.

DAVID STAYED SOMEWHERE ELSE TONIGHT, SO KAREN + I "WATCHED STAR TREK"
OOH BABY I GOT THE PONN-FAR SO BAD!
GROSS.

SORRY I HAVEN'T BEEN KEEPING YOU UP TO DATE, DEAR READERS. THE DOCTOR TOLD ME MY SPERM COUNT IS GREAT AND THAT WE NEED TO KEEP TRYING, ESPECIALLY SINCE I'VE QUIT SMOKING WEED.

MARCH OF THE S.O.D. - S.O.D.

4-16-15

IT'S A LITTLE TOUGH TO GET USED TO A MAC AT WORK.
I'VE ALWAYS HATED "MAC PEOPLE". I WISH I COULD STICK TO THE P.C.

STILL, THIS JOB IS AWESOME.

REASONABLE WORKLOAD, INTELLIGENT COWORKERS, GREAT ENVIRONMENT, ABOVE-AVERAGE PAY!

I CAME HOME AND PLAYED VIDEO GAMES.

CAROL - CHUCK BERRY

4-17-15

FIRST WEEK AT THE NEW JOB IN THE CAN!

I TOOK KAREN OUT TO OUR FAVORITE RESTAURANT.
THE WAITRESS ALREADY KNOWS OUR DRINK ORDER WHEN WE SIT DOWN!

I STAYED UP LATE JUST PLAYING VIDEO GAMES AND FUCKING OFF.

The only minority – Minutemen
4-18-15
A nice, quiet Saturday morning. I got some drawing done.
I also ran a few errands.
Stayed up late watching YouTube videos with David.
HA HA HA HA HA
Marriage – Descendents
4-19-15
Today was a nice Sunday. I went to lunch with Karen.
I got a haircut
And we BBQ'ed ribs in the back yard.
Moon Funeral – Artificial Brain
4-20-15
Back at work today, I still like it.
When I got home, the next-door neighbors were being forcibly evicted by the cops!
Karen + I watched Mad Men.
I'm glad this show got good again.
But its about to end.
I'm okay with that.
MEN
Recognize – Ol Dirty Bastard
4-21-15
Work was cool today.
I came home and watched TV with Karen.
Not the most exciting day I've ever had, but I don't care.
I'm really happy!

RAZORS IN THE NIGHT - BLITZ

4-22-15

ANOTHER FINE DAY AT WORK.

DAVID MADE DINNER FOR US AGAIN.

KAREN + I TOOK PEEBER FOR A WALK.

CLOUDED EYES - CHRONGEN

4-23-15

WORK WAS COOL AGAIN TODAY. I FEEL LIKE I'M REALLY GETTING INTO THE SWING OF IT.

CAME HOME AND HAD DINNER WITH KAREN.

HUNG OUT WITH DAVID FOR A LITTLE WHILE.

HA
HA
HA

TEETH TEETH TEETH - SHOWCASE SHOWDOWN

4-24-15

TODAY IS FRIDAY, BUT IT'S NOT THAT EXCITING -
I HAVE TO WORK TOMORROW.

KAREN + I WENT TO OUR MARGARITA SPOT.

THEN WE CRUISED THE CLEARANCE AISLE AT WAL MART.

#MANORLIFE!

I'M NOT A PUNK - DESENDENTS

4-25-15

I ONLY WORKED A HALF-DAY, IT WASN'T SO BAD.

AFTER THAT I WENT TO BAND PRACTICE.

KAREN WAS OUT WITH HER FRIENDS TONIGHT SO I PLAYED VIDEO GAMES.

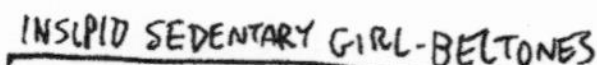
INSIPID SEDENTARY GIRL-BELTONES

4-26-15

TODAY WAS FUN. KAREN + I ATE BARBECUE.

THEN WE WALKED AROUND THE MANOR CEMETERY.

DAVID MOVED OUT YESTERDAY, WE FINALLY HAVE THE HOUSE TO OURSELVES AGAIN!
SORRY DAVE☹

LOUIE LOUIE- THE KINGSMEN

4-27-15

BACK TO WORK TODAY.

I CAME HOME AND STARTED A NEW WORKOUT REGIMEN.
I STUCK TO MY OLD ONE, BUT IT JUST WASN'T EFFECTIVE ENOUGH.

I KNOW MY BIGGEST PROBLEM IS DRINKING BEER.
I'M REALLY GONNA TRY TO STOP.

BACK FROM THE DEAD- DREAM DEATH

4-28-15

WORK WAS COOL TODAY.

I GOT SOMETHING REALLY COOL IN THE MAIL TODAY...
WHOA!

...A KLINGON HEADPIECE!
Q'PLAH!

HMMN TO A GAS GIANT- MORBID ANGEL

4-29-15

WENT TO WORK THIS MORNING.

AFTERWARDS I MET UP WITH MY PEN-PAL/COMIC BOOK FRIEND ADAM PASION.

WE HAD A COOL TIME HANGING OUT.
KANPAI!

VAGABOND DOG - NAKED RAYGUN
4-30-15
I'M STILL DIGGING MY JOB.
CAME HOME AND DID A WORKOUT.
THEN I WATCHED MAD MEN WITH KAREN.
WHAT IS THE DEAL WITH THIS WAITRESS?
GOOD MORNING SUN - JOHN HOLT
5-1-15
I GOT MY FIRST PAYCHECK TODAY. HOLY SHIT IT'S HUGE!
HOLY SHIT!
I TOOK KAREN OUT FOR CRAWFISH.
EAT ME!
THEN WE WENT TO HOME DEPOT AND BOUGHT A CEILING FAN FOR MY ROOM.
FAN
EXCORIATING ABDOMINAL EMANATION - CARCASS
5-2-15
TODAY I INSTALLED MY NEW FAN.
THEN KAREN + I WENT TO DAVE + JOETTA'S WEDDING.
IT WAS REALLY FUN!!!
WOO HOO!
SLUT MAN CITY - GWAR
5-3-15
THIS MORNING I DID THE LAWN.
THIS WEED EATER LOOKS LIKE SHIT. HOW DO YOU DRAW A WEED EATER?
RRRR
KAREN + I WENT TO COSTCO.
THIS PLACE ISN'T AS GREAT AS I'VE BEEN LED TO BELIEVE.
CRAP
IN LARGE AMOUNTS
THEN I BOUGHT A NEW DESK CHAIR ON EBAY.
SO LONG, BACK PAIN!

ORNAMENTS OF GOLD - SIOUXSIE + THE BANSHEES
5-4-15
BACK AT WORK. I LIKE MY JOB.
I CAME HOME AND DID NOT WORK OUT BECAUSE I AM A BIG HUGE FAT PIECE OF SHIT.
INSTEAD I WATCHED TV.
MAD MEN
MOTHER - DANZIG
5-5-15
WORK WAS COOL TODAY.
I MADE MYSELF DO A WORKOUT, EVEN THOUGH I DIDN'T WANT TO.
WE HAD A BAD THUNDERSTORM LAST NIGHT, PEEBER GOT SCARED.
AWW BUDDY
OWOWOWOWOW - DRAKULAS
5-6-15
TODAY I WENT TO WORK.
KAREN + I WENT OUT FOR TACOS
THESE DON'T LOOK LIKE TACOS AT ALL.
I WATCHED THE DANZIG LEGACY SPECIAL.
SO LAME BUT ALSO SO COOL AT THE SAME TIME!
CIRCLING ABOVE IN TIME BEFORE TIME - IMMORTAL
5-7-15
IT'S SO NICE TO HAVE A JOB THAT DOESN'T SUPER STRESS ME OUT.
MY NEW CHAIR CAME IN THE MAIL.
AWESOME!
I SAT IN IT AND PLAYED VIDEO GAMES.
CIVILIZATION V

CHEMICAL WARFARE - SLAYER

5-8-15

FRIDAY AT WORK WAS CHILL.

AFTER DINNER KAREN + I TOOK PEEBER FOR A WALK.

THEN I JUST GOT FATTER.
I HATE MYSELF

ROVING GAMBLER - SIMON + GARFUNKEL

5-9-15

TODAY I CLEANED THE HOUSE

I DID A GOOD WORKOUT.
GRRR

WHICH I THEN UN-DID BY TAKING KAREN OUT FOR ICE CREAM
OH THE SHAME. THE DELICIOUS SHAME.

THE JACK - AC/DC

5-10-15

TODAY I DID THE LAWN.

WASHED BOTH CARS.

AND GRILLED IN THE BACK YARD.

ROCK-N-ROLL SINGER - AC/DC

5-11-15

BACK AT WORK, I STARTED A REALLY TOUGH PROJECT TODAY.

I WENT AND BOUGHT SOME PICTURE FRAMES.
FINALLY, MY AUTOGRAPHED SLAYER POSTER IS FRAMED!

I ALSO DID A WORKOUT.
HATE-FUCKING MY BEER GUT.

OUTBREAK OF EVIL - SODOM
5-12-15
WORK WAS SUPER FRUSTRATING TODAY
BUT STILL BETTER THAN THE BEST DAY AT MY LAST JOB!
I TOOK PEEBER FOR A WALK
I DIDN'T DO A WORKOUT.
WHY IS IT SO HARD TO STAY MOTIVATED?
CHEESE DIP - JESUS CHRYSLER
5-13-15
WORK WAS MORE CHILL TODAY...
BUT I GOT NEW FILES FOR YESTERDAY'S HELL JOB. TOMORROW WILL SUCK.
WENT TO THE MARGARITA SPOT WITH KAREN.
CAME HOME AND PLAYED STUPID-ASS VIDEO GAMES.
SATURDAY'S CHILD - THE MONKEES
5-14-15
YEP. TODAY WAS PRETTY SUCKY AT WORK.
I GOTTA COME IN ON SATURDAY.
I ORDERED A PIZZA WHILE KAREN DID HER HOMEWORK.
DINNER TIME!
JUST A MINUTE
PIZZA
PIZZA
I THINK I'M GONNA BUY A SUIT THIS WEEKEND.
I'M TOO FAT TO WEAR MY OLD ONE.
THE ANCHOR - MINUTEMEN
5-15-15
WORK CHILLED OUT AGAIN. ITS MAINLY ONE PROJECT THAT'S KICKING MY ASS.
THESE COMPLICATED EXCEL FORMULAS ARE TOUGH.
IT WAS PAYDAY, SO I GOT SOME FANCY BEER
MY PAYCHECKS ARE SO FUCKING HUGE NOW!
I HAVENT WORKED OUT IN FOUR DAYS.
I'D REALLY LIKE TO LOSE THE EXTRA 30 POUNDS I'VE GAINED SINCE WE MOVED, BUT NOW THAT I KNOW HOW HARD IT IS AND HOW MUCH WORK ITS GONNA TAKE, ITS SUPER DISCOURAGING.

SUN CYCLE - BLUE CHEER

5-16-15

I GOT TO SLEEP IN FOR A LITTLE BIT TODAY.

YAWN

9:00

THEN I HAD TO GO TO FUCKING WORK.

AFTERWARDS I MET KAREN FOR BEERS.

THIS AINT SO BAD.

SLAVE TO CONVENTION - DOOM

5-17-15

TODAY KAREN + I DROVE OUT TO THE FANCY MALL.

FANCY MALL →

I BOUGHT A NEW SUIT.

OUCH!

400

CHEAP SUITS

WE SAW THE NEW MAD MAX MOVIE. IT WAS AWESOME!

ELECTRIC EYE - JUDAS PRIEST
5-18-15
BACK AT WORK, A 1-DAY WEEKEND WASN'T LONG ENOUGH.
LUCKILY I GET A THREE-DAY WEEKEND THIS WEEK!
I CAME HOME AND WATCHED THE FINAL EPISODE OF MAD MEN WITH KAREN.
THIS IS A NICE, FITTING END.
COKE
THEN I PLAYED MY DUMB ASS VIDEO GAME.
COME TO THE SABBATH - MERCYFUL FATE
5-19-15
WHEN I GOT HOME FROM WORK TODAY, KAREN HAD BAD NEWS
THE AIR CONDITONER IS BROKEN!
AFTER SOME GOOGLING, I FOUND THE PROBLEM, BUT HOME DEPOT DIDN'T HAVE THE PART I NEEDED.
WE DON'T CARRY ANYTHING LIKE THAT.
HOME DEPOT
LATER OUR NEIGHBORS CAME OVER FOR SOME BEERS.

NEVER KNOWING PEACE- TRAGEDY

5-20-15

WORK WAS OKAY TODAY.

I GOT THE PART I NEEDED FOR THE AC UNIT ON MY LUNCH BREAK.
I NEED A 370VAC RUN CAPACITOR.
HERE YOU GO

I PUT IT IN AND IT TOTALLY WORKS!!
WOW! I DIDN'T THINK I COULD DO IT!
RRRRRRRRRR

COLLIE AND WINE- GLEN BROWN

5-21-15

MY COMPUTER BROKE AT WORK TODAY, SO I WENT HOME EARLY.

I TOOK ADVANTAGE OF MY TIME OFF BY SITTING ON MY ASS LIKE THE WORTHLESS PIECE OF SHIT THAT I AM.

AND I PLAYED A VIDEO GAME.

CURSED REALMS OF THE WINTERDEMONS- IMMORTAL

5-22-15

WORK WAS PRETTY CHILL TODAY, FRIDAY BEFORE A 3-DAY WEEKEND.

I HAD A NICE DINNER WITH MY WIFE.

AND THEN WASTED THE REST OF MY NIGHT PLAYING THOSE DAMN VIDEO GAMES.
I JUST CONQUERED PERSIA!

THE POSTER- THE MONKEES

5-23-15

SATURDAY! I DID LAUNDRY AND MOWED THE LAWN.
IS IT WEIRD THAT I LOVE MOWING THE LAWN?
RRRRR

WE HAD A REALLY BAD STORM. THE POWER WENT OUT FOR A FEW HOURS.
I CAN'T BELIEVE HOW MUCH RAIN WE'VE BEEN GETTING THIS YEAR!
IT'S EL NIÑO.

WE LIT CANDLES AND I PLAYED MISFITS SONGS ON MY GUITAR.
DEMON I AM AND FACE I PEEL...

SOPHISTICATED BITCH- PUBLIC ENEMY
5-24-15
THE STORM LAST NIGHT BLEW DOWN A PIECE OF THE FENCE IN THE BACKYARD!
WHOA!
I WENT AND BOUGHT A NEW VIDEO CARD FOR MY COMPUTER.
MAN, THESE THINGS ARE CONFUSING.
GEFORCE 1150
GT 550
GEFORCE X1000
RADEON AT 7170
GEFORCE GT 890
GEFORCE GT 640
GX 770
RADEON GX 4748
IT WAS KINDA TOUGH + SCARY GETTING IT TO WORK, BUT I DID IT!
BOOT ERROR_
DIXIE DOODLE- LINK WRAY
5-25-15
I SPENT THE DAY ENJOYING MY NEW VIDEO CARD.
THERE WAS ANOTHER BIG CRAZY STORM!
KA-BOOM!
A LOT OF AUSTIN IS FLOODED. I'M GLAD OUR HOUSE IS ON TOP OF A HILL.
FLASH FLOOD WARNING!
LIVING IN THE PAST- CRIMPSHRINE
5-26-15
BACK AT WORK TODAY. IT WAS REALLY BUSY.
I'M GLAD I HAD A 3-DAY WEEKEND!
CAME HOME AND SCANNED SOME OLD FLYERS.
MAN, THE GOOD OL' DAYS. BEING PUNK IN THE PAST IS ALL I'VE GOT LEFT.
HMMMMM
THEN I PLAYED MORE OF THOSE DAMN VIDEO GAMES THAT I LOVE SO DAMN MUCH.
TELL HER NO- ZOMBIES
5-27-15
THIS IS SHAPING UP TO BE A PRETTY GRUELING WORK WEEK.
FOR THE PAST WEEK, I'VE BEEN TRYING A LOW-CARB DIET AT KAREN'S URGING.
I NEVER EVEN THOUGHT I LIKED BREAD UNTIL I COULDN'T HAVE IT ANYMORE.
MEAT
CHEESE
I HAVEN'T LOST ANY WEIGHT BUT MY POOP IS HORRIBLE
OH GOD!

I NEVER TOUCHED HER- HENRY FIAT'S OPEN SORE

5-28-15

WORK WAS REALLY BUSY AGAIN TODAY.
STILL, IT'S CHILD'S PLAY COMPARED TO MY LAST JOB.

AFTER WORK, KAREN + I WATCHED THE MOVIE PATTON.
I'VE ALWAYS BEEN CURIOUS ABOUT THIS MOVIE...

IT WASN'T AS GOOD AS I WAS HOPING IT WOULD BE.
GOD, THIS MOVIE IS SO LONG!
ZZZZ

NUMBER OF THE BEAST- IRON MAIDEN

5-29-15

WORK WAS STILL BUSY, I'M GONNA HAVE TO COME IN ON SATURDAY.

AFTER WORK I TOLD KAREN...
FUCK THIS DIET! TONIGHT WE ARE GETTING TACOS!

AND SO WE DID.
GLORIOUS CARBS!

ACE IN THE HOLE- BLACK OAK ARKANSAS

5-30-15

IT'S SATURDAY. I WENT TO WORK.

I STOPPED AT HOME DEPOT AFTERWARD AND GOT A NEW SHOWER HEAD.

I ALSO GOT A NEW DOOR KNOB FOR THE BATHROOM.

HEAD OUT TO THE HIGHWAY- JUDAS PRIEST

5-31-15

THIS MORNING I MOWED THE LAWN.

KAREN GRILLED SOME RIBS.

WE SAT ON THE BACK PORCH, DRINKING BEER AND PLAYING DOMINOES.

HEART OF THE SUNRISE- YES

6-1-15

BACK AT WORK AFTER MY 1-DAY WEEKEND.

"I FEEL SO REJUVENATED!"

WHEN I GOT HOME, KAREN WAS MAKING MARGARITAS.

ARE YOU THIRSTY?

YES!

MY WIFE IS SO AWESOME.

BABYCLINO- CAVES

6-2-15

WORK WAS OKAY TODAY

I FOUND OUT SOMETHING COOL.

CAVES IS PLAYING HERE ON THE 18TH!

WHEN I TOLD KAREN...

OH CRAP. I BOUGHT YOU TICKETS TO SEE NEIL DEGRASSE TYSON THAT NIGHT!

ITS COOL, WE CAN GO TO BOTH!

CINE LUBESTE SI LASA- ROTTING CHRIST

6-3-15

I WENT TO WORK TODAY. IT'S GETTING EASIER.

MET UP WITH BRYAN AFTERWARD FOR A BEER.

MY TIRE HAS A NAIL IN IT.

AH CRAP

HIGHWAY PIRATE- BLACK OAK ARKANSAS
6-4-15
WORK WAS A BREEZE TODAY.
I WENT TO BAND PRACTICE
THEN I GOT MY TIRE FIXED.
TIRE SHOP
TWELVE BUCKS
RAD!

SCHEME OF THINGS - LEATHERFACE

6-5-15

IT WAS A CHILL FRIDAY AT WORK.

KAREN + I WENT OUT TO DINNER.

I WATCHED KUNG FURY. IT WASN'T TOTALLY TERRIBLE.
JUST MOSTLY TERRIBLE.
ZZZ

D.M.V. - THE TEMPLARS

6-6-15

A NICE LAZY SATURDAY. I DID LAUNDRY.

I GOT A LOT OF DRAWING DONE.

KAREN + I ATE A PIZZA.
I'M GIVING UP ON THE STUPID-ASS LOW CARB DIET. ITS BEEN ALMOST 3 WEEKS AND I HAVEN'T LOST EVEN 1 POUND.

BLACK DIAMOND - KISS

6-7-15

GOT GROCERIES WITH KAREN THIS MORNING.

WE SAT OUT ON THE BACK PORCH AND DRANK BEERS.

SUNDAY EVENINGS WITH KAREN ARE MY FAVORITE.

P'UNCHAW KACHUN-TUTA KACHUN - ROTTING CHRIST

6-8-15

WORK WAS PRETTY GOOD TODAY.

I CAME HOME AND DID A LITTLE WORKOUT.

AND I WATCHED TV WITH KAREN.
RUPAUL'S DRAG RACE

NO LIFE, NO FUTURE - THE EXPELLED
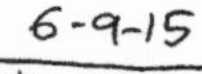
6-9-15

WORK WAS KINDA BORING.

I DROVE TO THE MALL TO PICK UP MY SUIT, ACROSS AUSTIN IN RUSH HOUR TRAFFIC

THE TRIP TOOK TWO HOURS.
ZZZ

THE ENDMILLS - PORTAL

6-10-15

WORK WAS OKAY TODAY.

CAME HOME AND WATCHED TV/ ATE DINNER WITH KAREN.

THEN WE TOOK THE DOG FOR A WALK.

ROOM OF GOLDEN AIR - MERCYFUL FATE

6-11-15

TEXT MESSAGE TO: KAREN
MARGARITAS ESTA NOCHE?

KAREN
MARGARITAS ESTA NOCHE?
SI SEÑOR

<3

GOING SOUTH - DEAD MOON

6-12-15

I LEFT WORK A LITTLE EARLY TODAY.

DRANK SOME BEERS AND WATCHED TV WITH KAREN.
THE SOPRANOS

PLAYED VIDEO GAMES ALL NIGHT.

WHAT TO EXPECT - FASTBACKS
6-13-15
THIS MORNING I MOWED THE LAWN.
AS OF TODAY, WE'VE LIVED IN THIS HOUSE FOR ONE YEAR!
KAREN+I GOT DRESSED UP AND WENT TO BEN W's WEDDING.
WE ATE HAMBURGERS AFTERWARD.
BURIED BY TIME AND DUST - MAYHEM
6-14-15
HOLY SHIT I'M 41 TODAY.
KAREN TOOK ME TO GET PUFFY TACOS.
THEN I BOUGHT A NEW THERMOSTAT.
HAPPY BIRTHDAY TO ME!
WIFI THERMOSTATS
RIPPER - CHRON GEN
6-15-15
BACK AT WORK TODAY. GLAD I HAVE A SHORT WEEK.
AFTER WORK I MET UP WITH MY OLD COWORKER FOR HAPPY HOUR.
THEN I SNUGGLED WITH KAREN.
CHILDREN GONE TO SHADOW - WORLD BURNS TO DEATH
6-16-15
WORK WAS PRETTY CHILL TODAY.
WE WERE SUPPOSED TO GET HIT WITH A HURRICAINE TONIGHT...
... BUT IT NEVER CAME.

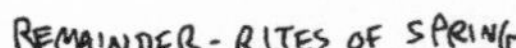
REMAINDER - RITES OF SPRING

WORK WAS PRETTY AVERAGE TODAY.

THE STREETS WERE FLOODING REALLY BAD!

6-17-15
IT RAINED ALL NIGHT.
THIS IS CRAZY!

DEATH AGONY + SCREAMS - G.I.S.M.

TODAY WAS AWESOME!
THIS FEELS LIKE MY REAL BIRTHDAY!

KAREN + I SAW NEIL DEGRASSE TYSON SPEAK!

6-18-15
THEN WE WENT TO HOTEL VEGAS AND SAW CAVES!
MINTY!
HAMISH!
LOU!

HYPNOTIC WINTER - JEFF THE BROTHERHOOD

CAVES STAYED OVER AT THE HOUSE LAST NIGHT. IT WAS FUN.

I MADE BREAKFAST FOR THEM. SOMETIMES I MISS THE TOURING LIFE.
BREAKFAST TACOS ARE THE BEST THINGS TO MAKE FOR TOURING BANDS.

6-19-15
I LIKE HAVING BANDS OVER NOW, IT'S LIKE A WAY TO PEEK INTO THAT LIFE AGAIN.
BEEP! BEEP!
BYE GUYS! DRIVE SAFE!

NOW EVERYBODY'S ME - DEAD MILKMEN

6-20-15

TODAY WAS PRODUCTIVE. I DID LAUNDRY + CLEANED THE KITCHEN.

I CAUGHT UP ON A LOT OF DRAWING.

AND I LAYED ON THE COUCH WATCHING TV AND EATING ICE CREAM.
SUCH A PRODUCTIVE DAY!

NATTY CHAMPION - PRINCE FAR I

6-21-15

TODAY WAS FUN. I MADE A CRAFTS PROJECT OUT OF BOTTLE CAPS.
EPOXY

I ALSO WENT INTO TOWN AND RAN SOME ERRANDS.
THIS WAY TO TOWN

THEN I WENT TO GHOST KNIFE PRACTICE!

ARRESTED FOR DRIVING WHILE BLIND - ZZ TOP

6-22-15

BACK AT WORK TODAY.

I CAME HOME AND DID A SMALL WORKOUT.
I GUESS A LITTLE HALF-HEARTED WORK-OUT IS BETTER THAN NOTHING.

WHICH I IMMEDIATELY UNDID WITH A LARGE BAG OF POPCORN.
OH YEAH SO MUCH BETTER.
ORVILLE REDENBACHER

OUTSIDE MY HEAD - OBITUARY

6-23-15

WORK. THERE ARE PARTS OF IT I LOVE AND PARTS OF IT I HATE.
I GUESS EVERY JOB IS LIKE THAT.

I CAME HOME AND DID NOT DO A WORKOUT.
BECAUSE I AM A GIANT HUGE PIECE OF SHIT AND I HATE MYSELF.

THEN I TOOK PEEBER FOR A WALK.

LARVAE - PORTAL

6-24-15

WORK WAS COOL TODAY.

I CAME HOME AND ATE SOME TAQUITOS BY MYSELF. KAREN IS DOING VOLUNTEER WORK TONIGHT.

I ALSO GOT DRUNK AND WATCHED T.V.
I DON'T LIKE IT WHEN KAREN'S NOT HERE.

STREAM OF CONCIOUSNESS- KREATOR
6-25-15
WENT TO WORK TODAY.
TOOK KAREN OUT FOR MARGARITAS.
TOOK A BATH AND CRASHED OUT SUPER EARLY.
8:30
ZZZ
YOU ALONE- MR. T EXPERIENCE
6-26-15
WORK GOT KINDA HECTIC TODAY.
GLAD IT WAS PAYDAY! I BOUGHT SOME FANCY BEERS.
THESE 8 BEERS ARE GOING TO COST YOU A SHAMEFUL AMOUNT OF MONEY.
THAT'S COOL.
AND I DRANK THEM.
FANCY BEER BRINGS ME JOY. I DON'T BUY DRUGS OR RECORDS OR ANYTHING FUN ANY MORE. I'M BUYING SOME FANCY BEERS DAMMIT!
CARNE VOODOO- RFTC
6-27-15
TODAY I MOWED THE LAWN.
I TRIED TO DO LAUNDRY BUT THE WASHER BROKE.
DAMMIT!! NOT AGAIN!
LATER I WAS PLAYING WITH PEEBER AND HE HIT HIS FACE ON THE SIDEWALK.
OH NO! BE CAREFUL BUDDY!
BONK
SATA A MISS GANA- PRINCE BUSTER
6-28-15
THIS MORNING I WENT TO WORK.
BUT IT'S SUNDAY!
THEN KAREN + I WENT TO HOME DEPOT AND BOUGHT A NEW WASHER.
I'M DONE WITH USED SHIT ON CRAIGSLIST.
THEN I DRANK SOME MICHELADAS.

CRYPTIC REMAINS- MASSACRE

6-29-15

WORK WAS ALL BUSY AND SHIT.

KAREN HAD VOLUNTEER WORK TONIGHT SO I ATE TAQUITOS AND WATCHED A SHITTY MOVIE.

RISE OF THE SILVER SURFER

I DIDN'T REALLY DO MUCH ELSE. MY LIFE IS KINDA BORING.

I'M OKAY WITH THAT.

ORBMORPHIA- PORTAL

6-30-15

WORK IS STILL SUPER BUSY.

KAREN + I ORDERED A PIZZA.

PEPPERONI EYES ♫

I FELL ASLEEP EARLY AGAIN. I WONDER WHY I KEEP DOING THAT?

ZZZZZZZZZ

THE NAIL THAT STICKS UP GETS HAMMERED DOWN- BORN AGAINST

7-1-15

WORK IS STARTING TO CALM DOWN.

BRANDON + CHELSEA CAME OVER TO HANG OUT.

THEN KAREN + I WATCHED THE FINAL EPISODE OF THE SOPRANOS.

AM I SUPPOSED TO HATE A.J. THIS MUCH?

JIM BOWIE- THE DICKIES

7-2-15

WORK WAS EASY AND GOOF-OFF TODAY. WE GOT A 3 DAY WEEKEND COMING UP.

I AM EXCITED TO HAVE A 3-DAY WEEKEND SINCE I HAD TO WORK LAST SUNDAY.

I'M GONNA DO SO MUCH SHIT THIS WEEKEND!

IN REALITY, I'M PROBABLY GONNA LIE AROUND THE HOUSE AND DO NOTHING.

OOH MY FREE TIME IS SO VALUABLE.

HEY LITTLE RICH BOY - SHAM 69

7-3-15

TODAY I CHANGED THE OIL IN MY VAN.

I GOT AN INFLATABLE KIDDIE POOL FOR $6.
AHH, WHY NOT?
ON SALE
FUN POOL

I SOAKED MY FEET IN IT WHILE I PLAYED GUITAR AND DRANK BEER.
THIS WAS A GOOD IDEA

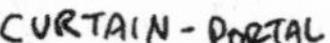
CURTAIN - PORTAL

7-4-15

THE 4TH OF JULY IS AWESOME IN OUR NEIGHBORHOOD.

WE WENT TO A LITTLE PARTY DOWN THE STREET

THEN WE SAT IN OUR DRIVEWAY AND WATCHED FIREWORKS!
I ♥ MANOR!

GAS CHAMBER - ANGRY SAMOANS

7-5-15

TODAY KAREN + I WENT TO THRIFT STORES.
I FOUND AN AWESOME BLAUER POLICE JACKET FOR $4.00!

WE RAN A FEW ERRANDS.
ERRAND PLACE

THEN I PLAYED VIDEO GAMES ALL NIGHT.

SOURLOWS - PORTAL

7-6-15

BACK AT WORK TODAY, IT WAS NICE BECAUSE MY BOSS IS ON VACATION.

I WENT OVER AND HUNG OUT WITH MY NEIGHBOR, GARY.
WOW, WHERE DID YOU LEARN TO DRAW SO WELL?

THEN I DRANK A COUPLE BEERS WITH KAREN.

#2 PENCIL-MELVINS
7-7-15
WORK GOT A LITTLE STRESSFUL TODAY.
BUT STILL NOTHING AT ALL LIKE MY OLD JOB!
KAREN + I ORDERED A PIZZA.
AND WE WATCHED A PBS DOCUMENTARY ABOUT MATH.
FUCKIN' WILD TIMES AT AGE 41!

EVERYBODY WANTS TO SEE HEAVEN, NOBODY WANTS TO DIE - BLACK OAK ARKANSAS
7-8-15
WORK WAS MUCH BETTER TODAY.
AFTER WORK I HUNG OUT AT GARY'S HOUSE.
I ATE LEFTOVER PIZZA.
I KINDA HATE IT WHEN KAREN DOES VOLUNTEER WORK.

SUBJUGATOR - ANTHRAX
7-9-15
TODAY I WENT TO WORK AT MY JOB.
THEN KAREN + I WATCHED A NEW TV SHOW CALLED MR. ROBOT.
THIS IS SO GOOD!
WE ALSO DRANK SOME BEERS
BEER

GET OUT OF THE WAY - THE MAGNIFICENT
7-10-15
FRIDAY AT WORK IS ALWAYS CHILL.
TOOK KAREN OUT FOR MARGARITAS.
MARGARITA PLACE
THE FAN ON MY NEW VIDEO CARD BROKE, SO MY COMPUTER IS SUPER LOUD.
ISN'T THAT INTERESTING?
WHRRRRRK

BURIED IN THE BACKYARD - CANNIBAL CORPSE

7-11-15

I MOWED THE LAWN THIS MORNING.

I BOUGHT A NEW TOY FOR PEEBER. HE BURIED IT IN THE YARD.

KAREN + I WENT OUT FOR ETHIOPIAN FOOD.

CLOCKOUT - DEVO

7-12-15

TODAY WAS NICE. KAREN AND I LAZED AROUND THE HOUSE ALL DAY.

I DREW THE COVER FOR THE BOOK THAT YOU ARE READING RIGHT NOW.
MANOR THREAT

LATER WE GRILLED IN THE BACK YARD.

MY HEART + THE REAL WORLD - MINUTEMEN

7-13-15

BACK AT WORK TODAY.

ANOTHER NIGHT WHERE KAREN IS VOLUNTEERING.

I ATE A SAD MEAL BY MYSELF.

WHAT DID I DO TO DESERVE YOU? - JOEY RAMONE

7-14-15

TODAY I WENT TO THE DENTIST AND GOT A NEW CROWN.

THE WHOLE SIDE OF MY HEAD WAS NUMB FOR HOURS.

I TOOK LIKE 700 IBUPROFINS.
OW

PALE BLUE EYES - VELVET UNDERGROUND

7-15-15

WORK WAS COOL TODAY.

AFTERWARD I WENT OVER TO GARY'S AND PLAYED THE DRUMS. IT WAS KINDA FUN.

THEN I HUNG OUT WITH MY BEAUTIFUL WIFE!

FAMILY LIFE - SHAM 69

7-16-15

WORK HAS BEEN REALLY SLOW LATELY.

TODAY ME + MY COWORKER BRUCE DITCHED OUT EARLY AND WENT TO GET BEERS.

I HAD FUN, HE'S A COOL GUY.
I GOT TO RIDE IN HIS SUPER-FANCY SPACE CAR.

LET'S BE TOGETHER TONIGHT - MR T EXPERIENCE

7-17-15

WORK WAS NORMAL TODAY... ...UNTIL...
HEY BEN!

...WE GOT A SUPER-HOT JOB AT 5 PM. I HAD TO STAY UNTIL 8:00 TO FINISH IT.

6134002 TO 6134602. WAIT, FUCK! THATS THE WRONG SEQUENCE.

I WAS WIPED OUT AFTER A 12-HOUR DAY.
BLEEEAARGH

I NEARLY MARRIED A HUMAN - GARY NUMAN

7-18-15

THIS MORNING I CLEANED AND RE-ARRANGED MY OFFICE.

THEN KAREN + I MET UP WITH MITCH + AMANDA FOR DINNER.
BAND

WE HAD A NICE TIME HANGING OUT.
BAND

ATATE-NGOZI FAMILY

7-19-15

KAREN + I BOTH WERE SUPER HUNGOVER.
WHY WE DRINK SO MUCH
CUZ WE DUMB

I DROVE TO ROUND ROCK.
ROUND ROCK ←
LATER WE GRILLED IN THE BACK YARD.
I LOVE SUNDAYS

SUN GOD - SQUIRREL BAIT

7-20-15

BACK AT WORK TODAY!

I HUNG OUT AT GARY'S PLACE AFTER.

AT THE END OF THE NIGHT I GOT TO EAT SOME GAS-STATION FRIED CHICKEN WITH MY DARLING WIFE.

LOVELOVELOVE - THE QUEERS

7-21-15

WORK WAS SLOW TODAY.

I WENT FOR A BEER WITH BRUCE AFTERWARD.

THEN I ATE A PIZZA WITH KAREN.
WTF?

STALKER SONG - DANZIG

7-22-15

WORK WAS COOL TODAY.

I TOOK PEEBER FOR A WALK...

..AND I DID SOME DRAWING.

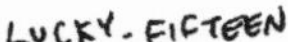
LUCKY - FIFTEEN

7-23-15

TODAY I WENT TO WORK.

AND I WATCHED TV WITH KAREN.
WHAT'S GOING ON, ARE YOU WEARING A HAT?
HUH?

AND I TOOK PEEBER FOR A WALK.

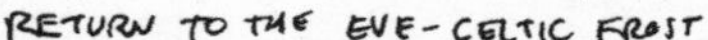
RETURN TO THE EVE - CELTIC FROST

7-24-15

ON THE WAY HOME FROM WORK TODAY MY CAR BROKE DOWN.

THE UPSIDE: IT BROKE DOWN RIGHT IN FRONT OF A MECHANIC SHOP, AN HOUR BEFORE THEY CLOSED.
AND TODAY IS PAYDAY SO I CAN AFFORD IT.

THE DOWNSIDE: IT COST $150
I MEAN, I CAN SORT OF AFFORD IT.

CHARLIE'S WATCHING - TOY DOLLS

7-25-15

TODAY WAS THE LAZIEST DAY EVER.
ZZZZ

I FELL ASLEEP ON THE COUCH.
ZZZ

AND I PLAYED A VIDEO GAME FOR A BUNCH OF HOURS.
I SPEND ALL DAY AT WORK LOOKING AT A COMPUTER SCREEN, SO OF COURSE I WANT TO DO IT ON MY DAY OFF, TOO.

GILGAMES - ROTTING CHRIST

7-26-15

ME + KAREN DROVE OUT TO ANDERSON MILL TODAY.
ANDERSON MILL
TEXAS
MANOR
AUSTIN

WE RAN SOME ERRANDS
STUPID BULLSHIT STORE
STUPID BULLSHIT STORE PLUS!
OH LOOK, IT'S THOSE STORES WE LIKE.

THEN WE SMOKED A PORK SHOULDER.
THIS WOULD WORK BETTER IF WE HAD A REAL SMOKER.
HMM

7-2?-15
STERILITY - ASSUCK
I WENT BACK TO WORK TODAY.
AFTER WORK I PLAYED MUSIC WITH GARY.
THIS IS SO LOW-PRESSURE AND GOOFING AROUND. IT MAKES ME FEEL LIKE A KID AGAIN.
AND I WATCHED HALT + CATCH FIRE WITH KAREN.
SEASON TWO!!
7-28-15
SHE SHE LITTLE SHEILA - GENE VINCENT
WORK WAS JUST FINE TODAY.
KAREN MADE SHRIMP TOSTADAS.
WE WATCHED MORE HALT + CATCH FIRE.
THIS SHOW HAS THE BEST MUSIC!
7-29-15
BREAK IT UP - RFTC
I LIKE MY JOB, SOME DAYS MORE THAN OTHERS.
NOT SO MUCH TODAY!
IT'S WEDNESDAY, SO I CAME HOME TO A KAREN-LESS HOUSE.
I PLAYED VIDEO GAMES ALL NIGHT.
7-30-15
NIH NIGHTMARE - G.I.S.M.
THINGS CALMED DOWN AT WORK TODAY.
I TOOK KAREN OUT TO OUR FAVORITE RESTAURANT.
"OUR FAVORITE"
restaur
THEN WE BOUGHT SOME STUFF AT WALMART.
"NOT OUR FAVORITE"
store

AUDRA LEE- FYP

7-31-15

IT WAS A NICE FRIDAY AT WORK

CAME HOME AND HAD A NICE DINNER WITH THE WIFE.

WE HAD A GREAT NIGHT GOOFING OFF + TALKING.

GET STRAIGHT- RADIOACTIVITY

8-1-15

TODAY I WENT AND BOUGHT A SMOKER.
I'M GONNA LEARN TO DO THIS RIGHT.
OFFSET SMOKER

I PUT IT TOGETHER. TOMORROW IT'S ON!!

I SPENT THE REST OF THE DAY PLAYING A VIDEO GAME.

FEATHERED FRIENDS- RFTC

8-2-15

WHEN I WOKE UP ON FRIDAY, I HAD THESE WEIRD WELTS IN MY ARMPITS.
EW

TODAY THEY ARE BLISTERED AND REALLY PAINFUL.
OW! JEEZ.

ANYWAY, KAREN TAUGHT ME HOW TO SMOKE MEAT TODAY.

I'M A PRETENDER- EXPLODING HEARTS

8-3-15

BACK AT WORK TODAY. MY ARMPITS HURT LIKE HELL.
OW

I CAME HOME AND SOAKED IN AN OATMEAL BATH.
SOAKING JUST YOUR ARMPITS IS HARDER THAN YOU'D THINK

I GUESS IT'S AN ALLERGIC REACTION TO DEODORANT?
WHATEVER IT IS, IT REALLY SUCKS.

NOT FUCKING DEAD - SEVERED HEAD OF STATE

8-4-15

TODAY I WENT TO THE DENTIST AND GOT MY NEW CROWN PUT IN.

I ALSO HAD MY FIRST REGULAR CHECKUP IN 17 YEARS.

YOU HAVE NO CAVITIES!

NO SHIT?

XRAY

UPDATE: MY ARMPITS ARE STILL FUCKED.

FEAR OF THE DARK - IRON MAIDEN

8-5-15

WORK TODAY.

CAME HOME TO AN EMPTY HOUSE. EXCEPT PEEBER. PEEBER WAS THERE.

I DON'T LIKE WEDNESDAYS.

COUNTER ATTACK - DRI

8-6-15

WORK WAS BUSY + STRESSFUL TODAY.

WENT FOR BEERS WITH BRUCE AFTERWARD.

HA HA HA WORK SUCKS

YES IT DOES

CAME HOME AND DRANK MORE BEERS WITH KAREN.

HA HA HA WORK SUCKS

YES IT DOES

WHAT IS A HOME WITHOUT LOVE - LOUVIN BROTHERS

8-7-15

TODAY WAS MY BOSS' LAST DAY AT WORK. SHE DIDN'T SEEM VERY HAPPY ABOUT IT.
PEACE OUT

KAREN + I WENT OUT TO DINNER.
FAVORITE SPOT

THEN WE WENT TO THE BOOK STORE.

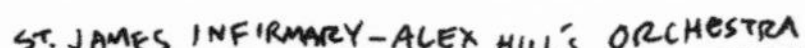
ST. JAMES INFIRMARY - ALEX HILL'S ORCHESTRA

8-8-15

THIS MORNING I GOT A HAIRCUT.
THEN I WENT TO GHOST KNIFE PRACTICE.

THEN I GOT MARGARITAS WITH KAREN.

I'LL BE YOUR MIRROR - VELVET UNDERGROUND

8-9-15

TODAY I SMOKED A RACK OF RIBS.

I MADE MUSIC WITH GARY AND MALACHI

THEN I WATCHED A MOVIE WITH KAREN.

DOWNBOUND TRAIN - CHUCK BERRY

8-10-15

WORK WENT BY SUPER FAST TODAY.
NOT HAVING A BOSS IS COOL!

I CAME HOME AND HUNG OUT WITH KAREN.

I PLAYED A VIDEO GAME.

6:00 - DREAM THEATER

8-11-15

WORK WAS CHILL TODAY.
zzz

I WENT TO A BASEBALL GAME WITH KAREN AND HER FRIENDS FROM WORK

IT WAS PRETTY FUN.

A MIND BESIDE ITSELF - I - EROTOMANIA - DREAM THEATER
WORK WAS VERY CHILL TODAY.

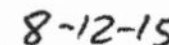
8-12-15

I CAME HOME AND DID SOME DRAWING.

THEN I TIDIED UP THE HOUSE. MY MOM IS COMING TO VISIT TOMORROW.

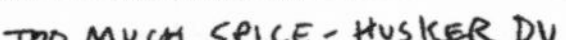
TOO MUCH SPICE - HUSKER DU

8-13-15

THIS MORNING I PICKED UP MY MOM AT THE AIRPORT.
HI MOM

WE HAD A NICE AFTERNOON TALKING + CATCHING UP.

KAREN MADE US A GREAT DINNER.

SHADOWS OVER TRANSYLVANIA - DARK FUNERAL

8-14-15

THIS MORNING I TOOK MY MOM SHOPPING ON SOUTH CONGRESS.
GOOFY STUFF
KEEP IT WEIRD
BUY SOME CRAP

THEN KAREN + I TOOK HER TO DINNER AT THE HULA HUT.

I LOVE MY MOM, BUT SHE CAN BE PRETTY EXHAUSTING.

BUT AFTER THE GIG - BALLAST

8-15-15

TODAY WE ALL WENT TO THE KYLE FLEA MARKET.
WHOA THIS FLEA MARKET IS COOL!

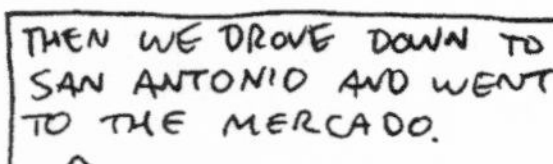
THEN WE DROVE DOWN TO SAN ANTONIO AND WENT TO THE MERCADO.

IT WAS A LONG, HOT DAY AND I GOT KINDA GRUMPY.

I LOVE MY MOM. I LOVE MY MOM.
I LOVE MY MOM. I LOVE MY MOM.
I LOVE MY MOM. I LOVE MY MOM.
I LOVE MY MOM. I LOVE MY MOM.

DELIVER- M.O.T.O.

8-16-15

THIS MORNING I DROPPED MY MOM OFF AT THE AIRPORT.
TERMINAL →

THEN I WENT TO GHOST KNIFE PRACTICE.

THEN I WENT HOME AND ENJOYED A FEW PRECIOUS MOMENTS TO MYSELF.

RIPE- SCREAMING FEMALES

8-17-15

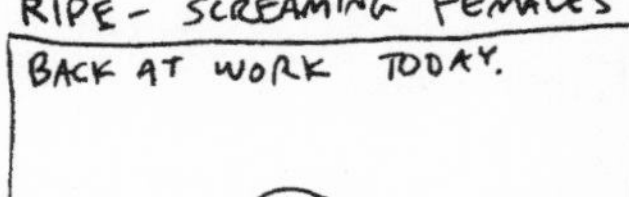
BACK AT WORK TODAY.

AFTERWARD I MADE MUSIC WITH GARY + MALACHI.

THEN I READ A BOOK.

NO FAIR- WIPERS

8-18-15

WORK WAS COOL TODAY.

KAREN + I WENT OUT TO DINNER. THIS WILL BE OUR ONLY NIGHT TOGETHER THIS WEEK.

WE WENT HOME AND TOOK ADVANTAGE OF THE FACT THAT THIS WILL BE OUR ONLY NIGHT TOGETHER THIS WEEK.

CENSORED

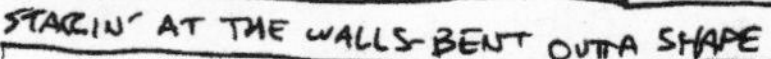
STARIN' AT THE WALLS- BENT OUTTA SHAPE

8-19-15

TODAY I WENT TO WORK.

I RECORDED A SONG WITH GARY.

THEN I ATE SOME CHIPS.
CRUNCH
CRUNCH
CHIPS

8-20-15
RED DYE NO. 9 - BILLY CLUB
WORK WAS PRETTY OKAY TODAY.
I CLEANED UP THE HOUSE TO GET READY FOR THE SCREAMING FEMALES.
THEY SHOWED UP AROUND 1:00.
MIKE!
JARRETT!
MARISSA
REBECCA
8-21-15
BEHIND THE WALL OF SLEEP - BLACK SABBATH
SO TIRED AT WORK.
THE SCREAMALES PICKED ME UP FROM WORK AND WE WENT DOWN TO THE SHOW!
GHOST KNIFE PLAYED WITH THEM AND IT WAS SUPER FUN!
THE ISLE - AHAB
8-22-15
VACATION (THE BAND) CAME BACK TO THE HOUSE LAST NIGHT. WE HUNG OUT, IT WAS FUN.
WOO HOO
I WAS SO WIPED OUT FROM TWO LATE NIGHTS IN A ROW.
SNAKEPIT GETS OLD.
I JUST OOZED INTO THE COUCH ALL DAY.
8-23-15
THE ANOINTED COMB - SHOWCASE SHOWDOWN
THE RECORD PLAYER THAT I'VE HAD FOR TWENTY YEARS FINALLY DIED TODAY.
..SO I WENT AND BOUGHT A NEW ONE!
I DON'T THINK I'VE OWNED A BRAND-NEW RECORD PLAYER SINCE I WAS A LITTLE KID.
SONY
PYLE
DENON
CROSLEY
ION
IT'S REALLY NICE.

PEACE OF MIND - BOSTON
8-24-15
BACK AT WORK TODAY...
I WENT TO HAPPY HOUR WITH BRUCE AFTERWARD.
THEN HE CAME OVER TO THE HOUSE FOR A FEW MORE BEERS.
OCTOBER REVOLUTION - ASSÜCK
8-25-15
WORK WAS PRETTY COOL.
I CAME HOME AND DIDN'T DO SHIT.
I HAVEN'T HAD A LOT OF TIME TO NOT DO SHIT LATELY.
THE INTERNET
PADDED CELL - BLACK FLAG
8-26-15
MY NEW BOSS IS SUPER COOL.
AFTER WORK KAREN + I WENT OUT FOR BURGERS.
THEN WE WATCHED TV.
ZZZ
ZZZ
XR3 - HARD SKIN
8-27-15
I'VE REALLY BEEN ENJOYING MY JOB THIS WEEK...
I WENT OVER TO GARY'S AND PLAYED SOME MUSIC.
KAREN + I WENT TO BED EARLY.
ZZZZZZ

FIRE IN THE RAIN- AGENT ORANGE
8-28-15
ANOTHER ENJOYABLE DAY AT WORK.
KAREN BROUGHT HOME CHINESE FOOD FOR DINNER.
AND MY PEANUTS BOOK THAT I ORDERED LAST WEEK ARRIVED TODAY!
I WANT TO OBTAIN THE WHOLE COLLECTION!
GOOD GRIEF!
EMERGENCY- CLOROX GIRLS
8-29-15
TODAY WAS AWESOME. I SMOKED A RACK OF RIBS..
.. I DREW A BUNCH OF COMICS...
...AND I LISTENED TO A BUNCH OF RECORDS.
BLACK LUNGS- FLESHMOTHER
8-30-15
TODAY WAS NICE. DID SOME YARD WORK.
RRRR
RAN A FEW ERRANDS.
ERRAND PLACE
ERRAND MOBILE
I'M STARTING TO FEEL NORMAL AGAIN.
KING OF FOOLS- SOCIAL DISTORTION
8-31-15
BACK AT WORK TODAY.
I LEFT EARLY TO GO TO THE DENTIST, AGAIN.
YOU'LL HAVE TO COME FOR THREE MORE VISITS AFTER THIS ONE.
???
I WONDER IF I'M BEING TAKEN FOR A RIDE.
THIS DENTIST HAS ALWAYS BEEN SUPER CHILL, BUT THIS IS SEEMING LIKE SOME BULLSHIT.

PHAROH HOUSE CRASH- PRINCE BUSTER

9-1-15

WORK WAS COOL TODAY

WENT TO GARY'S AND RECORDED SOME STUFF.

HUNG OUT WITH KAREN FOR A MINUTE.
NOW THAT SCHOOL HAS STARTED AGAIN I DONT GET TO SEE HER MUCH.

POOR BORN- DEAD MOON

9-2-15

WORK WAS PRETTY GOOD TODAY.

I CAME HOME AND PLAYED VIDEO GAMES.

THEN I PLAYED SOME VIDEO GAMES.
I'VE LITERALLY SPENT MY ENTIRE DAY LOOKING AT COMPUTER SCREENS.

I'M SORRY THAT I STOLE YOUR WEED- ME

9-3-15

WENT TO WORK THIS MORNING.
I'VE BEEN TRYING TO DRAW THIS DESK FOR MONTHS NOW, AND I'M FINALLY GETTING THE ANGLES RIGHT.

FINISHED UP MY SONG AT GARY'S.

I'M REALLY STOKED WITH HOW IT CAME OUT!

JOHNNY AND DEE DEE- TEENGENERATE

9-4-15

WORK DRAAAGGGEEED TODAY.
THREE-DAY WEEKEND IN JUST A FEW MORE HOURS.
ZZZ
ZZ

ALSO, TODAY IS PAYDAY!
WHEW! I WAS KINDA BROKE!

I TOOK KAREN OUT TO DINNER.

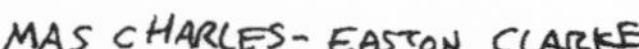
MAS CHARLES- EASTON CLARKE

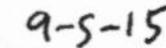
9-5-15

TODAY I SMOKED A RACK OF RIBS.

BUT I TOOK THEM OFF THE GRILL BEFORE THEY WERE DONE, AND HAD TO FINISH THEM IN THE MICROWAVE.
THESE AREN'T COOKED ALL THE WAY.

THEY TASTED LIKE SHIT. WHAT A FAILURE OF A DAY.
MAN, I SUCK AT BBQ-ING AS BAD AS I SUCK AT BREWING BEER. I WISH I COULD FIND A HOBBY I WAS GOOD AT.

TRUTH BE TOLD- OBITUARY

9-6-15

TODAY KAREN + I WENT TO THE FLEA MARKET.

THIS FLEA MARKET IS FUN, BUT IT KINDA SUCKS.

AFTER THAT WE HAD LUNCH AT BILLY'S.
I MISS THE DAYS WHEN WE COULD EAT HERE ALL THE TIME.

THEN WE SPENT THE REST OF THE EVENING RELAXING IN OUR FINE HOME.

PRIVACY INVASION- THE EXPLOITED

9-7-15

ITS LABOR DAY AND I DON'T HAVE TO WORK.

I PUT A GIANT MOON MONSTER MURAL ON MY OFFICE DOOR.

KAREN MADE CURRY AND WE WATCHED TV.
MOOOOOOOON MONSTER!
YOU'RE WEIRD

MISSISSIPPI QUEEN- MOUNTAIN

9-8-15

BACK AT WORK TODAY. I LIKE MY JOB.

I CAME HOME AND DID A WORKOUT.
I'VE BEEN LETTING IT SLIP TOO LONG. I'VE ALMOST GAINED BACK ALL OF THE WEIGHT I LOST IN '13.

I ONLY DRANK TWO BEERS.
I WANT TO DRINK MORE BUT I'M NOT GOING TO.

BLACK STEEL IN THE HOUR OF CHAOS - PUBLIC ENEMY
9-9-15
WORK WAS COOL TODAY.
I DID ANOTHER SOLID WORKOUT.
AND I ONLY DRANK ONE BEER!
JUST ONE!
THE NIGHTMARE CONTINUES - DISCHARGE
9-10-15
ANOTHER GOOD DAY AT MY GOOD JOB.
CAME HOME AND WORKED OUT.
NO BEERS AT ALL!!!
ALL MY FRIENDS HAVE FEET - SOCKEYE
9-11-15
WORK WENT BY SUPER FAST.
FRIDAAAYYY
KAREN MADE A HEALTHY DINNER.
I WENT TO BED KINDA EARLY
DON'T WORRY, I STILL DID A WORK-OUT TODAY.
ZZZ
WIRED OPPOSITES - ARTIFICIAL BRAIN
9-12-15
I RAN A TON OF ERRANDS TODAY.
HOLY SHIT! MY "CHECK ENGINE" LIGHT WENT OFF!
I SOLD SOME COMIC BOOKS AND MADE $200!
BUY·SELL·TRADE
IT WAS A GORGEOUS EVENING SO I TOOK PEEBER ON A LONG WALK.

AUTODRIVE- HERBIE HANCOCK

9-13-15

TODAY WAS REALLY NICE OUT. I TOOK A NAP IN THE HAMMOCK.
ZZZ

I WENT OVER TO GARY'S AND PLAYED SOME MUSIC WITH HIM+MIKE.

THEN I CAME HOME AND WATCHED STAR TREK WITH KAREN.

DOWN THE HIGHWAY- BOB DYLAN

9-14-15

BACK AT WORK. I LEFT EARLY TO GO TO THE DENTIST.

BUT I SAID FUCK THE DENTIST.
FUCK THE DENTIST.

FUCK THE DENTIST.
HARRY POTTER AND THE WHATEVER

BUMP-N-GRIND- BLACK OAK ARKANSAS

9-15-15

WORK WAS PRETTY CHILL TODAY.

I DID A WORKOUT WHEN I GOT HOME.

BUT THEN I ATE ICE CREAM.

EUROPE ENDLESS- KRAFTWERK

9-16-15

TODAY AT WORK I HAD TO HELP OUT DOWNSTAIRS IN THE MAIL ROOM.

IT WAS A NICE CHANGE FROM THE USUAL DESK-JOCKEYING.
WHEW

I STILL DID A WORKOUT AFTER WORK.

QUALITY OR QUANTITY - BAD RELIGION
9-17-15
ANOTHER WORK DAY DOWN IN THE MAIL ROOM.
I WAS SUPER TIRED AND SORE AT THE END OF THE DAY.
BLEH
DRANK 1 BEER AND FELL IMMEDIATELY ASLEEP.
ZZZ
EX-PUNK - DEFECT DEFECT
9-18-15
HAD TO COME IN EARLY FOR THE LAST DAY OF THIS BIG PROJECT.
NINE SOLID HOURS WITH NO LUNCH BREAK, WHEW!
KAREN AND I WENT OUT FOR A RELAXING DINNER AND DRINKS.
OVER AND OVER - MC5
9-19-15
IT'S SATURDAY, BUT I STILL HAD TO GO TO WORK TO CATCH UP EVERYTHING I'VE MISSED.
AFTERWARDS I WENT TO LUNCH WITH BRUCE.
I GOT KINDA TOO DRUNK.
HA HA
SUNKEN - PORTAL
9-20-15
TODAY KAREN + I WENT ON AN ADVENTURE TO ROUND ROCK.
ROUND O ROCK
WHEN WE GOT HOME, THE AIR CONDITIONER HAD STOPPED WORKING.
PANT PANT
WE SLEPT WITH THE WINDOWS OPEN AND A BUNCH OF FANS.
WRRR

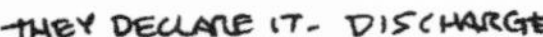
THEY DECLARE IT- DISCHARGE

9-21-15

WHILE I WAS AT WORK TODAY, KAREN GOT THE AIR CONDITIONER FIXED.
AWESOME!

SHE ALSO WENT TO THE DOCTOR TO HAVE AN IMPORTANT TEST.
WE SHOULD KNOW THE RESULTS IN A FEW DAYS.

WE SPENT THE EVENING SNUGGLING ON THE COUCH.

CRUMMY CRUMMY- MEAN JEANS

9-22-15

WORK WAS NORMAL TODAY.

KAREN HAD SOME NEWS.
MY TEST RESULTS CAME BACK. I'M GOING TO HAVE TO HAVE SURGERY TO REMOVE SOME PRE-CANCEROUS CELLS.

WE TALKED ALL NIGHT.
WE CAN GET THROUGH IT.

LOVE COMES ONCE - DEAD MOON

9-23-15

WHEN I TOLD MY COWORKERS WHAT IS GOING ON WITH KAREN TODAY, I CRIED IN FRONT OF THEM. IT WAS KINDA EMBARRASSING.
SOB

I CAME HOME AND ATE TACOS WITH KAREN.

I LOVE HER SO MUCH.

NOTHING IS SACRED- FUNERAL ORATION

9-24-15

WORK FELT PRETTY AWKWARD TODAY.
AHEM.

AFTERWORD I DID A WORKOUT (I'VE STILL BEEN DOING THEM ALL WEEK)

DID SOME DRAWING.

HOPING THAT YOU'RE HOPING - LOUVIN BROTHERS

WORK WAS OKAY TODAY.

I CAME HOME AND ATE DINNER.

9-25-15

I STAYED UP LATE AND WATCHED THE MOVIE "FARGO."

IM FROM WIDE BEAR LAKE, GO BEARS

SORRY, THIS DRAWING COMPLETELY FELL APART.

THE WRIT - BLACK SABBATH

MY ONLY DAY OFF THIS WEEK! I DID LAUNDRY.

CAUGHT UP ON SOME DRAWING.

9-26-15

HAD MARGARITAS WITH MY WIFE.

REPEATER - FUGAZI

I WENT IN TO WORK TODAY (SUNDAY) AND STARTED SLUGGING THROUGH THIS BIG JOB.

WHEN I GOT HOME, I HUNG OUT WITH KAREN.

9-27-15

WE WATCHED A MOVIE.

HAPPY BIRTHDAY KAREN - THE HAPPY BIRTHDAY KARENS
STILL WORKING ON THIS BIG ASS JOB ALL DAY LONG.
GRRR
I TOOK KAREN OUT TO KOME FOR HER BIRTHDAY.
9-28-15
AFTERWARDS WE WENT TO THE FANCY BEER STORE.
FANCY
BEER!

TOO HIGH TO DRIVE- SASS DRAGONS
9-29-15
THIS JOB AT WORK JUST KICKED MY ASS ALL DAY.
I PLAYED WITH THE DOG WHEN I GOT HOME.
WENT TO BED EARLY, I HAVE TO GO IN TO WORK EARLY AGAIN TOMORROW.
SIGH
BOUND TO ORDER- IMMOLATION
9-30-15
EARLY MORNINGS AND LONG DAYS ALL WEEK.
FUCK THIS JOB!
I DIDN'T DO MUCH WHEN I GOT HOME. I WAS TOO TIRED.
OH YOU KNOW WHAT, I FORGOT TO TELL YOU I GOT A RAISE LAST WEEK AT WORK.
DROWNING IN TORMENT- WHIPLASH
10-1-15
I FINALLY HAD A BREAKTHROUGH AT WORK WITH THIS BIG JOB...
I GOT IT!!!
I CAME HOME AND WATCHED THE MOVIE "COP CAR." IT WAS RAD!
HA HA WHOA!
I ALSO ATE A PIZZA.
BACK TO THE WOMB- MELT BANANA
10-2-15
WORK WAS AN EASY BREEZE TODAY.
AT DINNERTIME TONIGHT...
LET'S ORDER A PIZZA!
I JUST HAD PIZZA LAST NIGHT.
WHAT DO YOU WANT INSTEAD?
UH...

BLOOD TO GIVE- OBITUARY

10-3-15

I'M SO GLAD TO FINALLY HAVE A 2-DAY WEEKEND!

WHEW

I RAN INTO A BUNCH OF OLD FRIENDS TODAY.

WHOA, I FEEL LIKE I'M IN MY THIRTIES AGAIN!

THEN I TOOK KAREN OUT ON A LITTLE DATE.

HMK GREY- BLITZ

10-4-15

THIS MORNING I WASHED THE FLEET.

I BOLDLY MOVED INTO THE 1990'S AND REGISTERED A WEB DOMAIN.

BENSNAKEPIT.COM. SIGH.

THEN I WATCHED TV WITH KAREN.

DARK FADE- WARLOCK

10-5-15

BACK AT WORK TODAY. I WAS BRACED FOR THE SHIT-JOB TO COME BACK BUT IT NEVER DID.

I MET KAREN FOR LUNCH, SHE HAD TO GO TO THE HOSPITAL FOR HER PRE-OP VISIT.

I GOT HOME AND PLAYED WITH PEEBER.

I CAN'T GET OVER YOU- THE MONKS

10-6-15

WORK WAS PERFECTLY FINE TODAY.

I HUNG OUT WITH GARY AND MALACHI FOR A BIT.

THEN I PLAYED VIDEO GAMES.

FROM OUT OF NOWHERE - FAITH NO MORE
10-7-15
WORK WAS CHILL TODAY.
I BROUGHT HOME A NICE DINNER FOR KAREN.
WE WATCHED "MILLION DOLLAR BABY."
THE FIRST HALF OF THIS MOVIE IS GREAT!
POLITICS - BAD RELIGION
10-8-15
THIS MORNING MY VAN WOULDN'T START. I HAD TO JUMP IT.
SORRY.
AT LUNCH I TOOK IT TO THE MECHANIC.
YOST
AUTO
I JUST HAD A LOOSE BATTERY CONNECTION.
I FEEL STUPID FOR NOT CHECKING THAT FIRST MYSELF.
YEAR 1 - X
10-9-15
WORK WAS A SOFT BREEZE TODAY.
THE DEADLINE FOR THE HELL-JOB GOT PUSHED BACK 2 WEEKS. NOW I'M ON EASY STREET.
I CAME HOME AND PLAYED A BUNCH OF VIDEO GAMES.
MY COWORKER'S HUSBAND LENT ME A HARD DRIVE FULL OF NEW ROMS FOR MAME!
I ALSO GOT A LOT OF DRAWING DONE.
TELL US THE TRUTH - SHAM 69
10-10-15
TODAY I MOWED THE LAWN.
AND CLEANED OUT THE GARAGE.
AND WATCHED SOME TV.
THE Video Game HISTORIAN

AS HE CREATES SO HE DESTROYS - NILE
I RAN A FEW ERRANDS TODAY.
ERRAND MOBILE
NETFLIX + CHILL WITH KAREN.
10-11-15
WENT TO BED SUPER EARLY. GOTTA GET UP AT 4:00AM TOMORROW!
"ZZZ"
"ZZZ"
PAINKILLER - JUDAS PRIEST
GOT UP SUPER EARLY AND DROVE KAREN TO THE HOSPITAL.
THE SURGERY WAS FAST AND EASY, AND WE WERE ABLE TO GO HOME IN JUST A FEW HOURS.
THERE IS NOTHING MORE HEART-WRENCHING THAN SEEING YOUR LOVED ONE IN A HOSPITAL BED HOOKED UP TO A BUNCH OF STUFF
10-12-15
KAREN SLEPT FOR MOST OF THE DAY WHILE I LOOKED AFTER HER.
ZZZ
SYLVIA'S MOTHER - DR. HOOK
TODAY I STAYED HOME AND TOOK CARE OF KAREN.
SHE FELT PRETTY GOOD THIS AFTERNOON AND WE WENT OUT FOR A DRIVE.
10-13-15
WE GOT SOME HALLOWEEN DECORATIONS FOR THE HOUSE.
RIP
RIP
RIP
CREEP - THE DAMNED
BACK AT WORK TODAY...
I CAME HOME AND LOOKED AFTER KAREN.
10-14-15
I ALSO DID SOME DRAWING.

HIGH WATER EVERYWHERE - CHARLEY PATTON

10-15-15

WORK WAS OKAY TODAY.

KAREN SEEMS TO BE FEELING MUCH BETTER!

BRANDON + CHELSEA MOVED INTO THEIR NEW HOUSE TODAY, ITS RIGHT AROUND THE CORNER FROM US.

IT'S WASTED - MARKED MEN

10-16-15

A NICE, CHILL FRIDAY AT WORK.

KAREN MADE A BIG, FANCY EXTRAVAGANT DINNER.

I PLAYED VIDEO GAMES ALL NIGHT.

PARADISE LOST - SEWER TROUT

10-17-15

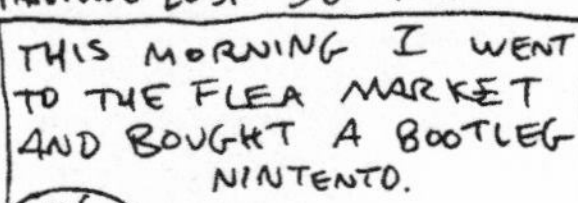
THIS MORNING I WENT TO THE FLEA MARKET AND BOUGHT A BOOTLEG NINTENTO.

POWER KRACKER

I HOOKED IT UP IN THE GARAGE TO THE FREE TV I FOUND A FEW MONTHS AGO.
1UP 290
HA HA!

THIS EVENING, KAREN AND I WENT OVER TO BRANDON'S HOUSE.
IT'S SO RAD TO HAVE FRIENDS LIVING IN THE NEIGHBORHOOD.

SOMETIMES - NAPALM DEATH

10-18-15

TODAY I GOT A SHITTY HAIR CUT.

THEN I WENT TO GHOST KNIFE PRACTICE.

I TOOK BRANDON OVER TO GARY + MALACHI'S PLACE TO MEET THEM.
UT

ON THE FLOOR- OBITUARY

10-19-15

OH GREAT IT'S MONDAY. BACK TO WORK!

KAREN MADE A BADASS DINNER.

AND I PLAYED SOME VIDEO GAMES.

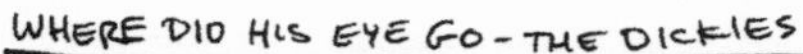
WHERE DID HIS EYE GO - THE DICKIES

10-20-15

WORK WAS OKAY TODAY.

AFTERWARD I GOT INTER-VIEWED BY JT HABERSAAT FOR HIS PODCAST.
BLAH BLAH BLAH

LATER I WENT TO THE MANOR SPORTS BAR WITH KAREN, BRANDON AND CHELSEA.

A NATION'S TEAR- ASSUCK

10-21-15

THE HELL JOB HAS RETURNED. I WAS ON THE CLOCK 10 HRS TODAY.

I GOT A BUNCH OF COOL STUFF IN THE MAIL.
OOOOH SHIT!
PLAY STATION 4

VIDEO GAMES!

TINKLIN- MAN- FLESHIES

10-22-15

WORK WAS LONG + BUSY TODAY.

I CAME HOME AND MADE DINNER FOR KAREN.
THIS IS TO IMPLY THAT I AM A BAD COOK

WE SNUGGLED AND WATCHED A MOVIE.

SCARE HIM - TOOTS + THE MAYTALS
10-23-15
WORK WAS HARD + SHITTY TODAY.
WHEN KAREN CAME HOME, SHE WAS BLEEDING LIKE CRAZY!
WE NEED TO CALL THE DOCTOR RIGHT NOW!!
THE DOCTOR SAID TO KEEP AN EYE ON IT, BUT SHE'S PROBABLY OKAY.
JESUS CHRIST THIS IS STRESSFUL.
DAYDREAM PARASITE - THE SPROUTS
10-24-15
KAREN SAID SHE FELT OKAY ENOUGH TO GO TO WORK TODAY.
ARE YOU SURE?
YEAH.
I DID LAUNDRY AND CLEANED UP THE HOUSE.
IT STARTED RAINING PRETTY HEAVILY. IT'S SUPPOSED TO LAST ALL WEEKEND.
PATENT LEATHER STOMP - SYD VALENTINE'S PATENT LEATHER KIDS
10-25-15
TODAY I HAD TO GO IN TO WORK A FULL SHIFT (IT'S SUNDAY)
I CAME HOME AND WATCHED TV WITH KAREN.
I GOT MY NEW SNAKEPIT T-SHIRTS IN TODAY!
SNAKE PIT FIEND CLUB
VELVET JANE - MIND FUNK
10-26-15
WORK WAS DAMN BUSY TODAY.
OOPS I FORGOT TO DRAW THE KEYBOARD
I WENT TO GHOST KNIFE PRACTICE.
I REALLY DO ENJOY PLAYING MUSIC.
CAME HOME AND DID SOME DRAWING.

GHOST ON THE HIGHWAY- GUN CLUB
WORK IS STILL REALLY BUSY
AT LEAST THE TIME GOES BY FAST!
CAME HOME AND ATE FROZEN TAQUITOS.
KAREN'S AT SCHOOL TONIGHT.
10-27-15
THEN I WATCHED A COOL DOCUMENTARY ABOUT JEFFREY LEE PIERCE + THE GUN CLUB
PACIFICOS- LENGUAS LARGAS
I'M CERTAINLY RAKING IN THE OVERTIME AT WORK.
KAREN + I WENT OUT FOR TACOS.
10-28-15
AFTERWARD WE BOUGHT SOME PUMPKINS.
I AINT TAKIN YOU OUT- PERSONAL + THE PIZZAS
ANOTHER STUPIDLY BUSY DAY.
I CAME HOME AND CARVED ONE OF THE PUMPKINS.
10-29-15
IT LOOKS COOL!
BOWL OF FLIES- LEATHERFACE
RIP DICKIE HAMMOND!
TODAY AT WORK I HAD TO DRIVE A TRUCK TO THE POST OFFICE.
IT'S BEEN CRAZY RAINING AND FLOODING AGAIN. IT TOOK OVER AN HOUR TO GET HOME.
10-30-15
KAREN MADE PORK CHOPS.

HALLOWEEN - HELLOWEEN
10-31-15
THIS MORNING I STARTED SETTING UP MY SPOOKY DRIVEWAY.
SPIDER WEB
LIGHTS
IT LOOKED PRETTY GOOD WHEN IT WAS ALL DONE. WE GOT TONS OF TRICK-OR-TREATERS!
RIP
RIP
RIP
WHEN WE RAN OUT OF CANDY, KAREN + I WENT INSIDE AND WATCHED HORROR MOVIES.
LET'S GO - THE CARS
11-1-15
TODAY KAREN + I CLEANED UP THE HOUSE
WE GOT GROCERIES AND RAN A FEW ERRANDS.
TO AUSTIN
THEN WE SNUGGLED ON THE COUCH AND WATCHED "THE HISTORY OF COUNTRY MUSIC".
YOU REALIZE THAT IN A WEEK AND A HALF, FALLOUT 4 WILL BE OUT AND YOU'LL NEVER SEE ME AGAIN, RIGHT?
UH HUH.
COW - M BLANKET
11-2-15
BACK AT WORK TODAY, THIS WEEK IS GONNA BE A LOT MORE CHILL THAN LAST WEEK.
I THOUGHT KAREN HAD CLASS TONIGHT, SO I ATE DINNER ON MY OWN.
SOME GROSS BULLSHIT
SOME BULLSHIT
BUT THEN SHE CAME HOME EARLY AND COOKED DINNER ANYWAY.
OOH!
NOT SUPERSTITIOUS - LEATHERFACE
11-3-15
WORK WAS A BREEZE.
I DID SOME DRAWING.
AND ALSO SOME GAMING.

LIE DETECTOR - DEAD KENNEDYS
11-4-15
WORK WENT BY FAST TODAY.
I GRABBED KAREN AND WE DROVE DOWNTOWN...
WHERE GHOST KNIFE PLAYED A SHOW WITH
SHELLSHAG
DON'T GO OUT IN THE RAIN - GROOVIE GHOULIES
11-5-15
I TOOK THE DAY OFF WORK TODAY. I'M GLAD I DID.
Z Z Z
I JUST LAYED AROUND THE HOUSE DOING NOTHING ALL DAY.
EGG SALAD
IT WAS AWESOME.
HERE LIES A GIANT FAT BLOB OF SHIT
DRÖMMUSIK - ANTI-CIMEX
11-6-15
WORK WAS BUSY BUT VERY CHILL TODAY.
WATCHED STAR TREK WITH KAREN.
PLAYED SOME DUMBASS VIDEO GAME.
ADDRESS - BITTER HOMES + GARDENS
11-7-15
TODAY IS SATURDAY. I HAD TO GO IN TO WORK FOR A FEW HOURS THIS MORNING.
GODDAMMIT
AFTERWARDS, KAREN + I GOT SOME GROCERIES.
LATER I PLAYED WITH PEEBER.

ANTI CIMEX - ANTI CIMEX
11-8-15
TODAY WAS AWESOMELY LAZY.
BLARF
I DIDN'T LEAVE THE HOUSE ALL DAY.
I GOT NOTHING ACCOMPLISHED.
WHOOO CARES
IF THIS LOOKS LIKE AN OWL.
TWITCH - PITCHFORK
11-9-15
BACK AT WORK. ONE GUY IS ON VACATION SO I'M EXTRA BUSY.
YEEP YEEP
WHEN I GOT HOME I SPENT SOME TIME WITH KAREN.
AFTER TOMORROW I'M GONNA BE "GONE" FOR A WHILE...
AND ALSO PEEBER.
WATCHIN' YOU - KISS
11-10-15
HOLY SHIT FALLOUT 4 CAME OUT TODAY!
HOLY SHIT HOLY SHIT HOLY SHIT
ITS SO AWESOME! YEAH!
RIDE ME DOWN EASY - WAYLON JENNINGS
11-11-15
WORK WAS PRETTY BUSY TODAY.
I CAME HOME AND SPENT A COUPLE HOURS IN THE WASTELAND.
THEN I WENT TO BED.
ZZZ

WHELAND- GIANT BAGS OF WEED

11-12-15

WORK WAS PRETTY STRESSFUL TODAY.
GGGGGG

PEEBER HURT HIS FOOT WHILE WE WERE PLAYING FETCH.

HE'LL BE OKAY, BUT IT MADE ME WORRY.

IT'S SO TERRIFYING TO THINK OF YOUR LOVED ONES BEING HURT.

EVEN HITLER HAD A GIRLFRIEND- MR 7 EXPERIENCE

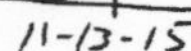
11-13-15

ANOTHER STRESSFUL DAY AT WORK. AT LEAST ITS FRIDAY.

KAREN + I TRIED OUT A NEW CAJUN RESTAURANT IN MANOR.

THEN I STAYED UP LATE PLAYING FALLOUT 4.

NIGHT + DAY- BILLIE HOLIDAY

11-14-15

TODAY I CLEARED SOME OLD DEAD BUSHES OUT OF THE YARD.

THEN I RODE WITH BRANDON INTO AUSTIN. I'M PLAYING FILL-IN GUITAR FOR HIS BAND'S SHOW ON TUESDAY.

ATX

WE PRACTICED AND LEARNED HALF THE SET TONIGHT
BEING IN A BAND IS FUN WHEN THERE'S NO COMMITMENT.

TRAPPED IN A SCENE- HERESY

11-15-15

THIS MORNING I PLAYED FALLOUT 4 FOR A LONG TIME.
I JUST SPENT TWO HOURS BUILDING A HOUSE

THEN I PRACTICED WITH PRINCE. I LEARNED 3 MORE SONGS.

THIS IS FUN!

THE SHOW IS GONNA BE FUN!

I JUST FOUND OUT THAT WORRIERS ARE PLAYING TOO!

ONCE UPON A... - MAN IS THE BASTARD
BACK AT WORK TODAY.
IMMEDIATELY AFTERWARD I WENT TO PRINCE PRACTICE.
LET'S RUN IT AGAIN
11-16-15
I GOT HOME SUPER LATE AND TIRED.
Z Z Z
LIFE IN A BOTTLE - RKL
WORK WENT BY FAST TODAY.
WE GOT TO THE SHOW EARLY + I GOT TO SEE A BUNCH OF OLD FRIENDS.
LOU!
LAUREN!
MIKEY!
11-17-15
I PLAYED PRETTY WELL FOR ONLY 3 DAYS PRACTICE.
I ONLY FUCKED UP ONE SONG!
BASKET CASE - VINDICTIVES
I WENT IN TO WORK LATE TODAY...
OH YES I AM HOLDING IT TOGETHER JUST FINE
...BUT I WAS STILL SUPER FUCKING HUNG OVER.
UH OH!
11-18-15
I CAME HOME AND MELTED INTO A PUDDLE.
ALL I NEED IS MONEY - EDDIE + THE HOT RODS
WORK WAS COOL TODAY.
I WATCHED ALL OF THE "W/BOB + DAVID" EPISODES.
WHY ARE THERE ONLY FOUR!?!
11-19-15
AND THEN I PLAYED FALLOUT.

PARTY AT GROUND ZERO- FISHBONE

11-20-15

WORK WAS VERY NICE TODAY.

KAREN + I WENT OUT FOR BURGERS + PIE.

THEN WE GOT STUFF TO GET READY FOR OUR THANKSGIVING TRIP.
WAL MART

ORION- METALLICA

11-21-15

TODAY I FINALLY GOT TO SPEND A BIG CHUNK OF HOURS PLAYING FALLOUT.

A "BIG CHUNK" ALRIGHT.

LATER I WENT OVER TO BRANDON'S AND RECORDED A SONG WITH HIM IN HIS GARAGE.

AFTER THAT I ATE PIZZA WITH KAREN.

NUCLEAR ARMED- GISM

11-22-15

SUNDAY! I CHANGED THE OIL IN MY VAN.

I WENT GROCERY SHOPPING.

I GOT A LOT OF DRAWING DONE.

THE MILLIONAIRE- DR. HOOK

11-23-15

BACK AT WORK TODAY. EVERYONE IS IN A GOOD MOOD BECAUSE ITS A SHORT WEEK.

I BROUGHT TACOS HOME FOR DINNER.
TACOS!

I PAID SOME BILLS, TOO!

SUSPIRIA - GOBLIN

11-24-15

IT GOT KINDA BUSY AT WORK.

AFTER LOOKING AT SOME D.I.Y. GUIDES ON THE INTERNET, I'VE DECIDED TO RE-TOLEX LANCE'S BEAT-UP OLD MARSHALL CABINET.
I THINK I CAN DO THIS.
RE-TOLEX A SPEAKER CA
I'M REALLY EXCITED TO START THIS PROJECT!
SOON YOU WILL BE AS GOOD AS NEW.

STORM WARNING - TAITT + THE COMETS

11-25-15

WORK WAS PRETTY RELAXED TODAY.

I TOOK PEEBER OVER TO BRANDON'S, HE'S STAYING THERE WHILE WE GO TO TULSA FOR THANKSGIVING.
???
THEN WE GOT ALL PACKED AND WENT TO BED EARLY.
Z Z Z

JUDICIAL SLIME - NAPALM DEATH

11-26-15

WE GOT UP EARLY THIS MORNING + HIT THE ROAD FOR TULSA.

THE EIGHT-HOUR DRIVE WASN'T TOO BAD.

WE GOT TO KAREN'S PARENTS' HOUSE AND HUNG OUT WITH HER DAD.

NOCTURNAL FEAR - CELTIC FROST

11-27-15

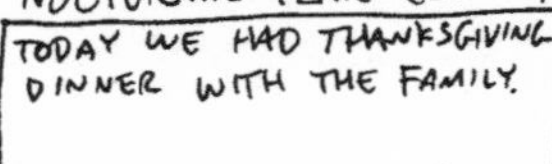
TODAY WE HAD THANKSGIVING DINNER WITH THE FAMILY.

KEITH (MY FATHER-IN-LAW) TOOK ME + ZAC (MY BROTHER-IN-LAW) TO HIS COUSIN'S LIQUOR STORE. THEY HAVE A PHENOMINAL BEER SELECTION!

I HAD FUN PLAYING WITH MY NEPHEW, WYATT.

DESPERATION STREET- HARD SKIN
11-28-15
THIS MORNING WE PAID A QUICK VISIT TO KAREN'S GRANDMA.
THEN WE HIT THE ROAD FOR HOME.
IT FELT GREAT TO SLEEP IN OUR OWN BED.
THE OLDER I GET, THE MORE I APPRECIATE MY HOME.
THE RED AND THE BLACK- MINUTEMEN
11-29-15
I'M GLAD WE HAD A DAY OFF BEFORE GOING BACK TO WORK.
WHEW
I RAN A BUNCH OF ERRANDS.
IT LOOKS LIKE THE LIGHT-UP STAR TREK CHRISTMAS ORNAMENT I GOT LAST YEAR SOMEHOW CAUSED EVERY BULB ON THE TREE TO BLOW OUT. YIKES!
BRANDON CAME OVER AND HUNG OUT FOR A BIT.
HUH HUH HUH
DON'T LET 'EM GRIND YA DOWN- MOTORHEAD
11-30-15
I REALLY DIDN'T WANT TO GO BACK TO WORK THIS MORNING.
BEEP BEEP BEEP BEEP BEEP BEEP
6:30
BUT I DID, BECAUSE I HAD TO, BECAUSE THAT'S THE WAY THE WORLD WORKS.
I CAME HOME AND CAUGHT UP ON SOME DRAWING.
I'M LETTING 'EM GRIND ME DOWN.
TOYS- THE EPOXIES
12-1-15
TODAY I WENT TO WORK.
THEN I CAME HOME AND PLAYED VIDEO GAMES.
I ALSO PLAYED WITH PEEBER

CRIMINAL IMAGE- SCREAMING FEMALES
12-2-15
TODAY I BOUGHT KAREN'S CHRISTMAS PRESENT.
I GOT HER A NEW DESK. I HOPE SHE DOESN'T READ THIS BEFORE X-MAS.
BUY NOW
OH YEAH I WENT TO WORK TOO.
I ATE SUSHI WITH KAREN
ARSENIC CHICK- WARLOCK PINCHERS
12-3-15
WORK WAS OKAY TODAY. MY WORK DAYS GO BY REALLY FAST
JUST BUSY ENOUGH, NOT TOO BUSY.
WHEN I GOT HOME I WRAPPED A LITTLE XMAS GIFT FOR KAREN.
THEN IT WAS FALLOUT TIME!
VULNERABILITY- OPERATION IVY
12-4-15
A NICE, EASY FRIDAY AT WORK.
I ATE A SHITTY SALAD FOR DINNER.
AND WAS A PIECE OF SHIT.
HA HA HA
SORRY DEAR- KING DIAMOND
12-5-15
I GOT SO MUCH DONE TODAY. I CLIMBED ON THE ROOF AND PUT UP CHRISTMAS LIGHTS.
BRANDON + I DROVE TO ELGIN TO GET BBQ FROM SOUTHSIDE MARKET.
AUSTIN
REAL TEXAS
LATER I WENT ON A DATE WITH KAREN.

LET ME ENTERTAIN YOU- QUEEN
12-6-15
TODAY OUR WATER HEATER BROKE.
AHH FUCK!
WE WENT TO HOME DEPOT AND GOT A NEW ONE. THE PLUMBER IS COMING TO INSTALL IT ON TUESDAY.
WATER HEATER
$500
GOD DAMMIT.
$700
WHEN WE GOT HOME, OUR NEXT-DOOR NEIGHBOR WAS GETTING ARRESTED!
THEY DECLARE IT- DISCHARGE
12-7-15
BACK TO WORK. IT'S BUSY, BUT I REALLY LIKE MY JOB.
I WATCHED THE DOCUMENTARY 'DARK STAR', ABOUT H.R. GIGER.
HOLY SHIT! HIS PERSONAL ASSISTANT IS TOM G. WARRIOR!
I GOT TO STAY UP LATE. TOMORROW MORNING I HAVE TO HELP INSTALL THE NEW WATER HEATER.
YEAH IT'S 10:30PM! PARTY!
THE TIDE IS HIGH- THE PARAGONS
12-8-15
THIS MORNING I HELPED HASSAN INSTALL OUR NEW WATER HEATER.
OOF!
THEN I WENT TO WORK.
THEN I CAME HOME AND DRANK WINE WITH KAREN.
WIG WAM BAM- THE DONNAS
12-9-15
WORK WAS COOL TODAY.
I ATE DINNER WITH KAREN.
TONIGHT IS HER LAST NIGHT of HOMEWORK FOR THE SEMESTER!
I CAN'T WAIT TO GET MY WIFE BACK!

WAR NEVER CHANGES - RAMLA UT
12-10-15
WORK WAS JUST FINE TODAY.
WHEN I CAME HOME I PLAYED FALLOUT FOR A REALLY LONG TIME.
KAREN GOT HOME LATE. SHE IS OFFICALLY FINISHED WITH THIS SEMESTER OF SCHOOL!
PEPE TO - ROLAND ALPHONSO
12-11-15
FRIDAY AT WORK IS COOL.
KAREN MADE A PIZZA FOR DINNER.
I HUNG OUT AT BRANDON'S.
ANGELS WE HAVE HEARD ON HIGH - BAD RELIGION
12-12-15
THIS MORNING I GOT ALL MY CHRISTMAS SHOPPING DONE.
XMAS THING
XMAS STORE
I TOOK KAREN OUT TO HER FAVORITE RESTAURANT TO CELEBRATE BEING DONE WITH THE SEMESTER.
WE DRANK WHITE RUSSIANS AND LISTEND TO CHRISTMAS MUSIC.
GHOULASH - SATAN'S PILGRIMS
12-13-15
KAREN'S CAR HAD A FLAT TIRE THIS MORNING.
WOMP WOMP
WE WENT GROCERY SHOPPING.
I'M SO EXCITED FOR YOU TO START COOKING AGAIN!
ME TOO!
KAREN MADE AN AWESOME DINNER!

AMERICAN NIGHTS- THE RUNAWAYS

BACK AT WORK TODAY...

KAREN HAD SPENT HER DAY OFF MAKING TONS OF COOKIES!

12-14-15
I ATE VERY MANY OF THEM

DON'T STOP ME- QUEEN

WORK WAS COOL TODAY.

MY COMPUTER AT HOME IS BROKEN.
DAMMIT.

12-15-15
I WORKED ALL NIGHT ON FIXING IT.
STUPID WINDOWS 10.
INSTALLING 21%

SIVA- SMASHING PUMPKINS

WE HAD A CHRISTMAS PARTY AT WORK TODAY.

I CAME HOME AND DID MORE FIXING MY COMPUTER.
INSTALLING 78%
GRR.

12-16-15
I ATE COOKIES WITH KAREN.

NIGHT CRAWLER- JUDAS PRIEST

ANOTHER COOL DAY AT WORK!

I TOOK KAREN OUT FOR MARGARITAS.

12-17-15
WE CAME HOME AND WATCHED A MOVIE.

HAPPY SEGOIA - THE FUCKING CHAMPS
12-18-15
A VERY CHILL DAY AT WORK...
I CAME HOME AND RELAXED WITH A FANCY BEER.
THEN I PLAYED WITH MY (NEW) COMPUTER.
I'M JUST GOING TO DRAW MYSELF TYPING ON A COMPUTER OVER AND OVER AGAIN EVERY DAY FOR THE REST OF MY LIFE.
THEY LIE WE DIE - FLUX OF PINK INDIANS
12-19-15
THIS MORNING I PLAYED FALLOUT FOR A LONG TIME.
I JUST SPENT TWO HOURS BUILDING A HOUSE.
THEN I DID A BUNCH OF YARD WORK, I TRIMMED THE HEDGES AND EVERY-THING!
KAREN + I WATCHED RETURN OF THE JEDI.
I BOUGHT TICKETS FOR THE NEW MOVIE TOMORROW!
PARANOID CHANT - F.Y.P.
12-20-15
TODAY KAREN + I SAW THE NEW STAR WARS MOVIE.
THEN I GOT A HAIRCUT.
SNIP
SNIP
IT WAS A NICE DAY.
GOOD KING WENCENSLAUS - BUTTHOLE SURFERS
12-21-15
BACK TO WORK, EVERYTHING AT MY JOB IS GREAT!
I WATCHED "MAKING A MURDERER" ON NETFLIX WITH KAREN
DO YOU THINK HE DID IT?
I DUNNO
AFTER THAT I GOOFED OFF.

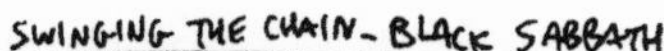
SWINGING THE CHAIN- BLACK SABBATH

12-22-15

WORK WAS PRETTY CHILL TODAY.

I RAN SOME ERRANDS ON THE WAY HOME
ERRAND STORE

KAREN WAS SUPPOSED TO GET HER NEW TATTOO FINISHED, BUT HAD TO RESCHEDULE.
BUMMER.

LYDIA-BASEMENT BENDERS

12-23-15

I WENT TO WORK TODAY.

KAREN+I WENT OUT TO DINNER...

AND GOT SOME LAST-MINUTE XMAS SHIT AT THE STORE.
LAST MINUTE XMAS SHIT

ROTTEN APPLE- SCREAMING FEMALES

12-24-15

I ONLY WORKED FOR 4 HOURS TODAY.

I CAME HOME AND MOWED THE BACK YARD.
RRRRRRRR

KAREN+I WATCHED DIE HARD AND SCROOGED.
MMM NICE!

BLACK DEATH- DESTRUCTION

12-25-15

HOLY SHIT ITS CHRISTMAS!

AFTER WE EXCHANGED GIFTS, KAREN+I MADE A RACK OF RIBS ON THE SMOKER.

MERRY CHRIBSMAS!

THEN WE DRANK FANCY BEERS AND HAD A FANCY TIME.

READY 2 RIP – MEAN JEANS

12-26-15

THIS MORNING I PUT KAREN'S NEW DESK TOGETHER FOR HER.

THESE ARE LIKE IKEA INSTRUCTIONS, ONLY MUCH SHITTIER.

THEN I BEGAN THE HERCULEAN TASK OF SCANNING ALL THE COMICS FOR THE BOOK YOU ARE READING RIGHT NOW.

RRRRRRRR
RRRRRRRRR.

NOT AS LAZY A DAY AS I WOULD'VE LIKED

ZZZ

EVOLVED AS ONE – NAPALM DEATH

12-27-15

I SPENT MOST OF THE DAY SCANNING AND DOING OTHER WORK FOR THE NEW BOOK.

ZZZ

SNAKEPIT 2013
SNAKEPIT 2014
SNAKEPIT 2015

KAREN + I WENT TO HER WORK'S CHRISTMAS PARTY.

BOOZE
BOOZE
BOOZE
BOOZE

I HAD A LOT OF FUN!

IT'S NICE TO GO TO A PARTY AND JUST CHILL AND NOT GET ALL HAMMER-DRUNK.

DOCTOR DAN – MARKED MEN

12-28-15

BACK AT WORK TODAY, WE'RE STARTING TO GET A LOT BUSIER.

I CAME HOME AND ATE A PIZZA WITH KAREN.

WE WATCHED TV AND TALKED AND HAD A NICE EVENING TOGETHER.

EUROPEAN SON – VELVET UNDERGROUND

12-29-15

WORK WAS STEADY BUT COOL TODAY.

SHE READ A BOOK WHILE I PLAYED FALLOUT.

SNIF SNIF

THEN I WORKED A LONG TIME ON THE FILES FOR MY NEW BOOK.

I SURE HOPE YOU FUCKIN APPRECIATE IT!

DUMB- NIRVANA

12-30-15

WAIT A SECOND. THIS ISN'T A LEAP YEAR, WHY ARE THERE TWO DAYS ON THIS PAGE? A YEAR ALWAYS ENDS WITH A FULL-PAGE COMIC.

LET'S FLIP BACK THROUGH THE YEAR... HOLY SHIT, I DREW FEBRUARY 17TH TWICE! I GUESS I'D FORGOTTEN THAT I'D DONE IT AND DREW IT AGAIN. NOW THE WHOLE BOOK IS MESSED UP.
SHARE DIT 2015

WOW, THIS IS HANDS-DOWN THE DUMBEST MISTAKE I'VE EVER MADE IN 15 YEARS OF DRAWING THESE COMICS. I TRULY AM A COMPLETE FUCKING DUMBASS.

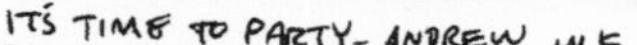
IT'S TIME TO PARTY- ANDREW W.F.

12-31-15

IT'S NEW YEARS EVE! BRANDON CAME OVER AND WE DRANK BEERS IN THE DRIVEWAY, WATCHING THE FIREWORKS.